CHILTON'S *New* Repair and Tune-Up Guide

Honda Singles

ILLUSTRATED

Prepared by the

Automotive Editorial Department

Chilton Book Company

401 Walnut Street
Philadelphia, Pa. 19106

215—WA 5-9111

managing editor **JOHN D. KELLY;** assistant
managing editor **PETER J. MEYER;** senior
editor, motorcycles **SVANTE E. MOSSBERG;**
editor **MICHAEL S. YAMPOLSKY**

Member

Motorcycle
Industry
Council

CHILTON BOOK COMPANY   PHILADELPHIA   NEW YORK   LONDON

Published in Philadelphia by Chilton Book Company
and simultaneously in Ontario, Canada,
by Thomas Nelson & Sons, Ltd.
Manufactured in the United States of America

Library of Congress Cataloging in Publication Data

Chilton Book Company. Automotive Editorial Dept.
  Chilton's new repair and tune-up guide: Honda
singles.

    1. Honda motorcycle.   I. Title.   II. Title:
New repair and tune-up guide: Honda singles.
TL448.H6C47   1973   629.28'7'75   72-10384
ISBN 0-8019-5739-7

ACKNOWLEDGMENTS

AMERICAN HONDA MOTOR COMPANY, INC.
Gardena, California

COLOSIMO'S HONDA
Philadelphia, Pennsylvania

CHIACCIO MOTORS
Riverton, New Jersey

Contents

1 · Model Identification and Description

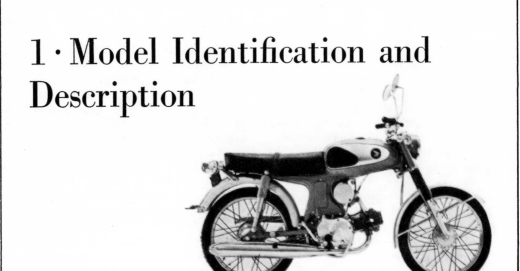

Introduction

This book is intended to serve as a guide for the maintenance, tune-up, and repair of the following Honda models:

C50
C50M
S50
C65
C65M
S65
CL70 (K1-K3)
C70M
C70
SL70
S90
CL90
CL90L
CD90
C90
CT90 (K1-K4)
CB100 (K1-K2)
CL100 (K1-K2)
SL100 (K1-K-2)
CB125S
CD125S
SL125 (K1)

To use it properly, one must approach each operation logically and read the recommended procedures thoroughly before actually beginning the work. It is also nec-

essary, of course, to have the required tools and a clean, uncluttered place in which to do the work. Cleanliness is one facet of mechanics that cannot be overstressed and will be emphasized throughout the text. If your particular model is not mentioned above do not despair. Most Honda models in the same displacement class use exactly the same engine and transmission, and only the final drive and frame components vary. Therefore, if you have a CT70, for example, this guide will supply the necessary information to tune, maintain, and overhaul your engine.

Each chapter is constructed so that descriptions, procedures, and specifications can be easily located, thus allowing experienced mechanics to isolate only the information they require, and yet providing the inexperienced mechanic with background data necessary to his understanding of the machine.

Development History

In 1948, when the Honda Motor Company was formed, Soichiro Honda was in the right place at the right time, and he made the right move. Post-war Japan was desperately in need of inexpensive transportation and Honda's first product, a cheap, reliable, motorized bicycle, filled this need admirably. The little mo-ped incorporated a small Imperial Army surplus two-stroke engine that ran on a fuel extracted from the roots of pine trees. It sold very well, and Honda's supply of engines was soon exhausted. Consequently, he designed his own engine, a 50 cubic centimeter (cc), two-stroke, mo-ped that proved to be so successful that production could not satisfy the demand.

By 1949 the success and growth of his company enabled Honda to produce a completely Honda-designed motorcycle, and in August of that year, the 100 cc D model, which became known as the Dream, was introduced. The Dream featured a pressed steel frame with rigid rear suspension and telescopic front forks. Its 2.3 Horsepower two-stroke engine drove through a two-speed transmission and a chain final drive. Unfortunately, Japan was hit by an economic recession at about this time and the Honda Motor Company suffered to near bankruptcy. Honda wisely hired a sales and financial director, since this was the weakest area in his organization, and the company was again showing increasing growth by 1950. Japan began her astounding industrial growth and the Honda Motor Company increased its production accordingly. By the end of 1950 Honda was producing 300 Dream models each month, compared to the 1,600 units per year that all other Japanese motorcycle manufacturers combined were producing.

Honda's first four-stroke motorcycle, the E model, was introduced early in the 1950s. Its 5.5 hp engine was mounted in a pressed steel frame much like that of the earlier D model and it had a top speed of 50 miles per hour. The E model was a huge success; 32,000 were sold in 1953.

May of 1952 saw the introduction of a new Honda mo-ped, the 50 cc Cub. Production was soon up to 65,000 units per month, and the fantastic sales of the Cub enabled Honda to plow an ever-increasing amount of money back into the company for research and development.

The 90 cc four-stroke Benly was designed and produced in 1953. The Benly was a much more modern bike than its predecessors, with a 3.8 hp engine and a three-speed foot-shift transmission. The pressed steel frame was all new, and it had telescopic suspension up front and torsion bar suspension at the rear.

The Honda Motor Company spent over one million dollars in 1953 on modern, efficient machine tools in anticipation of entry into the world market. Toward this end, Honda fielded a team for the 1954 Isle of Man TT races, hoping to compete with the European machines and pave the way for sales of Honda motorcycles in other countries. Honda's racing bikes were clearly uncompetitive and were beaten badly. All efforts were turned, for a time, on improving the line of street machines, and in 1955 several new models appeared. One of the most notable, the SA model, was an OHV 250 with swing-arm rear suspension.

The most famous Honda motorcycle, and the one which was responsible for catapulting Honda into the world market was the 50 cc Super Cub which was introduced in 1958. It was soon followed by the overhead-cam twins, which solidified Honda's position and helped to make Honda one of the largest motorcycle manufacturers in the world. Honda avenged their earlier defeat at the Isle of Man by building a series of extremely complex and powerful GP motorcycles that, during the early and middle 60s, won every class of international road racing.

The present line of single-cylinder Hondas carries on the tradition of excellence that characterizes all of their models. There are machines designed for a casual romp through the boonies, serious dirt riding, and the traditional street and street/scrambler models. All of Honda's bikes are fast, smooth, and very reliable, and are designed to please the most demanding of customers.

General Specifications

Model	C50	C50M	S50
DIMENSIONS			
Overall length (in.)	70.67	70.67	69.45
Overall width (in.)	25.19	25.19	24.21
Overall height (in.)	38.4	38.4	35.95
Ground clearance (in.)	5.12	5.12	4.92
Wheelbase (in.)	46.65	46.65	45.28
Net weight (lbs)	152.0	166.6	168.0
ENGINE			
Type		ohc, air-cooled, four-stroke	
Bore and stroke (mm)	39 X 41.4	39 X 41.4	39 X 41.4
Compression ratio	8.8 : 1	8.8 : 1	8.8 : 1
Displacement (cc)	49	49	49
Valve train		chain-driven, overhead-cam	
Lubrication system		pressure and splash, wet sump	
Horsepower @ rpm	4.8 @ 10,000	4.8 @ 10,000	5.2 @ 10,000
Torque (ft lbs @ rpm)	2.7 @ 8,200	2.7 @ 8,200	4.75 @ 8,200
Carburetion (Keihin)		piston valve type, manual choke	
DRIVE TRAIN			
Clutch type		automatic, wet, multiple-disc, centrifugal type	wet, multiple-disc type
Transmission		constant meshed-gear type	
Power reduction (primary)	gear/3.722	gear/3.722	gear/3.300
Power reduction (secondary)		chain and sprocket	
	3.000	3.000	3.154
Gear ratio (total)	NA	NA	12.2
1st	3.364	3.364	3.000
2nd	1.722	1.722	1.765
3rd	1.190	1.190	1.300
4th	——	——	1.043
5th	——	——	——
ELECTRICAL SYSTEM			
Ignition		battery and coil, high-voltage electrical spark	
Starting system	kick	kick and electric	kick
Charging system		flywheel magneto	
Battery (volts/amp hr)	6/2	6/11	6/2
Fuse (amps)	10	10	10

General Specifications (cont.)

Model	C65	C65M	S65
DIMENSIONS			
Overall length (in.)	70.67	70.67	69.13
Overall width (in.)	25.19	25.19	24.02
Overall height (in.)	38.4	38.4	35.83
Ground clearance (in.)	5.12	5.12	4.92
Wheelbase (in.)	46.65	46.65	45.28
Net weight (lbs)	161	174	170
ENGINE			
Type		ohc, air-cooled, four-stroke	
Bore and stroke (mm)	44 X 41.4	44 X 41.4	44 X 41.4
Compression ratio	8.8 : 1	8.8 : 1	8.8 : 1
Displacement (cc)	63	63	63
Valve train		chain-driven, overhead-cam	
Lubrication system		pressure and splash, wet sump	
Horsepower @ rpm	5.5/9,000	5.5/9,000	6.22/10,000
Torque (ft lbs @ rpm)	3.32/7,000	3.32/7,000	3.47/8,500
Carburetion (Keihin/mm)		piston valve type, manual choke	
DRIVE TRAIN			
Clutch type		automatic, wet, multiple-disc, centrifugal type	wet, multiple-disc type
Transmission		constant meshed-gear type	
Power reduction (primary)		gear/3.300	
Power reduction (secondary)		chain and sprocket	
	3.154	3.154	3.308
Gear ratio (total)	12.4	12.4	11.4
1st	3.364	3.364	3.000
2nd	1.722	1.722	1.765
3rd	1.190	1.190	1.300
4th	——	——	1.043
5th	——	——	——
ELECTRICAL SYSTEM			
Ignition		battery and coil, high-voltage electrical spark	
Starting system	kick	kick and electric	kick
Charging system		flywheel magneto	
Battery (volts/amp hr)	6/2	6/11	6/2
Fuse (amps)	10	10	10

General Specifications (cont.)

Model	CL70	C70	C70M
DIMENSIONS			
Overall length (in.)	70.1	70.7	70.7
Overall width (in.)	29.7	25.2	25.2
Overall height (in.)	39.2	38.4	38.4
Ground clearance (in.)	5.1	5.1	5.1
Wheelbase (in.)	46.5	46.7	46.7
Net weight (lbs)	174.2	165.0	174.2
ENGINE			
Type		ohc, air-cooled, four-stroke	
Bore and stroke (mm)	47 X 41.4	47 X 41.4	47 X 41.4
Compression ratio	8.8	8.8	8.8
Displacement (cc)	72	72	72
Valve train		chain-driven, overhead-cam	
Lubrication system		pressure and splash, wet sump	
Horsepower @ rpm	6.5/9,500	6.2/9,000	6.2/9,000
Torque (ft lbs @ rpm)	3.83/8,000	3.83/7,000	3.83/7,000
Carburetion (Keihin/mm)		piston valve type, manual choke	
DRIVE TRAIN			
Clutch type	wet, multiple-disc type	automatic, wet, multiple-disc, centrifugal type	
Transmission		constant meshed-gear type	
Power reduction (primary)	gear/3.722	gear/3.722	gear/3.722
Power reduction (secondary)		chain and sprocket	
	3.615	2.786	2.786
1st	2.692	3.364	3.364
2nd	1.824	1.722	1.722
3rd	1.300	1.190	1.190
4th	0.958	——	——
5th	——	——	——
ELECTRICAL SYSTEM			
Ignition		battery and coil, high-voltage electrical spark	
Starting system	kick	kick	kick and electric
Charging system	flywheel magneto	flywheel magneto	AC generator
Battery (volts/amp hrs)	6/5.5	6/4	6/11
Fuse (amps)	10	10	10

General Specifications (cont.)

Model	CD90	C90	CT90	CT90 (from F. no. 000001A)
DIMENSIONS				
Overall length (in.)	70.72	72.10	70.92	73.6
Overall width (in.)	25.22	25.22	25.61	26.8
Overall height (in.)	37.63	39.20	38.61	41.0
Ground clearance (in.)	5.12	5.12	5.40	6.9
Wheelbase (in.)	45.39	46.89	46.81	47.9
Net weight (lbs)	——	187.00	179.30	200.00
ENGINE				
Type		ohc, air-cooled, four-stroke		
Bore and stroke (mm)	50 X 45.6	50 X 45.6	50 X 45.6	50 X 45.6
Compression ratio	8.2 : 1	8.2 : 1	8.2 : 1	8.2 : 1
Displacement (cc)	89.6	89.6	89.6	89.6
Valve train		chain-driven, overhead-cam		
Lubrication system		pressure and splash, wet sump		
Horsepower @ rpm	7.5	7.5	7.0	7.0
Carburetion (Keihin/mm)		piston valve type, manual choke		
DRIVE TRAIN				
Clutch type	wet, multiple-disc type	automatic, wet, multiple-disc type		
Transmission		constant meshed-gear type		
Power reduction (primary)	gear/3.722	gear/3.722	gear/3.722	gear/3.722
Power reduction (secondary)		chain and sprocket		
	3.000	2.857	3.000	3.000
1st	2.540	2.538	2.538	(4.738)*
2nd	1.610	1.555	1.611	(3.008)*
3rd	1.190	1.000	1.190	(2.222)*
4th	0.96	——	0.958	(1.789)*
5th	——	——	——	——
Sub transmission total ratio			1.000	(1.867)
ELECTRICAL SYSTEM				
Ignition		battery and coil, high-voltage electrical spark		
Starting system	kick	kick	kick	kick
Charging system		AC generator		
Battery (volts/amp hrs)	6/6	6/6	6/5.5	6/5.5
Fuse (amps)	10	10	10	10

* The figures in parenthesis indicate a sub-transmission ratio

General Specifications (cont.)

Model	CL90, CL90L	S90	SL90
DIMENSIONS			
Overall length (in.)	72.1	74.47	73.6
Overall width (in.)	31.9	26.5	31.5
Overall height (in.)	41.3	38.61	43.3
Ground clearance (in.)	6.3	5.71	9.8
Wheelbase (in.)	47.2	47.08	48.8
Net weight (lbs)	202.9	190.73	216.1
ENGINE			
Type		ohc, air-cooled, four-stroke	
Bore and stroke (mm)	50 X 45.6	50 X 45.6	50 X 45.6
Compression ratio	8.2	8.2	8.2
Displacement (cc)	89.6	89.6	89.6
Valve train		chain-driven, overhead-cam	
Lubrication system		pressure and splash, wet sump	
Horsepower @ rpm	①	8.0 @ 9,500	8.0 @ 9,500
Torque (ft lbs @ rpm)	②	4.70 @ 8,000	4.77 @ 8,000
Carburetion (Keihin)		piston valve type, manual choke	
DRIVE TRAIN			
Clutch type		wet, multiple-disc type	
Transmission		constant meshed-gear type	
Power reduction (primary)	gear/3.72	gear/3.72	gear/3.72
Power reduction (secondary)		chain and sprocket	
	3.21	3.21	3.28
1st	2.54	2.54	2.54
2nd	1.61	1.53	1.61
3rd	1.19	1.09	1.19
4th	0.96	0.88	0.96
5th	——	——	——
ELECTRICAL SYSTEM			
Ignition		battery and coil, high-voltage electrical spark	
Starting system	kick	kick	kick
Charging system		AC generator	
Battery (volts/amp hrs)	6/6	6/6	6/5.5
Fuse (amps)	10	10	10

① CL90: 8.0/9,500
   CL90L: 4.9/8,000

② CL90: 4.7 @ 8,000
   CL90L: 14.24 @ 3,500

General Specifications (cont.)

Model	CB100	CL100	SL100
DIMENSIONS			
Overall length (in.)	74.2	71.6	75.4
Overall width (in.)	29.5	32.5	31.9
Overall height (in.)	40.0	40.5	42.9
Ground clearance (in.)	NA	NA	NA
Wheelbase (in.)	47.4	47.8	49.4
Net weight (lbs)	191.8	191.8	211.7
ENGINE			
Type		ohc, air-cooled, four-stroke	
Bore and stroke (mm)	50.5 X 49.5	50.5 X 49.5	50.5 X 49.5
Compression ratio	9:5 : 1	9.5 : 1	9.5 : 1
Displacement (cc)	99	99	99
Valve train		chain-driven, overhead-cam	
Lubrication system		pressure and splash, wet sump	
Horsepower @ rpm		11.5 @ 11,000	
Carburetion (Keihin)		piston valve type, manual choke	
DRIVE TRAIN			
Clutch type		wet, multiple-disc type	
Transmission		constant meshed-gear type	
Power reduction (primary)		gear/4.055	
Power reduction (secondary)		chain and sprocket	
	2.857	3.071	3.142
1st	2.500	2.500	2.500
2nd	1.722	1.722	1.722
3rd	1.333	1.333	1.333
4th	1.083	1.083	1.083
5th	0.923	0.923	0.923
ELECTRICAL SYSTEM			
Ignition		battery and coil, high-voltage electrical spark	
Starting system	kick	kick	kick
Charging system		AC generator	
Battery (volts/amp hrs)	6/6	6/6	6/6
Fuse (amps)	15	15	15

General Specifications (cont.)

Model	CB125S	CD125S	SL125
DIMENSIONS			
Overall length (in.)	74.8	74.8	78.5
Overall width (in.)	29.5	29.5	31.9
Overall height (in.)	40.0	39.4	44.3
Ground clearance (in.)	NA	NA	NA
Wheelbase (in.)	47.4	47.2	50.2
Net weight (lbs)	220.0	196.2	209.5
ENGINE			
Type		ohc, air-cooled, four-stroke	
Bore and stroke (mm)		56 X 49.5	
Compression ratio		9.5 : 1	
Displacement (cc)		122	
Valve train		chain-driven, overhead-cam	
Lubrication system		pressure and splash, wet sump	
Horsepower @ rpm		12.0 @ 9,000	
Carburetion (Keihin)		piston valve type, manual choke	
DRIVE TRAIN			
Clutch type		wet, multiple-disc type	
Transmission		constant meshed-gear type	
Power reduction (primary)		gear/4.055	
Power reduction (secondary)		chain and sprocket	
	3.267	2.800	3.267
1st	2.500	2.769	2.769
2nd	1.722	1.722	1.722
3rd	1.333	1.272	1.272
4th	1.083	1.000	1.000
5th	0.923	——	0.815
ELECTRICAL SYSTEM			
Ignition		battery and coil, high-voltage electrical spark	
Starting system	kick	kick	kick
Charging system		AC generator	
Battery (volts/amp hrs)	6/6	6/6	6/6
Fuse (amps)	10	10	15

2 · Maintenance

Introduction

The importance of maintaining a motorcycle conscientiously and carefully cannot be overstressed. Apart from the obvious benefits of safety and economy, a well-maintained bike will generally be ridden with more care and consideration than a dirty, out-of-tune motorcycle. When something is wrong with a machine, even something very minor, most riders tend to become annoyed and treat the bike more harshly than they normally would. This, naturally, does nothing but aggravate the problem and may lead to component failure sooner than expected.

To counter the tendency toward frustration and anger when one's motorcycle is not right, a special attitude toward maintenance must be developed. If you stay aware and actually take notice of what you are doing, you can gain a sensitivity for your machine and know beforehand when something is wearing out or needs attention. Aircraft maintenance crews and professional racing mechanics use maintenance checklists and logbooks to make certain that no operations are overlooked and that no component is stressed beyond its maximum working life. They view maintenance as preventive action, rather than corrective action.

Motorcycle maintenance should be ap-proached in basically the same manner. Keeping a machine properly serviced need not be excessively time-consuming, but services should be performed regularly and in a professional manner. This means that the owner/mechanic should have:

1. An adequate supply of good quality tools.

2. A fairly clean place to work.

3. Enough time to do the job properly.

4. Necessary working specifications and procedures.

Just as in breaking-in a bike and getting acquainted with it, a feel should be developed for the maintenance needs of the various components. The conditions under which the machine is used will have a great bearing on how often attention is necessary. It may be beneficial to modify the maintenance schedule after a few thousand miles have been covered and the bike's peculiarities have become known.

Daily Inspection

A daily inspection doesn't have to involve more than a quick "confirmation" check of the bike and should take no more than a few seconds. Items to be checked before each ride include:

1. Operation of the lights (especially the brake light).

2. Brake adjustment.
3. Engine oil level.

Weekly Inspection

In addition to the items that are checked daily, inspect and adjust, if necessary:

1. Tire pressure.
2. Chain adjustment.
3. Battery electrolyte level.
4. Clutch adjustment.
5. Lubricate control cables and pivots.
6. Tightness of critical nuts and bolts such as axle nuts, engine mounting bolts, and control fasteners.

It would be a good idea to clean the bike as thoroughly as time permits, even if it is only to hose it down and wipe it dry. A motorcycle can accumulate an amazing amount of dirt in a short time and, if it is allowed to build up for more than a few weeks, it will take hours to clean. If the bike is taken to a car wash with high-pressure spray equipment, be careful to keep the spray away from the air filter, carburetor, and wheel bearings—hot water under pressure can work itself into all kinds of places where it shouldn't be. Remember to check the brakes after washing, as water can make them useless on the first few applications. Drag them slightly, if necessary, to dry them out. Start and run the engine for at least ten minutes to evaporate any water that has accumulated in vital areas.

Periodic Maintenance

ENGINE

Oil Changes (1,000 mi / 60 days summer, 30 days winter)

In any high-performance engine, the oil plays a vital part in maintaining smooth, trouble-free running and component longevity. Not only does the oil lubricate moving parts but it must also act as a coolant, which is especially important in an air-cooled engine.

Honda recommends that the oil initially be changed at 200–600 miles and thereafter at 1,000 mile intervals. Frequent oil changes are excellent life insurance for any engine, however, and some discretion should be exercised on the part of the rider as to when the oil *needs* to be changed. For example, during the first 2,000 miles, the engine will be tighter, run hotter, and have more abrasive particles in the oil than at any time in its life. Accordingly, changing the oil at say, 500 mile intervals during this period would be wise. If the motorcycle is ridden in stop-and-go traffic or cold weather, the oil should again be changed more frequently to prevent acids and condensation that accumulate during this kind of service from corroding the engine or diluting the oil.

Change the oil after the engine has been run long enough to reach operating temperature. This ensures that the oil is fluid enough to drain completely and that impurities suspended in the circulating oil will be removed. Honda recommends that SAE 10W-40 or 10W-50 oil of SD (previously MS) service rating be used. For even better protection, you can use the new SE-rated oils, which are able to withstand more heat than SD-rated oil before breaking down. If a single-viscosity oil is to be used, it must be a high-detergent (heavy-duty) oil of SD service rating. For temperatures above 60° F, use SAE 30W-30 oil; between 32 and 60° F, use SAE 20W-20; and below 32° F, use SAE 10W-10 oil. Do not use vegetable-based or non-detergent oil.

SAE GROUPS	OUTSIDE TEMPERATURE	SAE GROUPS
#30	°C °F	
#20or	15 — 60	#10W-30
#20W		
#10W	0 — 32	

Specified grades of oil

Remove the drain plug from the crankcase sump and remove the filler cap to assist draining. When most of the oil has drained, kick the engine over a few times to remove any oil remaining in the delivery system. Replace the drain plug and refill the engine with the correct grade and amount of oil. Start the engine and let it idle for a minute or so to circulate the oil.

Crankcase drain plug

1. Drain plug

Turn the engine off and check the oil level with the filler dipstick. To obtain a true reading on the dipstick, three precautions must be observed:

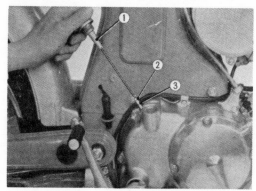

Oil level dipstick

1. Dipstick
2. High level mark
3. Low level mark

1. Allow the oil a few seconds to drain down into the crankcase.

2. Place the machine on its center stand, on a level surface.

3. Do not screw the dipstick/filler cap into the case when checking the oil level or a false (high) reading will be obtained. Add oil if necessary to bring the level to the upper mark on the dipstick.

Oil Filter (3,000 mi)

A centrifugal oil filter is used on all models other than the 90 cc bikes, and all of the engines have an oil screen filter which must be cleaned periodically. The filters need not be cleaned at every oil change, but they should be attended to about twice a year, or about every sixth oil change on machines that are used daily and accumulate high mileage. Bikes used in the dirt should be serviced more often, and the oil filter should be cleaned more frequently.

1. Clean the oil filter in conjunction with an oil change. Drain the oil, but do not reinstall the drain plug yet.

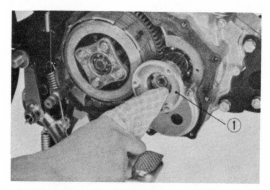

Cleaning the centrifugal oil filter

1. Centrifugal oil filter

2. Remove the right crankcase cover on all models and pull out the oil screen. On 100 and 125 cc models, remove the right crankcase cover to get at the centrifugal oil filter, and the left-side filter cap to get at the pump screen.

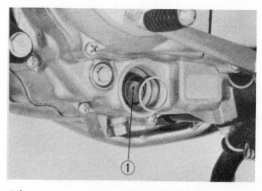

Oil pump screen (100 and 125 cc models)

1. Oil pump screen assembly

3. Clean centrifugal oil filters by wiping all dirt and grit from the surface with a clean rag. Remove the centrifugal oil filter cap (100 and 125 cc models) and wipe out the inside of the filter with a clean rag.

4. Pull out the oil filter screen and clean it thoroughly with gasoline, blow it dry with compressed air, and replace it. The screen must be installed with the narrow portion toward the inside, and so the screen fin is to the bottom (all 50, 65, and 90 cc models). The filter on the 100 and 125 cc models fits in vertically.

5. Install the drain cap and the filter covers, then replenish the oil supply.

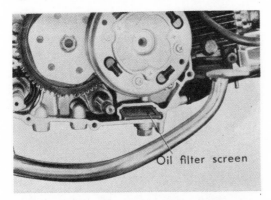

Oil pump screen (90 cc and smaller engines)

Air Filter (3,000 mi / 6 mo)

The air filter element should be serviced without fail at the prescribed intervals, or more frequently when the machine is used under dusty conditions. A dirty filter can cause poor running, excessive fuel consumption, carbon buildup, and, ultimately, overheating.

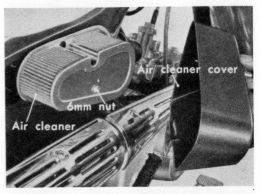

Removing the air filter element (shown is the S50 model)

On most models, the filter element is located under a right-side panel, but on step-through machines, it is located on the frame tube. Clean paper elements with compressed air (directed from the inside

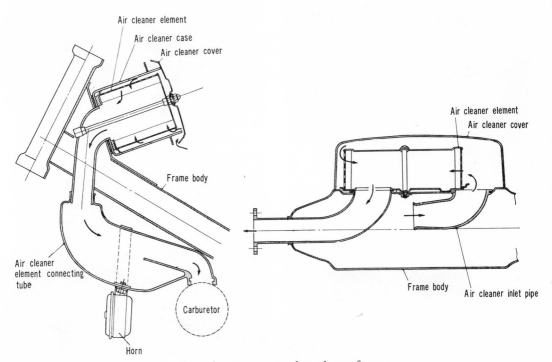

Air cleaner location on step-through type frames

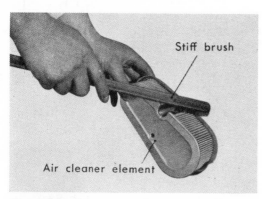

Cleaning the element

out) or by tapping the element lightly and brushing away the dirt with a stiff brush. Replace the element if it is torn or wet with oil or water. Clean rubber foam filter elements in solvent and wet the elements with a light-grade oil. Wring out any excess oil before reinstallation. Foam elements must be replaced if torn.

Clutch Adjustment (3,000 mi / 6 mo)

The clutch release mechanism should be adjusted at the prescribed intervals, or whenever the clutch begins to drag or slip and satisfactory operation cannot be obtained by adjusting (if applicable) free-play at the lever. At the time of adjustment, lubricate the grease fitting using one or two strokes of the grease gun.

S50, S65, CL70, AND SL70 MODELS

1. Adjust the clutch cable at the lever by loosening the cable adjuster locknut and rotating the cable adjuster until there is about 0.4–0.8 in. of free-play at the lever, then secure the locknut.

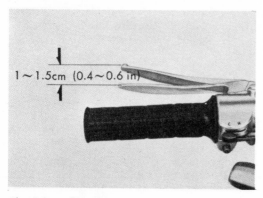

Clutch lever free-play

2. Check the operation of the clutch with the motor running. The gears should engage quietly and smoothly, and the bike should not tend to creep while in first gear with the clutch engaged. Go on to the next step if the clutch drags or slips.

3. If you can't arrive at a suitable adjustment, remove the clutch cover, loosen the adjusting screw locknut, and rotate the adjusting screw to the right until you feel tension on it, then rotate the screw $1/8$–$1/4$ turn to the left. This should be the correct adjustment give or take $1/8$ of a turn. Secure the locknut while holding the adjusting screw and check the adjustment with the motor running. It may be necessary to readjust the cable at this time.

Adjusting the clutch

C50, C50M, C65, C65M, C70, C70M, C90, AND CT90 MODELS

1. Loosen the clutch adjusting screw locknut located on the right-side crankcase, then rotate the screw to the left until there is tension on it. Rotate the adjusting screw about $1/8$ of a turn to the right and secure the locknut while holding the screw steady.

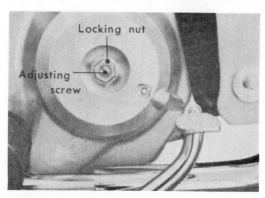

Adjusting the clutch

2. Check the adjustment by starting the motor and placing the transmission in first gear. The adjustment determines how fast the clutch will engage when the throttle is opened. If the bike starts to creep before the throttle is opened, the adjustment will have to be done again and the screw will have to be turned about 1/8 turn to the right. If it takes too long for the clutch to engage when the throttle is opened, the adjusting screw will have to be turned slightly to the left. If the initial adjustment is not correct, you will have to make small adjustments until you arrive at a suitable adjustment.

S90, CL90, CL90L, AND CD90 MODELS

1. Adjust the clutch cable until there is about 0.4–0.6 in. of free-play at the lever by loosening the knurled locknut at the lever and rotating the upper adjuster of the clutch cable.

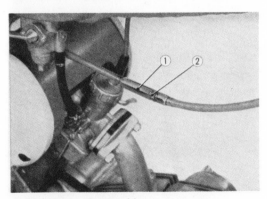

Adjusting the clutch cable

1. Clutch cable adjuster   2. Adjuster locknut

2. Start the motor and put the transmission in first gear. If the clutch is properly adjusted, the gear change will be quiet and smooth, and the bike will not creep or stall. If the clutch performs well, secure the locknut. If you were unable to arrive at the proper amount of free-play, check to see if there is another adjuster near the bottom of the cable. This can be used to take up excessive slack, or allow for more free-play, and is adjusted by loosening the locknut and rotating the adjuster.

ALL 100 AND 125 CC MODELS

1. Loosen the locknut at the clutch lever and rotate the cable adjuster until there is excessive play at the lever, then loosen the

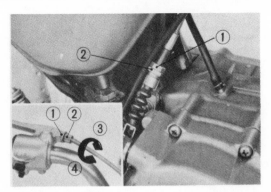

Adjusting the clutch cable

1. Adjuster locknut   3. To increase play
2. Cable adjuster   4. To decrease play

locknut located near the kick-start lever. Rotate the adjuster screw counterclockwise until a slight resistance is felt, then rotate the screw clockwise about 1/8–1/4 of a turn and secure the locknut.

Adjusting the clutch push rod

1. Locknut   2. Adjusting screw

2. Rotate the cable adjuster until there is about 0.4–0.8 in. of free-play still left at the lever, then secure the cable adjuster locknut.

3. Start the engine and place the transmission in first gear. If the clutch is adjusted correctly, the engagement will be quiet and smooth. If the bike tends to stall, creep, or if the clutch slips, start over and change the adjustment about 1/8 turn. Minor adjustments can be made entirely at the clutch lever if doing so doesn't make the cable too loose or tight. If you have trouble getting the transmission back into neutral, don't worry because that's common to most Hondas. Just slip the clutch a little while lifting up on the shift lever and the transmission should go into neutral.

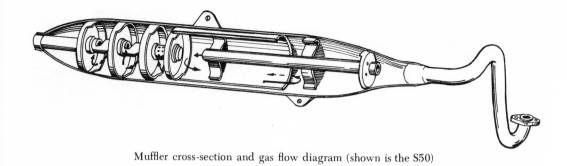

Muffler cross-section and gas flow diagram (shown is the S50)

MUFFLER (3,000 MI)

Whatever doesn't get burned completely in the combustion chamber winds up somewhere as a carbon deposit. The baffle (diffuser pipe) in your muffler is a favorite meeting place for these carbon particles and, consequently, must be cleaned periodically. A carbon-clogged baffle can cause your machine to lose power and overheat, so periodically, or whenever you think it needs it, clean out the baffle.

The baffle is located in the tip of the muffler (on models on which the baffle can be removed), and is removed by removing the securing nut and pulling out the baffle.

muffler can eat away the walls of the muffler and cause it to leak. A muffler or exhaust pipe with as much as a pin hole in it can cause a popping in the muffler that will be most noticeable when decelerating. The muffler itself can also be decarbonized by running a length of chain through it repeatedly. This, however, is not as important as keeping the baffle clean.

BATTERY

The battery is located behind the left-side panel and has the fuse carrier connected to it. The electrolyte level can be checked through the clear battery case.

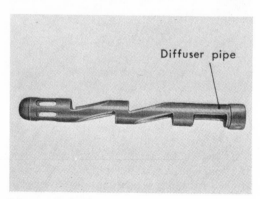

Exhaust pipe baffle

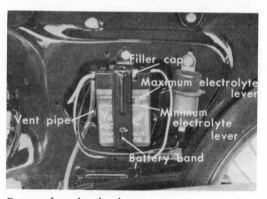

Battery electrolyte level

It may be difficult to remove if it has gotten caked in, so you may have to remove the entire muffler and poke it out. Clean the baffle as well as possible in kerosine or gasoline, then place it in an open area and set it on fire. When the fire burns out and the baffle cools off, tap it against a hard surface. All of the now well-fried carbon should flake off. If the baffle is damaged beyond redemption it should be replaced.

Inspect the muffler at this time for signs of rot or damage. The acids built up in the

If necessary, add distilled water to raise the electrolyte level to a position between the upper and lower marks. Do not overfill as this may cause the electrolyte to boil over and ruin your paint and chrome. Be very careful when working with a battery because electrolyte will strip off skin, clothing, etc., as well as paint and chrome, in a matter of seconds. Baking soda can be used as a neutralizer if necessary, but if the stuff gets on your skin or near your eyes, consult a physician immediately.

Check the condition of the battery

breather tube. It must extend to a point below the frame where relatively little damage can be done if the battery spills or boils over. Make sure that the tube is not pinched or closed off, or the battery may build up enough pressure to explode.

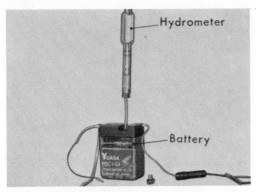

Measuring specific gravity

The state of the battery's charge should be checked periodically with a hydrometer. If the specific gravity reading on any cell is below 1.200 (at 68° Fahrenheit), the battery should be recharged. Do not use a high-output battery charger unless absolutely necessary. If the battery must be charged quickly, observe these precautions:

1. Do not charge the battery at an amperage rate greater than its rated amp/hr capacity.

2. Never allow the electrolyte temperature to exceed 110° Fahrenheit (110° F) while charging.

3. Do not quick-charge a fully discharged battery.

4. Do not quick-charge a battery in which the specific gravity of one or more cells is noticeably lower than the others.

5. Do not charge the battery in a confined room or near heat, since hydrogen gas is released during the charging.

6. Disconnect the positive battery lead if the battery is to be charged while on the motorcycle.

7. Thirty minutes is usually adequate charging time at maximum charging rate.

An adjustable, low-output (trickle) charger is an alternative to the high-output charger, and is available at most automotive supply stores at a reasonable cost. A battery that is charged at a low rate will take and retain a fuller charge, and plate

damage due to high current is less likely to occur. When charging a battery at a low rate, observe item six above and do not exceed the following charging rates:

6 AH battery—2.0 amps
9 AH battery—2.7–3.0 amps
12 AH battery—3.6–4.0 amps

Do not charge a battery for an extended period of time at a rate of charge greater than $\frac{1}{10}$ its amp/hr (AH) rating.

When rechecking the specific gravity of the cells after charging, allow sufficient time for the gas bubbles to be released or a false (low) reading will be obtained. A good battery should have a specific gravity reading of 1.260–1.280 in all cells at 68° F. The battery is in need of replacement if one or more of the cells is excessively low. If a charging system fault is suspected as the reason why the battery goes dead, consult chapter seven for additional information.

Do not neglect to keep the battery case and terminals clean. A solution of baking soda and water works well to remove corrosion, but take care to keep the baking soda from entering any of the cells or the electrolyte will be neutralized. Petroleum jelly can be used as a corrosion inhibitor on the terminals after they have been cleaned.

Check the level of the battery every week. Electrolyte evaporates rapidly in the summertime and you may wind up with a dry battery after only a few weeks.

FUEL SYSTEM (3,000 MI/6 MO)

The fuel filter, located in the fuel tap, should be removed and cleaned at the pre-

Petcock

scribed intervals or whenever fuel feed problems are encountered. Simply turn the fuel tap to "stop" and unscrew the cup to gain access to the filter. Fuel flow at both the "on" and "reserve" positions can be checked at this time. If the tap allows any gasoline to pass while in the "stop" position, the tap should be repaired or replaced, as gasoline may leak into the crankcase and dilute the oil.

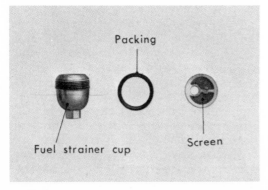

Fuel strainer

Clean the filter screen and reinstall the cup and filter on the fuel tap. Use a new O-ring if necessary. Do not overtighten the cup. Examine the fuel lines for leakage and for restriction caused by kinks or sharp bends. Check to see that the vent hole in the tank filler cap is not plugged to preclude the possibility of fuel starvation.

Do not start the engine until all spilled gasoline has evaporated or has been wiped off the engine. Use a can or jar to catch the gasoline when testing the fuel flow.

FRONT SUSPENSION AND STEERING (6,000 MI/12 MO)

Steering Head Bearings

Precision steering and stable handling are very much dependent upon the steering head bearings. To check the bearings, place the bike on its center stand and swing the forks slowly through their full steering travel from stop to stop. Movement should be smooth, light, and free from any binding. Check for play in the bearings by grabbing the bottom of the forks and trying to move them back and forth in line with the motorcycle. Play can be removed by tightening the steering head main nut. Tighten the main nut no more than necessary to remove play, and

then recheck the forks' motion. If the steering movement remains unsatisfactory, the bearings should be replaced.

Fork Oil

The oil in the forks should be changed regularly to ensure proper fork operation and extend seal life. The models with a leading link front end have self-contained damping units which must be replaced if defective.

Fork leg filler caps (shown is the CB100)

1. Filler caps

Remove the small drain plug at the bottom of each fork leg and work the suspension until all the oil has been expelled. Remove the top filler plugs, replace the drain plugs, and fill the fork leg with the proper amount and grade of oil. (Consult the specifications at the end of the chapter.)

Fork leg drain plugs (shown is the CB100)

1. Drain plug

After the oil has been poured into the forks, work them up and down to expel any air in the hydraulic passages before replacing the filler caps.

The recommended lubricant need not be

used. There are many oils designed strictly for front fork use that will provide efficient fork operation, but any good engine oil may be used. You may wish to beef up the suspension by trying out various viscosities of oil. The only thing to avoid is overfilling the forks, as this may cause the seals to blow. It is a good idea, however, to add about 10 cc more oil than is recommended to compensate for the oil which remains in the container used to pour the oil.

REAR SUSPENSION (3,000 MI/6 MO)

Lubricate the swing arm pivot grease fitting(s) using a high-pressure grease gun. Wipe off any excess grease. There should be absolutely no side-play and the swing arm must not be bent or weakened from cracked welds or else handling (especially at high speeds) will become erratic. Check to see that the bushings at the shock absorber mounting eyes are in good condition by attempting to move the swing arm up and down by hand and watching for play. Consult the "Chassis" chapter for additional information.

WHEELS, TIRES, AND BRAKES (3,000 MI/6 MO)

Wheels

Check the tightness of the spokes, but unless a spoke is obviously too loose, do not attempt to tighten it or the wheel may become distorted. Tighten a loose spoke until it is approximately as taut as the neighboring spokes. If any spokes are broken, or if a large number are loose, the wheel should be removed for complete servicing. Consult chapter eight for additional information.

Check the adjustment of the wheel rim with a dial indicator if the tire is wearing unevenly or if a wobble is apparent at low speeds and grows progressively worse as speed is increased. If the run-out exceeds 0.08 in. (2 mm), the wheel must be trued or replaced.

Tires

Examine the tires for casing damage (splits, bubbles, etc.,) and for objects lodged in the tread. Replace the tires before the tread is completely worn off or if the tread becomes unevenly worn, because it may prove more costly to repair the bike

if you dump it. Always maintain the correct tire pressure and always check the pressure before riding since heat causes the air inside to expand. If you plan to do some high-speed riding, if you weigh a lot, or if you plan to do most of your riding with two aboard, it is a good idea to increase the pressure a couple of pounds. A good rule of thumb is to increase the pressure by 2 lbs for every weight increase of 50 lbs over the norm (usually considered as a rider of 150 lbs).

Brakes

Brake lining wear on drum brakes can be determined by observing the angle formed by the brake operating lever and rod (at the drum) while the brake is applied. When the lever and rod move past perpendicular as the brake is applied, the brake shoes should be replaced.

The brakes on all of the models are adjusted by rotating the adjusting nut at the hub (for front brakes), or at the brake rod (for rear brakes). Rotating the adjuster clockwise will decrease the amount of

Front brake adjuster

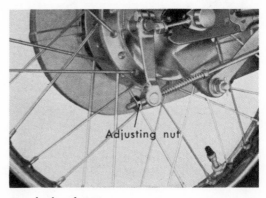

Rear brake adjuster

free-play at the brake lever or pedal, and rotating it counterclockwise will increase the amount of free-play. Make sure the cutaway portion of the adjusting nut is seated against the lever or a false adjustment will result. Minor adjustments can be made at the handlever on the 100 and 125 cc models by loosening the knurled locknut and rotating the adjuster until a satisfactory adjustment is obtained. Free-play should be about ¾–1¼ in. at both brakes but this is mostly a matter of personal preference. Check the adjustment by raising the wheel and rotating it. If you can hear the brakes dragging or if the wheel does not spin freely, back off on the adjuster until there is sufficient clearance between the brake shoes and the drum.

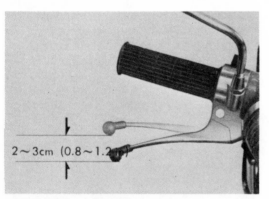

Front brake lever free-play

Rear brake pedal free-play

Sooner or later you'll come to the point where there is no more room left for adjustment since the shoes have worn down. Unless the shoes are worn past their serviceable limit (consult the "Brakes" section for procedures and specifications), the brake actuating lever itself can be adjusted

so that what remains of the shoes can be used. Remove the lever by removing the pinch bolt and prying the lever open. When it is spread sufficiently, it will be able to be slipped off the shaft. Rotate the lever a few degrees to the rear for rear brakes and to the front for front brakes, slip it back on the shaft, and secure it with the pinch bolt. The brakes can now be adjusted according to the information given in the previous paragraph. Never do this without taking down the brake and inspecting the shoes, as you may be placing the hub in jeopardy; if the shoes are too thin they may wear down to the rivets quickly, and rivets score brake drums almost immediately.

FINAL DRIVE

Chain Adjustment and Lubrication

To check the chain adjustment, place the bike on the center stand and move the chain up and down at the midpoint of either run. On models with a fully enclosed chain, remove the inspection hole cap and check the adjustment through the hole. If the total movement exceeds 1.5 in., the chain is too loose and must be adjusted.

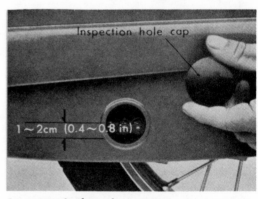

Inspecting the drive chain tension

The procedure is as follows:
1. Loosen the rear axle nut until it can easily be turned by hand.
2. Rotate the adjuster nuts evenly until the play is reduced to within ½–¾ in. Turning the adjusters an unequal amount will adversely affect wheel alignment, so make sure the adjusters are both aligned with the same punch marks on the swing arm.

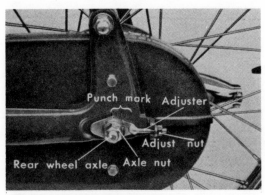

Adjusting the drive chain

3. Secure the axle nut firmly and re-check the alignment and chain adjustment to make sure you haven't moved the axle while tightening the nut. Inserting a screwdriver through the rounded end of the axle will hold it in place while the nut is secured.

NOTE: *A dry chain should be lubricated before adjustment so that the links will not bind and restrict chain movement, making it seem tighter than it really is. If tension varies alternately between too loose and too tight as the chain is rotated, remove it and inspect for excessive wear after it has been thoroughly cleaned and lubricated. If the rear suspension has been modified it is a good idea to adjust the chain with someone sitting on the rear portion of the seat so the swing arm is in its riding position.*

It is very important to keep the drive chain lubricated at all times. It will be necessary to use a special-purpose motorcycle chain lubricant, as regular engine oil doesn't penetrate the rollers or cling adequately. A wax-based product is probably the best bet unless you're into periodically soaking the chain in a liquified grease and graphite solution. Depending upon riding speed, mileage, weather, and chain and sprocket condition, it may be necessary to lubricate the chain as much as one or more times a day (especially if you are riding in sand which is a notorious chain and sprocket killer). To avoid excessive oil fling-off after the chain has been lubricated, allow the machine to sit for at least 10 minutes before riding it. Most chain lubricants contain a thin compound to aid accurate delivery and complete penetra-

tion that will evaporate in a few minutes, leaving a thick lubrication compound that will not be thrown off.

A dry chain can cause a noticeable drop in performance and as much as a 25 percent increase in fuel consumption. It can also wear out sprockets prematurely and, of course, the risk of chain breakage is increased, an occurence which is never to be encouraged as it takes a heavy bite out of spokes, crankcases, chainguards, and legs. To prevent this, it is wise to replace the chain when it begins to give indications of becoming tired; i.e., stretching quickly after adjustment, tight and loose spots along the run, and being worn to a point where a link can be lifted more than about $1/4$ in. or $1/2$ of a tooth away from the rear sprocket after adjustment. The chain is the weakest link in the drive train and should be given the attention necessary to keep it in good condition.

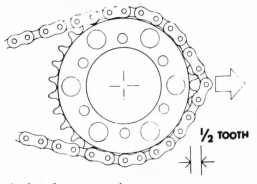

Checking for excessive chain wear

Sprockets (3,000 mi / 6 mo)

Sprockets should be examined for wear. If the rear wheel is out of alignment, the sprocket teeth will show wear on their sides. If the sprocket is worn due to age or a worn chain, the teeth will be slightly

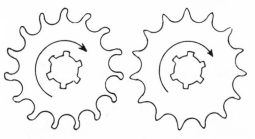

Sprocket with wear spots   Unworn sprocket

Checking the sprockets for wear

hooked, with the hook facing away from the direction of rotation. If either sprocket is damaged or worn noticeably, both sprockets should be replaced. A worn sprocket can ruin a good chain, and a worn chain can ruin a good sprocket. Sprocket life will also be reduced considerably by an improperly adjusted or lubricated chain.

Storage Procedure

WINTER STORAGE

A few precautions should be taken when the motorcycle is to be out of use for a relatively short period of time, as during the winter season. If the following procedures are carried out, there will be very little likelihood of damage to the machine.

1. Wash the bike thoroughly and ride it until the engine is fully warmed and all water has evaporated.

2. Change the engine oil and clean the oil filters.

3. Run the engine a minute or two to circulate the fresh engine oil.

4. Top up the tank with the brand of gasoline normally used.

5. Turn off the fuel tap, remove the air filter element, start the machine, and squirt a few shots of oil into the carburetor to thoroughly lubricate the valves, rings, and cylinders. Switch off the ignition and reinstall the filter element.

6. Remove the drain plug or float bowl (if applicable) and allow the carburetor to drain thoroughly. Don't allow the gas to spill onto the hot engine.

7. Check the battery electrolyte level and state of charge. Recharge it thoroughly if necessary and top it off with distilled water. Clean off the battery and coat the terminals with petroleum jelly. Disconnect the positive lead during storage and store the battery in a cool dry place.

8. Lubricate all points on the machine: grease fittings, lever pivots, cables, chain, etc.

9. Apply a heavy coat of wax on all metal surfaces, taking special care with the chrome. If the wax is the type that can be allowed to dry before polishing, it is not necessary to buff it before storage. Dust can be removed later by buffing the dry, unpolished wax.

10. Place the bike on its center stand and throw a protective cover over it. Make sure that the cover is made of a porous material (an old blanket or a piece of canvas will do), because a material such as plastic will encourage the formation of condensation on the inner surface. If the machine is to be stored outside you can see the problem that will be caused by moisture. You should in this case go out and wipe it down frequently to prevent rusting.

When taking the bike out of storage, go over it completely, checking all points of maintenance (lubrication, battery charge, tightness of nuts and bolts, etc.,) and engine tune. Reconnect the battery and check the oil level. It may be necessary to replace the spark plugs as they often become irrevocably fouled during storage.

LONG-TERM STORAGE

In addition to the winter storage procedures, a machine that is to be out of use for a period of time much longer than two months should be given the following attention;

Eliminate steps four and seven above, and substitute;

4. Turn off the fuel tap, disconnect the fuel lines, and drain all but about one quart (1 qt) of gasoline from the tank. Pour half a cup of oil into the tank and rock the bike back and forth to coat the walls of the tank. Seal the fuel lines and fuel tap tubes.

7. Remove and fully charge the battery. It should be stored in a cool, dry environment and given a refresher charge every two months.

Periodic Maintenance Chart

This chart is concerned with those maintenance operations which should be performed with some regularity in order to maintain a high level of mechanical efficiency. If the machine is used severely or under strenuous conditions, the service intervals should be reduced considerably according to need. It can never hurt to perform these operations, but you may do your engine a considerable injustice if you neglect them.

Periodic Maintenance Chart

Service Required	Months or Miles, whichever occurs first			Thereafter Repeat Every	
	First	Second	Third		
Month	——	6	12	6	12
km	300	5,000	10,000	5,000	10,000
Mile	200	3,000	6,000	3,000	6,000
Engine Oil—change	O	Every 1,000 Miles (1,600 km)			
Oil Filter—clean	O		O		O
Spark Plug—clean and adjust or replace		O	O	O	
Contact Breaker Points—check or service		O	O	O	
Ignition Timing—check or adjust	O	O	O	O	
Valve Tappet Clearance—check or adjust	O	O	O	O	
Cam Chain—adjust	O	O	O	O	
Air-Cleaner—clean		O			O
Throttle Operation—check		O	O	O	
Carburetor—check or adjust		O	O	O	
Fuel Valve Strainer—clean		O	O	O	
Fuel Tank and Fuel Lines—check		O	O	O	
Clutch—check or adjust	O	O	O	O	
Drive Chain and Sprockets—adjust and lubricate or replace	O	O	O	O	
Front and Rear Brake—adjust	O	O	O	O	
Front and Rear Brake Shoes—check or replace			O		O
Front and Rear Brake Links—check		O	O	O	
Wheel Rims and Spokes—check	O	O	O	O	
Tires—check or replace		O	O	O	
Front Fork Oil—check and		O			O
change			O		O
Steering Head Bearings—check or adjust			O		O
Steering Handle Lock—check for operation			O		O
Side Stand Spring—check		O	O	O	
Battery Electrolyte Level—check and replenish if necessary	O	O	O	O	
Lights, Horn, Speedometer and Tachometer— check for operation or adjust		O	O	O	

Maintenance Data

Model	C50	C50M	S50
CAPACITIES			
Engine Oil (pt)	1.7	1.7	1.7
Fork Oil (cc)	——	——	——
Gas Tank (pt)	6.3	6.3	11.6
Fuel Reserve Tank (pt)	NA	NA	NA
TIRES			
Front Tire Size	2.25 X 17	2.25 X 17	2.25 X 17
Front Tire Pressure (psi)	24.2	24.2	24.2
Rear Tire Size	2.25 X 17	2.25 X 17	2.25 X 17
Rear Tire Pressure (psi)	30.0	30.0	30.0

Model	C65	C65M	S65
CAPACITIES			
Engine Oil (pt)	1.7	1.7	1.7
Fork Oil (cc)	——	——	——
Gas Tank (pt)	9.5	9.5	13.7
Fuel Reserve Tank (pt)	NA	NA	NA
TIRES			
Front Tire Size	2.25 X 17	2.25 X 17	2.25 X 17
Front Tire Pressure (psi)	24.2	24.2	24.2
Rear Tire Size	2.25 X 17	2.25 X 17	2.25 X 17
Rear Tire Pressure (psi)	30.0	30.0	30.0

Model	CL70	C70	C70M	SL70
CAPACITIES				
Engine Oil (pt)	1.5	1.5	1.5	1.5
Fork Oil (cc)	100–105	——	——	130–140
Gas Tank (pt)	12.8	9.6	9.6	NA
Fuel Reserve Tank (pt)	NA	NA	NA	NA
TIRES				
Front Tire Size	2.50 X 17	2.25 X 17	2.25 X 17	NA
Front Tire Pressure (psi)	25.6	24.2	24.2	NA
Rear Tire Size	2.50 X 17	2.50 X 17	2.50 X 17	NA
Rear Tire Pressure (psi)	28.5	30.0	30.0	NA

Model	S90	CL90,CL90L	SL90
CAPACITIES			
Engine Oil (pt)	1.9	1.9	1.9
Fork Oil (cc)	170–175	170–175	170–175
Gas Tank (pt)	14.80	15.9	17.6
Fuel Reserve Tank (pt)	NA	NA	4.2
TIRES			
Front Tire Size	2.50 X 18	2.50 X 18	2.75 X 19
Front Tire Pressure (psi)	22.0	22.0	25.6
Rear Tire Size	2.50 X 18	2.75 X 18	3.25 X 17
Rear Tire Pressure (psi)	28.0	29.5	28.5

Maintenance Data (cont.)

Model	CD90	C90	CT90	CT90 (from F. no. 000001A)
CAPACITIES				
Engine Oil (pt)	1.9	1.9	1.9	1.9
Fork Oil (cc)	——	——	——	130–140
Gas Tank (pt)	15.0	11.6	13.7	12.8
Fuel Reserve Tank (pt)	NA	NA	NA	NA
TIRES				
Front Tire Size	2.50 X 17	2.50 X 17	2.50 X 17	2.75 X 17
Front Tire Pressure (psi)	25.6	25.6	25.6	26.0
Rear Tire Size	2.50 X 17	2.50 X 17	2.75 X 17	2.75 X 17
Rear Tire Pressure (psi)	28.5	28.5	29.5	29.5

Model	CB100	CL100	SL100
CAPACITIES			
Engine Oil (pt)	2.1	2.1	2.1
Fork Oil (cc)	130–140	130–140	180–190
Gas Tank (pt)	16.0	16.0	16.0
Fuel Reserve Tank (pt)	2.5	2.5	2.5
TIRES			
Front Tire Size	2.50 X 18	2.50 X 18	2.75 X 19
Front Tire Pressure (psi)	22.0	22.0	25.6
Rear Tire Size	2.75 X 18	3.00 X 18	3.25 X 17
Rear Tire Pressure (psi)	26.5	28.0	28.5

Model	CB125S	CD125S	SL125
CAPACITIES			
Engine Oil (pt)	2.0	2.0	2.0
Fork Oil (cc)	130–140	130–140	180–190
Gas Tank (pt)	16.0	16.0	14.4
Fuel Reserve Tank (pt)	2.6	2.6	3.2
TIRES			
Front Tire Size	2.75 X 18	2.50 X 18	2.75 X 21
Front Tire Pressure (psi)	23.6	22.0	26.4
Rear Tire Size	3.00 X 17	2.75 X 18	3.25 X 18
Rear Tire Pressure (psi)	27.0	26.5	28.0

3 · Tune-Up

When performing a tune-up, you are restoring to peak efficiency certain engine components that are subject to changes in operating efficiency during use. A tune-up is nothing more than a series of adjustments performed in logical order, one at a time, to predetermined specifications. There is no guess work involved. There are no complicated disassembly procedures and it is not necessary for you to have years of experience in diagnosing engine problems and speed tuning. All tune-up operations are quite straightforward.

A tune-up involves the following procedures, in the order shown:

1. Valve clearance adjustment.
2. Spark plug service and compression check.
3. Contact points service.
4. Ignition timing.
5. Carburetor adjustment.

There are no special tools that are necessary to perform a tune-up other than the tool kit which came with the bike and a continuity tester which can be made out of a taillight bulb with two wires soldered to it.

Bear in mind that items not covered in this chapter such as air and fuel filter servicing, cleaning and checking the battery, etc., can have an effect on the results of a tune-up. It is assumed that you have maintained your bike at least passably well. If not, refer to chapter two and carry out all the engine-related maintenance procedures before beginning the tune-up.

Valve Clearance

Valves should be set with the engine stone cold. Since the clearances you will be working with are relatively small, take care to adjust the valves as closely as possible to specification. Excessive clearance can cause unnecessary noise and accelerated cam lobe wear, and insufficient clearance can be responsible for hard starting, rough running, and, ultimately, burned valves and valve seats. Take your time and make sure you've done it right. Make sure the surface of your feeler gauges is smooth and unmarred or an accurate adjustment may not be attained. After the first or second time, you will develop a feel for the correct clearance and the job will go much faster.

ADJUSTMENT

1. Remove the left crankcase cover and the tappet adjusting cap. It will be necessary to remove the seat and tank on 100 and 125 cc models. The cam chain should also be adjusted at this time.

2. Rotate the engine until the flywheel "T" timing mark is in alignment with the timing mark scribed on the crankcase.

Aligning the "T" timing mark (50, 65, and 70 cc models)

Aligning the "T" timing mark (90, 100, and 125 cc models)

3. Check the tappet clearance with a suitable feeler gauge. If there is no clearance at the tappet, the engine is on the exhaust stroke and it will be necessary to rotate it 360° to bring it to the top of the compression stroke. If the clearance is too tight or loose, checked by using the next oversize and undersize feelers, the tappet must be adjusted.

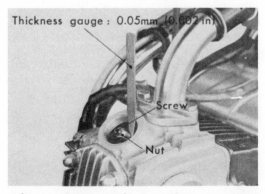

Adjusting the tappet clearance (shown is a 50 cc engine)

4. To adjust the tappet, loosen the locknut and rotate the adjusting screw in to decrease the clearance and out to increase it. The adjustment is correct when a slight tugging pressure is required to remove the feeler. When you tighten the locknut the clearance will probably tighten also, so try setting the clearance slightly loose and hold the adjusting screw with a screwdriver while securing the locknut. Recheck the clearance after the locknut is tight by comparing the fit of the next over- and under-size feeler gauge. The correct clearance for the intake and exhaust valves is 0.05 mm (0.002 in.).

5. Perform the above operations on the remaining valve.

6. Put the machine back in order before starting it. Listen to the valves by placing the tip of a screwdriver against the inspection cap and your ear against the handle of the screwdriver. You should be able to hear each valve distinctly. If you can't hear a valve, it's probably too tight and the adjustment should be performed again. Remember to wait until the engine is cold if readjustment becomes necessary.

Spark Plug Service

The condition of the spark plug has a great deal of influence upon how the engine runs. Regardless of what it looks like, the spark plug, if it has many thousands of miles on it, should be replaced at this time as a matter of course. The spark plug high-tension lead and connector should also be checked, and any component which appears to be in a less-than-perfect

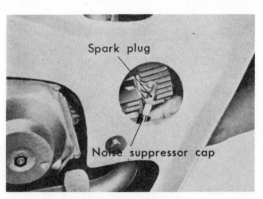

Checking a spark plug for good spark

condition should be replaced. Check the ignition coil by grounding the spark plug —while still in the high-tension lead— against the cylinder and rotating the engine. If a good healthy spark isn't produced, the coil connections should be thoroughly checked and the coil replaced if necessary. Don't hold the lead while doing this as you may get a nasty shock.

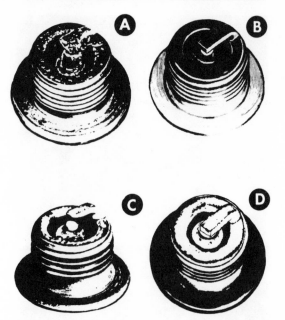

Spark plug deposits

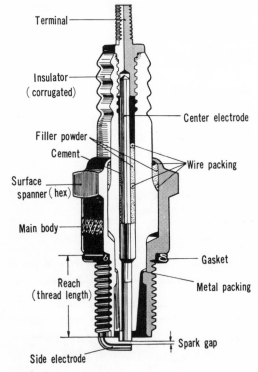

Spark plug construction

Examine the tip of the plug and decide which plug in the illustration it most closely resembles. Check also for a cracked insulator or damaged threads. Light carbon deposits can be removed in a spark plug cleaning machine (which most garages have and will probably let you use) or by carefully scraping them off with a small, sharp instrument. Heavy carbon (B) deposits are indicative of either a rich fuel mixture or a too-cold plug heat range for the conditions in which it is being used. Be wary, however, of using a hotter plug unless actual plug fouling is occurring. Heat range does not refer to spark intensity, but to the ability of a spark plug to dissipate heat. A cold plug will dissipate heat rapidly, while a hotter plug will dissipate heat more slowly. The danger in

using a plug that is too hot is that it will retain enough heat to cause preignition and, eventually, severe overheating and piston failure. Generally, you should use the plug recommended by the manufacturer, or select the coldest heat range that is possible to use without fouling. A plug which appears to have a tan, milky deposit (D) on the electrode is indicative of a well-balanced, healthy engine.

Oil fouling (A) indicates excessive oil consumption, caused by worn or sticking piston rings, worn valve stems and guides, or faulty valve stem oil seals. Do not attempt to cure oil fouling by using spark plugs of a hotter heat range. The cause of oil burning should be determined and corrected. Run a compression check as directed in the following section.

Burnt electrodes (C) indicate a fuel mixture that is too lean or a spark plug heat range that is too hot. Check for air leaks at the carburetors and intake tubes, and check the fuel tap and lines for restrictions. Try using a plug which is one step colder in heat range.

Replace any spark plugs that have damaged insulators or threads. If the old plug is to be reused, thoroughly clean the threads and insulator before installing it. Gap the electrode to about 0.025 in. and lubricate the threads lightly with graphite or engine oil before installing either a new

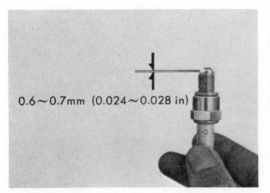

Spark plug gap

Standard compression values

or used plug, then tighten the plug down to 11–14 ft lbs in the cylinder head. Make sure to use a gasket on the plug. If you don't have a torque wrench, tighten the plug about ¼ turn past finger-tight. Threads in an aluminum cylinder head can be easily cross-threaded or stripped, and great care should be exercised when starting the plug into the threads. If you plan to run a compression check, do so before installing the plugs.

Compression Check

A compression check will tell you whether or not you have trouble in the top end. Compression pressure in the cylinder should be about 170 psi. To obtain an accurate reading, make sure the compression gauge is properly seated in the spark plug hole, and hold the throttle open all the way while cranking the engine until the needle on the gauge stops advancing.

Checking cranking compression (shown is an S50)

Low readings can indicate a leaking head gasket, valves that are too tightly adjusted or are burnt, or worn piston rings.

If you obtain a low reading, squirt a couple of shots of oil into the spark plug hole and recheck the compression. If the pressure increases significantly, the indication is that the rings are worn. If it does not increase and there is evidence of a cylinder head gasket leak, the chances are that the head gasket is blown and must be replaced. If there is no evidence of a bad head gasket or worn rings, the process of elimination points its dirty little finger at the valves. To make certain that it is not merely insufficient valve clearance that is doing you in, back out the valve adjusters a couple of turns and recheck the compression. Do this even if you have just adjusted the valves because you may have goofed. If you still don't have good compression, button it up and make a date for a top-end overhaul because a tune-up is not going to help you at this point. Be sure to reset the valves if you plan on doing any riding in the meantime.

Cam Chain Adjustment (100 and 125 cc Models)

1. Remove the tappet covers and rotate the engine until the piston is on the compression stroke and both valves are closed (play at the rocker arms). If there is no clearance at the tappets, rotate the engine 360° to bring the engine from the exhaust stroke to the compression stroke.

Cam chain adjuster

1. Adjuster locknut   2. Adjusting screw

2. Loosen the cam chain adjuster lock-nut and loosen the adjuster screw a few turns to free the tensioner. Turn the screw clockwise until there is a noticeable tension on the screw and secure the locknut while holding the screw steady. Be careful not to place too much tension on the chain.

3. Replace the tappet covers.

Contact Breaker Points Service and Adjustment

Examine the contact points for pitting, misalignment, and excessive wear of the rubbing block that rides on the breaker cam. If the points are in good condition except for a slight amount of pitting, they may be cleaned with an ignition points file. Allow the points to spring shut on the file and move the file back and forth without exerting any pressure against the

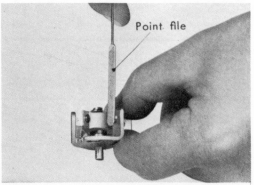

Filing contact points (It is not necessary to remove the points to perform this)

points' surface. Remove dirt and grit from between the points by pulling a thick piece of paper, such as a business card, through the points two or three times. Remember the object is to restore the points to a serviceable condition, not a like-new condition. You don't want to remove too much of the point surface. Make sure the point surfaces are seating evenly, and correct if necessary by bending the fixed point.

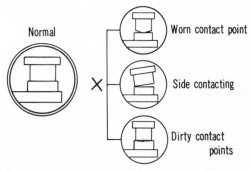

Breaker point seating conditions

If the points are heavily pitted, replace the points and condenser. These can be obtained as a unit already mounted on a base plate, or as separate components which can be mounted in place of the worn units. Disconnect the electrical leads, taking care to note where everything goes, unscrew the components from the base plate or remove the base plate assembly (depending on which method you have chosen for replacement), and mount the new parts. If single components are to be used, be sure to insulate the points properly with insulating washers which must be used in their original positions. Tighten things down firmly, but avoid using excessive pressure which may crack the insulating washers and cause unwanted grounding of the points. When the new parts are mounted, reconnect the electrical leads.

Place a drop or two of gasoline or other non-oily solvent on a piece of paper and pull it through the points to remove any dirt or preservative coating on the contact surfaces. Put a small daub of distributor cam lubricator or another high-melting-point grease on the contact breaker cam. This will prevent the points' rubbing block from wearing excessively and thereby reducing the points' gap.

BREAKER POINT GAP ADJUSTMENT

The breaker point arrangement on all of the single-cylinder engines is basically the same, except that on the 50 and 65 cc models the points are located inside the rotor rather than being separate assemblies as on the larger models.

1. Rubbing block   2. Breaker cam

1. Rotate the engine until the points are open as far as they will go. This is the point where the rubbing block is on the highest point of the breaker cam.

2. Check the point gap with a 0.3–0.4 mm (0.012–0.016 in.) feeler gauge. If the gap is incorrect, adjust it by loosening the breaker arm retaining screws so there is just a slight drag created by the pressure of the screws. (If the screws are loosened too much, the points will spring shut instead of holding an adjustment.) Pry the points to open or close them by prying with a screwdriver at the adjusting position. Secure the retaining screws when you are satisfied with the adjustment and then check it again to make sure tightening the screws hasn't altered the gap.

3. Run a business card through the points to remove any deposits which may have come off the feeler gauge.

IGNITION TIMING

Honda engines are designed to provide the same accuracy in ignition timing whether the engine is statically (without the engine running) or dynamically (with the engine running) timed. The main advantage of dynamic timing is that any defects in the automatic advance mechanism, which would not become immediately noticeable to the naked eye, become very obvious under the strobe light.

To time an engine statically, you may resort to a multitude of hack methods and still come up with a pretty accurate adjustment. The 50, 65, and 70 cc models require that such a method be used, but on the other models, a timing light is recommended.

A timing light can be made out of a tail-light bulb and two pieces of wire. Solder the leads to the bulb—one to the casing and one to the contact on the bottom of the bulb—then attach alligator clips to the lead ends. The bulb will light when the points open and thereby indicate whether the timing is advanced or retarded. A more sophisticated timing light can be made by adding a flashlight battery wired in series to the bulb. (On test lights with a battery, the light will go out when the points open.) A word of caution: if you use a light with a battery wired in series to it, the motorcycle's power source cannot be used without burning out the test light bulb. If you use just a bulb with two leads, you must use the machine's power source.

To time an engine dynamically, you need a strobe light which should be attached as directed by the manufacturer of the light. The engine should be timed while at normal operating temperature, and while running at about 2500–3000 rpm.

Static Timing

50, 55, and 70 cc Models

1. Remove the left crankcase cover. Remove the spark plug and ground it against the cylinder head while it is still attached to the high-tension lead and turn on the ignition switch. The engine can be rotated easily (on hand clutch models) by placing the machine on its center stand, shifting the transmission into high gear, and rotating the rear wheel in its normal direction.

2. Rotate the engine until the spark plug fires and then stop immediately. Observe where the "F" mark on the rotor is. If the "F" mark is aligned with the crankcase timing mark, the engine is correctly timed. If plug fired before the "F" mark reached the crankcase timing mark, the timing is advanced and must be corrected by loosening the breaker lockscrew and shifting the breaker base to the left. If the timing is retarded it must be corrected by shifting the base to the right. Try to move

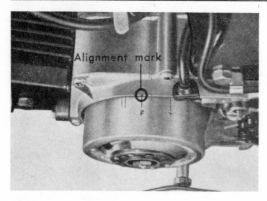

Aligning the "F" mark

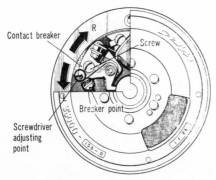

Adjusting the ignition timing (shown is a 100 cc engine)

the base a comparable distance between where the "F" mark was when the plug fired and the crankcase timing mark.

3. Secure the breaker lockscrew and re-check the timing. If the timing seems correct, replace the spark plug and the left crankcase cover.

90, 100, AND 125 CC MODELS

1. Remove the covers from the points and the left crankcase, attach one test light lead to the contact breaker arm spring and the other lead to ground (i.e., the cylinder cooling fins), and turn on the ignition switch (if applicable to the type of light in use). The engine (on all hand clutch models) can be easily rotated by placing the machine on the center stand, shifting the transmission into high gear, and rotating the rear wheel in its normal direction.

2. Rotate the engine until the test light goes out (for the type of test light that uses the machine's power source) and observe the location of the "F" mark and the crankcase timing mark. The two marks should be aligned if the timing is correct.

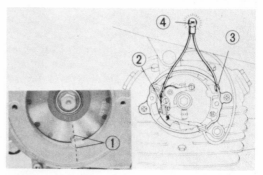

Adjusting the ignition timing and aligning the "F" mark

1. "F" aligning mark 3. Ground
2. Breaker arm spring 4. Test light

3. If the light goes off before the timing marks are aligned, the timing is advanced and can be remedied by loosening the breaker base securing screws and shifting the base clockwise to retard it. If the timing light stays on after the marks are aligned, the timing is retarded and the breaker base must be shifted counterclockwise to advance it.

Adjusting the breaker base plate

1. Base plate mounting screws 2. Base plate

4. Secure the breaker base and recheck the timing before installing the points and left crankcase covers.

Dynamic Timing

50, 65, AND 70 CC MODELS

1. Remove the left crankcase cover and connect the strobe light as directed by the manufacturer of the light.

2. With the engine running at its normal operating temperature at approximately 2500–3000 rpm, train the strobe light at the crankcase timing mark. If the timing is

Strobe timing

correct, the timing mark will appear to be between the two parallel lines on the rotor to the left of the "F" timing mark.

3. If the crankcase timing mark doesn't line up correctly, turn off the engine and shift the breaker base to the right to advance the timing and to the left to retard it. Start the motor and check for a proper adjustment again.

90, 100, AND 125 CC MODELS

1. Remove the points and left crankcase covers, and attach the strobe light according to the manufacturer's instructions.

Strobe timing

1. Timing light   2. Tachometer

2. With the engine running at its normal operating temperature at approximately 2500–3000 rpm, observe the timing marks on the rotor.

3. If the timing mark falls between the two parallel lines to the right of the "F" mark, the timing is correct. If the timing is retarded, shift the breaker base counterclockwise; clockwise if the timing is advanced. This can be done with the engine running.

4. Secure the breaker base while watching the timing marks then mount and secure the points and left crankcase covers.

Carburetor Adjustments

Carburetor tuning is largely a matter of patience and feel, the latter being developed with practice. Take your time and work with the procedures until you feel confident that the bike is responding properly. Do not hesitate to check and recheck your settings until you know they're right. After you have done it a few times, you'll be able to tune the carburetor rapidly and accurately.

It is a good practice to check the mixture after you've set it. The best way to do this is to clean the spark plug, install it, and then run the engine up to a high speed, pull in the clutch (if applicable), and cut the power. Do not allow the machine to come back to an idle or to run at low rpm before turning it off. (On centrifugal clutch models, you can only check the average operating mixture.) Remove the plug and check its condition. If you've done a good job, providing that you are using the correct heat range plug, the electrode will look tan or milky. If the mixture is too rich, the tip will look black and sooty. If the mixture is too lean, the plug will look bleached and white. Repeat the above process, while making small ($\frac{1}{8}$–$\frac{1}{4}$ turn) adjustments until the plug looks right.

If you should ever see your exhaust pipe turn yellow or blue, you can be sure that the mixture is way too lean and you should correct the situation immediately. If the bike blows dark smoke out the exhaust pipe and you are fairly sure that everything is all right inside, check for too rich a mixture and correct it immediately. It's safest to have the mixture slightly rich, but if it gets too rich it will cause accelerated carbon build up, and may cause damage to the top end because the fuel cleans the protective oil coating off the cylinder walls.

ADJUSTMENT

1. Run the engine until the normal operating temperature is reached, then set the idle speed as desired. A normal idle speed

for models with a traditional clutch set up is about 1200–1350 rpm; a normal speed for models with an automatic clutch is about 1400–1600 rpm. Idle speed is increased by turning the throttle stop screw in; decreased by turning the stop screw out.

2. Adjust the mixture by turning the air screw slowly in until the engine runs irregularly, then back it out until it begins to run irregularly again. The correct adjustment is at that point where the engine runs its smoothest and fastest, and that point is somewhere in the middle. The "Tune-Up Specifications" chart indicates the factory setting which may be used but, due to variations in the manufacturing, this may not always be the most accurate method. The chart indicates the number of turns off its seat the air screw should be turned. Take care not to bevel the seat of the adjuster by applying pressure on it.

3. Readjust the throttle stop screw if the adjustment has changed. Avoid using an idle speed very much slower than that recommended by the factory as this may cause hard starting and poor low-speed operation.

Adjusting the carburetor (50–70 cc C series models)

Adjusting the carburetor (90 cc models)

1. Throttle stopscrew   2. Air screw

Adjusting the carburetor (50–70 cc S series models)

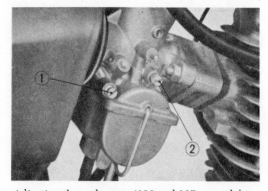

Adjusting the carburetor (100 and 125 cc models)

1. Air screw   2. Throttle stopscrew

Tune-Up Specifications

	C50 C50M S50 C65 C65M S65 CL70 C70 C70M SL70
VALVE CLEARANCE (cold)	
Intake (in./mm)	0.002/0.05
Exhaust (in./mm)	0.002/0.05
CRANKING COMPRESSION	
Pressure range (psi)	115–170
IGNITION	
Spark plugs:	
Standard make*	NGK
Type	C-7HS
Gap (in./mm)	0.024–0.028/0.6–0.7
Point gap (in./mm)	0.012–0.016/0.3–0.4
CARBURETION	
Idle speed (rpm)	1,000–1,200
Air screw opening	$1\frac{1}{8} \pm \frac{1}{4}$

Model	S90	CL90, CL90L	SL90
VALVE CLEARANCE (cold)			
Intake (in./mm)		0.002/0.05	
Exhaust (in./mm)		0.002/0.05	
CRANKING COMPRESSION			
Pressure range (psi)		115–170	
IGNITION			
Spark plugs:			
Standard make *		NGK	
Type	D-6HS	D-6HS	D-8HS
Gap (in./mm)		0.024–0.028/0.6–0.7	
Point gap (in./mm)		0.012–0.016/0.3–0.4	
CARBURETION			
Idle speed (rpm)		1,250–1,350	
Air screw opening	$1\frac{1}{4} \pm \frac{1}{8}$	$1\frac{3}{8} \pm \frac{1}{8}$	$1\frac{1}{4} \pm \frac{1}{8}$

* Other reputable makes are also acceptable. Be sure to select plugs of the correct heat range, reach, and diameter. Most spark plug application charts also have conversion tables and a heat range chart, enabling you to select the spark plug that best suits your needs. Following the specifications charts is a NGK heat range chart that will enable you to choose a plug to fit the conditions.

Tune-Up Specifications (cont.)

Model	CD90	C90	CT90	CT90 (from F. no. 000001A)
VALVE CLEARANCE (cold)				
Intake (in./mm)			0.002/0.05	
Exhaust (in./mm)			0.002/0.05	
CRANKING COMPRESSION				
Pressure range (psi)			115–170	
IGNITION				
Spark plugs:				
Standard make°			NGK	
Type	D-6HS	D-6HS	D-8HS	D-8HS
Gap (in./mm)			0.024–0.028/0.6–0.7	
Point gap (in./mm)			0.012–0.016/0.3–0.4	
CARBURETION				
Idle speed (rpm)	1,250–1,350		1,400–1,060	
Air screw opening	$1\frac{1}{4} \pm \frac{1}{8}$	$1 \pm \frac{1}{8}$	$1\frac{3}{8} \pm \frac{1}{8}$	$1\frac{1}{8} \pm \frac{1}{8}$

Model	CB100 CL100 SL100 CB125S CD125S SL125
VALVE CLEARANCE (cold)	
Intake (in./mm)	0.002/0.05
Exhaust (in./mm)	0.002/0.05
CRANKING COMPRESSION	
Pressure range (psi)	115–170
IGNITION	
Spark plugs:	
Standard make°	NGK
Type	D-8ES
Gap (in./mm)	0.025–0.028/0.6–0.7
Point gap (in./mm)	0.012–0.016/0.3–0.4
CARBURETION	
Idle speed (rpm)	1,200–1,300
Air screw opening	$1\frac{1}{2} \pm \frac{1}{8}$

° Other reputable makes are also acceptable. Be sure to select plugs of the correct heat range, reach, and diameter. Most spark plug application charts also have conversion tables and a heat range chart, enabling you to select the spark plug that best suits your needs. Following the specifications charts is a NGK heat range chart that will enable you to choose a plug to fit the conditions

Spark Plug Size and Heat Range Chart

Diameter	Reach	Wrench Size	Heat Range	NGK	DENSO
14 mm	12.7 mm	20.6 mm ($^{13}\!/_{16}$ in.)	Hot ↑	B6H	W17F
				B7H	W22F
	19.0 mm			B7E	W22E
				B7ES	W22ES
				B8E	W24E
				B8ES	W24ES
				B9E	W27E
				B10E	W31E
			Cold	B12E	W37E
12 mm	12.7 mm	18 mm	Hot ↑	D4H	X17F
				D6H	X20F
				D6HS	X20FS
				D8H	X22F
				D8HS	X22FS
				D9H	X24F
				D10H	X31F
				D10HS	X24FS
				D12H	X34F
				D13H	X37F
				D14H	X40F
	19 mm			D6E	X20E
				D7E	X22E
				D7ES	X22ES
				D8E	X24E
			Cold	D8ES	X24ES
10 mm	12.7 mm	16.0 mm	Hot ↑	C4H	U17F
				C6H	U20FB
				C7HW	U22F
				C7HS	U22FS
				C9H	U24F
				C10H	U31F
				C12HA	U34F
				C13H	U37F
			Cold	C14H	U40F

4 · Engine and Transmission

When preparing to do any work on the engine it is essential that cleanliness is maintained and that an area suitable to work in is available. Naturally, the tools and parts necessary to accomplish the task are also required. It is best, when performing a job for the first time, to familiarize yourself as much as possible with the components and procedures with which you will be working. The time spent here will be well rewarded through an increase in knowledge and confidence, and a decrease in needless mistakes and aggravation. In addition, the satisfaction gained in knowing that the job was done right is immeasurable.

Cleanliness and a careful approach are imperative. A quick ring job could become a complete engine disassembly if simple precautions are not taken. Lay out and mark all parts in sequence as they are removed; this way the correct order of reassembly will be obvious. If possible, clean the engine parts in solvent and blow them dry with compressed air. When cleaning ball or roller bearings, don't spin them until they have been thoroughly cleaned and dried because particles in the solvent bath often get caught in the bearing races and can only be removed with high-pressure air.

A good general rule to follow when disassembling an unfamiliar engine is to restrain yourself. When a nut or bolt seems to require an inordinate amount of pres-

sure to remove it, don't just give it the old heave-ho effort. Instead, sit back, relax for a few minutes, and then survey the situation. More engine damage is caused by swinging a heavy wrench than most other causes combined, and the reason is usually a mechanic who is blinded with frustration. These engines are made primarily with aluminum alloy, so you have to be careful. Use the best tools you can get your hands on, and try to avoid hammer-and-chisel techniques. An impact driver with a variety of screwdriver bits will prove to be incredibly valuable when it comes to removing side covers and all the other screws that hold the engine together.

Remember that once you've rebuilt the engine it's like new and must be broken in again. How you treat it for the first thousand miles is going to determine how well and how long it's going to keep running. Don't push a tight engine more than it wants to go. All those new parts have to wear in properly and that takes time. New engines run extra hot so it's important to keep them well timed and to not run them at constant high speeds for extended periods of time. Stop and let your engine cool off every so often if you're going a great distance. Back off while riding once in a while to get that extra oil up to the top end. If the plug starts to foul while you're riding, stop immediately and clean it off or replace it. Never try to clear it by revving the engine since it probably won't work

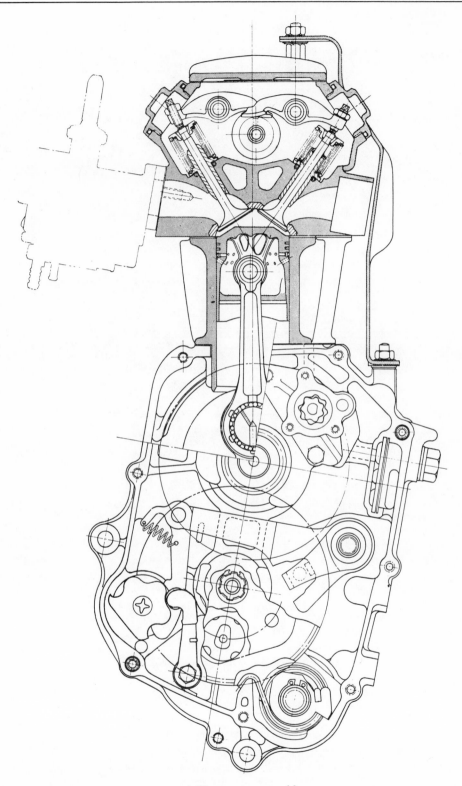

A 50 cc engine assembly

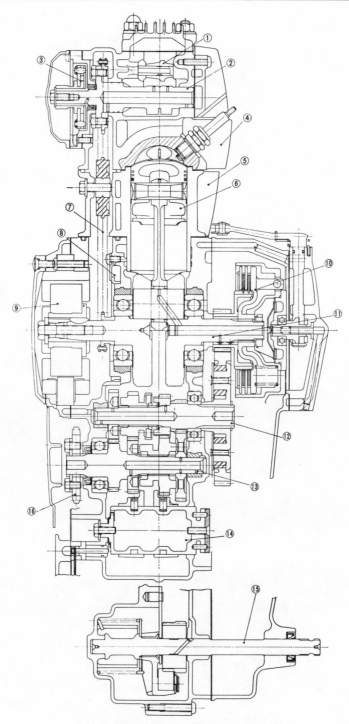

The S90, CL90, and CL90L engine assembly

1. Valve rocker arm
2. Camshaft
3. Spark advancer
4. Cylinder head
5. Cylinder
6. Piston
7. Cam chain
8. Cam chain tensioner
9. AC generator rotor
10. Clutch assembly
11. Crankshaft
12. Transmission mainshaft
13. Transmission countershaft
14. Gearshift drum
15. Kick-starter spindle
16. Drive sprocket

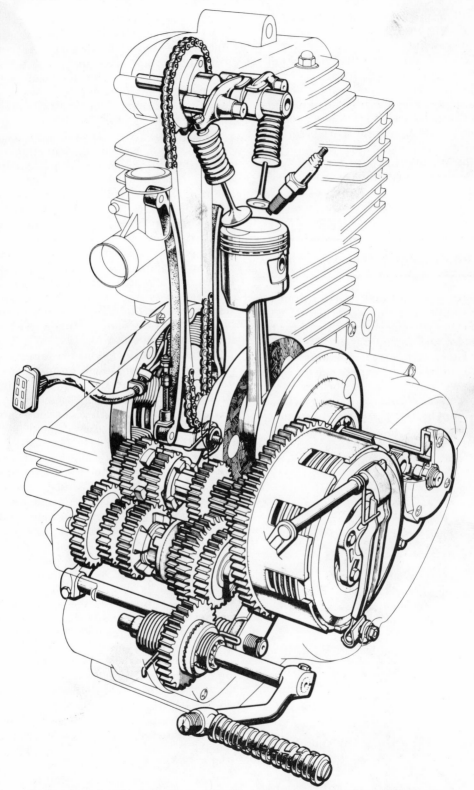

The 100 and 125 cc engine assembly. The 125 cc unit is a bored-out 100 cc engine

and will only fill the combustion chamber with oil, not the most ideal situation for your new engine.

Do the following after the first 500 miles and then again at 1,000 miles:

1. Drain the oil and replace it with fresh oil. Don't be alarmed by all the little metal filings (unless it was only a top-end job you just did), because that's natural for a new or rebuilt motor.

2. Inspect all hardware for a tight fit.

3. Replace the spark plug, set the point gap, adjust the timing, and check the carburetion.

Operational Description

Honda engines and gearboxes have earned quite a reputation for themselves as being extremely efficient and sophisticated in design, and highly durable in application. The factory's racing efforts in the mid-60s provided the experience necessary to squeeze a great deal of horsepower out of a small-displacement engine without sacrificing the reliability necessary to remain competitive in a long grueling race. The advances made with their racing engines went to producing a new breed of

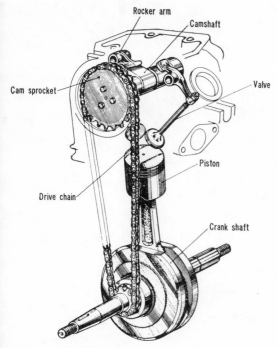

Valve mechanism

machine suitable for the general public.

All of the engines covered in this guide are overhead-cam, four-stroke, overhead-valve units that are capable of turning at very high rpms. The overhead valves are actuated by a chain-driven overhead-cam that is driven directly off the crankshaft. All but the 100 and 125 cc models come equipped with an automatic chain tensioner that is hydraulically operated. (The 100 and 125 cc models have a tensioner that is mechanically adjusted periodically.) The large particles circulating in the oil are trapped by either an oil screen, a centrifugal oil filter, or both. Two types of clutch are used on these models, an automatic or centrifugal clutch, and a more traditional type unit which is actuated by a handlever. All clutches are multiple, wet-disc types that provide smooth and accurate gear changes in conjunction with the sturdy, Honda constant-mesh transmission.

The four-stroke engine requires four complete cycles of the piston to complete one power stroke. During the intake stroke, the intake valve opens and the fuel mixture is drawn into the cylinder as a result of the sudden vacuum created in the combustion chamber by the piston's downward motion. As the piston moves toward the top of its travel on the compression stroke, both valves are closed and the combustible materials are compressed. When the breaker points are opened by the action of the breaker cam, the spark plug fires and ignites the charge. The resulting combustion forces the piston down in the power stroke. As the piston moves down toward its lowest point of travel, the exhaust valve opens. As the action of the flywheels sends the piston back up on the exhaust stroke, the remains of the previous charge are forced out through the exhaust valve. Just before the piston reaches the top of its travel the intake valve opens and the exhaust flow induces the intake flow which continues while the exhaust valve closes. The process now repeats itself since each of the four cycles has been completed.

The power flow is as follows: The energy from the combustion of the fuel mixture is transmitted to the piston which is forced down in the power stroke. The pulse travels through the connecting rod to the crankshaft and then to the clutch.

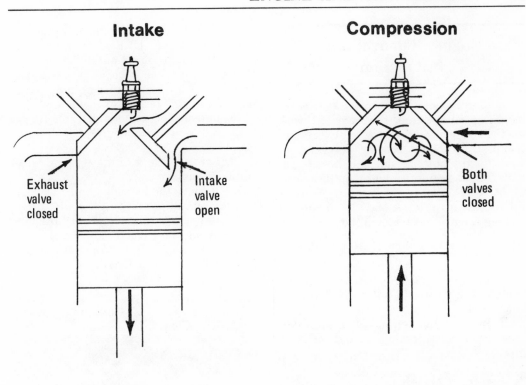

Intake

Exhaust valve closed

Intake valve open

Compression

Both valves closed

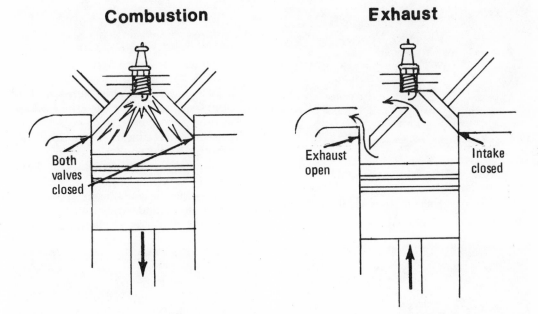

Combustion

Both valves closed

Exhaust

Exhaust open

Intake closed

Four-cycle engine operation

From the clutch it flows through the primary drive gear to the primary driven gear, through the transmission mainshaft to the mainshaft gear, and then to the countershaft gear. The energy goes through the countershaft to the drive sprocket next. From there, the power runs through the drive chain to the rear wheel, and the rear wheel puts the power onto the ground to get things rolling.

Engine Removal and Installation

On most models it is not necessary to remove the engine from the frame to work on the top end, carburetor, clutch, or oil pump. If it should become necessary to work on the bottom end, it is best to remove the engine intact and then disassemble it. Don't remove unnecessary items as this is just more work and the chance of making a costly mistake will be increased.

ALL 50, 65, AND 70 CC MODELS EXCEPT FOR THE CL70 AND SL70

1. Remove the air cleaner assembly (all models except S50 and S65), and drain the engine oil.
2. Remove the fairing (if applicable).
3. Remove the muffler and exhaust pipe.

Removing the muffler (shown is a C50)

4. Remove the footpeg assembly.
5. Remove the tool box.
6. Remove the oil lines (S50 and S65 models).

Disconnecting the oil lines

7. Remove the carburetor from the cylinder head on all "C" models and also remove the intake pipe from all "S" models. Pinch the fuel line with a hose clamp or block the line to prevent gasoline leakage onto the engine of the "C" models.
8. Disconnect the clutch cable at the lever and then at the engine (all "S" models).
9. Remove the kick-starter and gearshifter levers.
10. Remove the left-side crankcase cover and disconnect the electrical leads.
11. Rotate the rear wheel until the master link is positioned as shown, and remove the master link. Connect the ends of the chain with a length of mechanic's wire as an aid in reassembly.

Disconnecting the drive chain

12. Disconnect the high-tension lead from the spark plug and place the lead out of the way.
13. Remove the high-tension lead clip from the right-side crankcase cover.
14. Remove the brake pedal and stoplight switch return springs.
15. Remove the nuts from the engine mounting bolts and draw out the bolts while taking care not to allow the engine

Engine mounting bolt positions

to fall onto the floor. Remove the engine.

16. Installation is in the reverse order of removal. Note the following:

a. Installation can be made easier by temporarily securing the engine by inserting a screwdriver in the mounting holes while inserting the mounting bolts.

Temporarily mounting the engine

b. The brake pedal spring and the stoplight switch are mounted together.

c. Make sure the master link is in excellent condition, and mount it so the closed end is in the direction of normal wheel rotation.

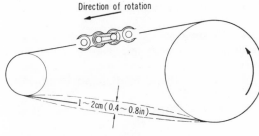

Direction of normal rotation

CL70 AND SL70 MODELS

1. Run the engine until its normal operating temperature is reached, then drain all the engine oil.

2. Remove the shifter lever, the footpeg assembly, the left-side crankcase cover, and disconnect the drive chain as described in the previous section.

3. Remove the exhaust system.

4. Disconnect the carburetor intake manifold at the cylinder head.

5. Disconnect the clutch cable at the release lever.

6. Remove the spark plug and move the high-tension lead out of the way.

7. Remove the battery cover and disconnect the three wires at the wiring harness. (The leads should be white, yellow, and pink.)

8. Disconnect the brake pedal return spring at the pedal.

9. Remove the engine mounting nuts and bolts, then remove the engine, taking care not to let it fall out of the frame.

10. Installation is in the reverse order of removal. Take care to have the closed portion of the master link facing in the direction of normal chain rotation.

S90, CL90, CL90L, AND CD90 MODELS

1. Run the engine until the normal operating temperature is reached and then drain the oil.

2. Remove the footpeg assembly, the muffler, and the left-side crankcase cover. Remove the chain as described in the previous section.

3. Disconnect the clutch cable at the release lever.

Disconnecting the clutch cable

1. Clutch cable   2. Clutch actuating lever

4. Disconnect the carburetor intake manifold at the cylinder head and place the assembly out of the way.

5. Disconnect the spark plug high-tension lead and place it out of the way.

6. Disconnect the brake pedal return spring.

7. Remove the engine mounting nuts and bolts, and lift the engine out of the frame.

8. Installation is in the reverse order of removal. Note the following:

Disconnecting the intake manifold

1. Intake manifold   2. Flange mounting bolt

a. Block up the engine under the frame.

b. Route the wiring harness up to the battery box and suspend the engine from the frame by inserting a screwdriver into a frame and engine mounting point.

c. Insert the engine mounting bolts from the left side, then secure and torque the mounting nuts.

d. Connect the brake pedal return spring to the lower mounting bolt.

e. Connect all the wiring harness leads.

f. Connect the battery leads to the battery terminals, push the wires up into the top of the battery box, install the battery, taking care not to pinch any of the wires, and route the battery overflow tube down through the bottom of the battery box.

g. Connect the clutch cable to the release lever.

h. Install the intake manifold onto the carburetor and mount the assembly to the cylinder head, taking care to correctly position the O-ring between the manifold and the cylinder head.

i. Attach the high-tension lead to the spark plug. The lead should be secured by the clip under the right-side intake manifold mounting bolt.

j. Install the muffler assembly.

k. Connect the drive chain, taking care to have the closed portion of the master link facing the direction of chain rotation. The master link must be in excellent condition.

l. Install the chaincase, the rear crankcase cover, and the footpeg assembly.

C90 AND CT90 MODELS

1. Remove the fairing or mudguard (as applicable), and drain the oil.

2. Remove the footpeg assembly.

3. Remove the chaincase rear cover and disconnect the master link after wiring the chain halves together.

4. Remove the muffler and exhaust pipe.

5. Disconnect the intake manifold at the cylinder head.

6. Disconnect the electrical leads at the connectors.

7. Remove the high-tension lead from the spark plug and place it out of the way.

8. Disconnect the brake pedal return spring.

9. Remove the engine mounting bolts and remove the engine from the frame, taking care not to drop it.

10. Consult step no. eight of the previous section for installation procedures.

SL90 MODELS

1. Run the engine until its normal operating temperature is reached, drain the oil, and then remove the muffler and exhaust pipe.

2. Remove the left crankcase rear cover and disconnect the drive chain master link. Wire the two chain halves together.

3. Disconnect the clutch cable at the release lever.

4. Disconnect the high-tension lead from the spark plug and place it out of the way.

5. Remove the intake manifold at the cylinder head.

6. Remove the kick-starter and gear-shifter levers.

7. Disconnect the electrical leads at the connectors.

Disconnecting electrical leads

Engine mounting bolt positions

8. Remove the engine mounting nuts and bolts and remove the engine from the frame.

9. Consult step no. 8 of the "S90, CL90, CL90L, and CD90 Models" section for installation procedures.

100 AND 125 CC MODELS

1. Run the engine until its normal operating temperature is reached, then drain the oil.

2. Remove the exhaust pipe and muffler.

3. Remove the footpeg assembly.

4. Disconnect the clutch cable at the release lever. It will probably be necessary to loosen the adjuster at the handlever to provide the necessary slack in the cable.

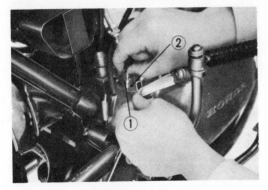

Disconnecting the clutch cable

1. Clutch cable   2. Clutch actuating lever

5. Disconnect the carburetor at the intake manifold.

6. Remove the gearshifter lever.

7. Remove the left-side, rear crankcase cover, then disconnect the drive chain and wire the halves together.

8. Disconnect the coupler from the wiring harness.

Disconnecting the electrical couplers

1. Electrical couplers

9. Remove the engine support nuts and bolts, then remove the engine from the frame.

Engine mounting bolt positions

10. Install the engine in the reverse order of removal. Note the following:

a. Hang the engine on the frame by inserting a screwdriver through the frame and engine mounting points.

b. Temporarily install the exhaust system before performing the final torquing.

c. Make certain that the closed portion of the master link is facing in the direction of chain rotation, and that the link is in excellent condition.

Top-End Service

50, 65, AND 70 CC MODELS
Cylinder Head
REMOVAL AND DISASSEMBLY

1. Run the engine until normal operating temperature is reached, then drain the oil.

2. Remove the left-side crankcase cover, and remove the right- and left-side cylinder head covers.

Cylinder head covers

3. Remove the flywheel using either the Honda puller (tool no. 07016-00102) or a suitable substitute, then remove the stator.

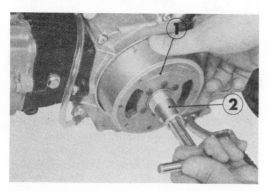

Removing the flywheel

   1. Flywheel generator   2. Flywheel puller

4. Rotate the engine until the key of the left crankshaft is pointing toward the cylinder head, and so the "O" mark on the cam sprocket is at its topmost position.

Removing the cam sprocket

5. Remove the AC generator rotor and stator from C70M models, then remove the circlip securing the starter motor sprocket, and remove the starter chain, starter motor sprocket, and the starting sprocket.

6. Remove the three bolts which secure the cam sprocket to the cam, and remove the sprocket.

Cam sprocket and sprocket mounting bolts

   1. Cam sprocket   2. Sprocket mounting bolts

7. Remove the nuts securing the cylinder head to the cylinder, and remove the cylinder head. Tap the head gently with a hammer and wood block if it is reluctant to come off.

8. Remove the cam chain guide roller pin, then remove the roller.

9. Remove the rocker arms and the cam from the cylinder head. Use a 6 mm bolt for pulling out the rocker arm pin.

10. Using either the Honda valve spring compressor (tool no. 07031-20001) or a suitable substitute, compress the valve springs until the keepers can be removed, then remove the valve assemblies. Keep the assemblies separate for reassembly in their original positions.

Removing the cam chain roller assembly

1. Cam chain roller guide   3. Roller pin
2. Sealing washer (8 mm)

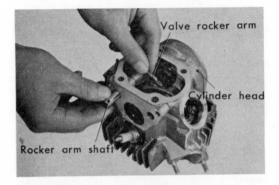

Valve rocker arm

Cylinder head

Rocker arm shaft

Disassembling the rocker arms

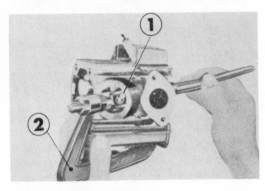

Disassembling the valves

1. Valve collar   2. Valve spring compressor

INSPECTION AND REPAIR

1. Clean all parts in a suitable solvent and blow them dry. Carbon deposits on the piston and head can be softened with a decarbonizing solvent and scraped off with a blunt instrument such as a butter-knife. Do not use a caustic soda solution to clean aluminum parts. Avoid gouging the piston crown or removing any metal. It is not necessary to restore the components to a like-new condition. Perodically, as you work, wipe the surface clean with a clean rag soaked in clean gasoline. If this is done with the cylinder still in place, you can catch the carbon flakes by pressing a line of grease around the piston on top of the rings. Rotating the piston will leave the grease ring with the carbon trapped in it on the cylinder, and it can then be wiped out. The cylinder head assemblies should be disassembled before being decarbonized.

2. Inspect the cylinder head for warpage on the gasket surface by laying a straightedge across the head and measuring the distance between the straightedge and the gasket surface with feeler gauges. If the clearance exceeds 0.002 in. (0.05 mm), the head must be repaired or replaced. Repair the head in the following manner:

a. Place a sheet of fine grit emery paper on a flat surface and move the head around in a figure-eight motion

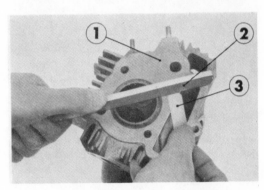

Checking the cylinder head for warpage

1. Cylinder head   3. Feeler gauge
2. Straightedge

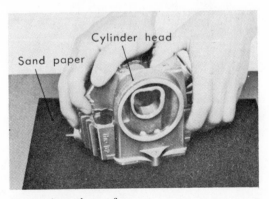

Cylinder head

Sand paper

Truing the gasket surface

while applying mild pressure. It is better to work slowly with mild pressure than quickly with heavy pressure. Don't remove any more metal than is necessary.

b. An alternative method is to use a piece of glass and a fine valve grinding compound instead of the emery paper.

c. Check the results with Prussian blue or red lead. To do this, lay out some very fine sandpaper on a flat surface. Coat the gasket surface of the head with the dye and allow it to dry. Move the head very gently over the sandpaper just long enough to remove the dye, then look at the gasket surface. If the head is flat all of the dye will have been removed. If there is still dye on the head, repeat the entire process or consult your dealer.

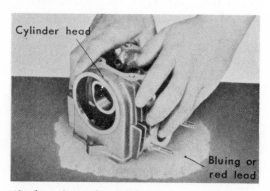

Checking the results with dye

3. Inspect the valve seat for a contact surface in excess of 0.080 in. (2.0 mm) and cut the seat if necessary until the seat width measures 0.040–0.051 in. (1.0–1.3 mm). For the valve seat contact area, 30° and 60° cutters are used; a 45° cutter is used for the valve contact area. This should not be attempted by those inexperienced with aluminum heads as it is too easy to remove too much metal. Consult

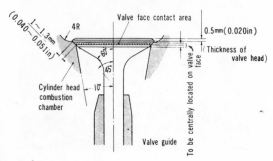

Valve seat contact area

Cutting a new valve seat

your dealer for the name of a qualified machinist. Valve faces and stems may be reground if necessary, but replacement is advised. Valves with a stellite face must be replaced as they cannot be ground. Always lap in a new valve.

4. If the seat has just been cut, or if the seat looks alright and you just want to ensure a good seal between the seat and valve, lap the valves in at this time in the following manner:

a. Lightly oil the valve stem and insert it in the guide.

b. Apply a light coat of lapping compound to the seat. It is best to apply a few evenly spaced daubs rather than a random application.

c. Slip a gas line over the valve stem and rotate it back and forth in your hands while applying mild pressure against the seat by pulling on the gas line.

d. Clean the seat area when smooth and assemble the valve. Pour some gas into the spring-side of the head and allow the head to sit. If there is no leakage through the seat, the lapping has been successful.

5. Measure the clearance between the valve stem and guide with a dial indicator, then measure the diameter of the valve with a micrometer. Measure the valve in several places and replace it if worn or unevenly worn. Replace the guide if worn or damaged in the following manner:

a. Remove the guide from the head with either the Honda valve guide remover (tool no. 07047-04001) or a suitable drift. If drifting, heat the head in an oven to about 200° F to loosen the guide.

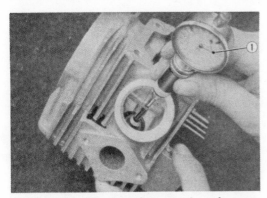

Measuring the clearance between the valve stem and guide

1. Dial indicator

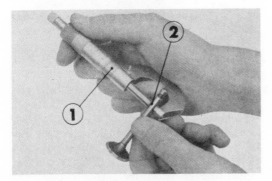

Measuring the valve stem

1. Micrometer   2. Valve

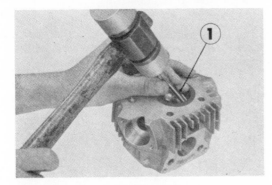

Drifting out the valve guide

1. Valve guide drift

b. Install a new guide that is one size over the previous one, then ream it to size with either the Honda reamer (tool no. 07008-24001) or a suitable substitute. Take care not to deform the guide, and oil the reamer lightly when it encounters interference. Remove metal chips as soon as they occur, and always continue to rotate the reamer when removing or installing it.

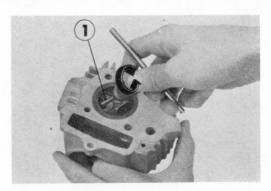

Reaming the valve guide

1. Valve guide reamer

6. Inspect the valve springs for a worn, collapsed, or damaged condition, and replace them if necessary. If a spring is noticeably shorter than a new one, or if it is shorter than the serviceable limits listed in the specifications charts at the end of this chapter, replace the spring set.

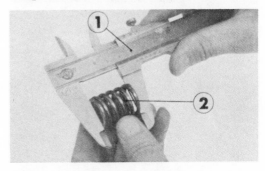

Measuring the valve springs

1. Vernier caliper   2. Valve spring

7. Inspect the cam for worn spots or damage and replace it as necessary. Measuring the cam with a micrometer will indicate if it is worn past its serviceable limit.

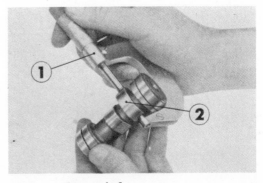

Measuring the camshaft

1. Micrometer   2. Camshaft

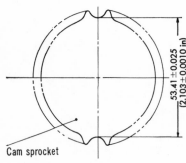

Cam sprocket

Cam sprocket teeth base contour

8. Inspect the cam sprocket for a worn or damaged condition and replace it as necessary.

9. Inspect the rocker arms for a worn or damaged condition, or for excessive play on their shafts. If the shaft is scored, the rocker arm may hang up and interfere with normal valve operation. Rockers should be replaced on the valve and shaft from which they came.

Rocker arm

1. Slipper face   2. Shaft bore

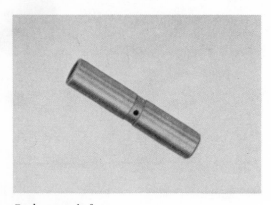

Rocker arm shaft

ASSEMBLY

1. Assembly is in the reverse order of disassembly. Make sure you use new inlet seals if they have been disturbed—regardless of how they appear. Use a new head gasket and valve keepers also, as these parts will fail easily if reused.

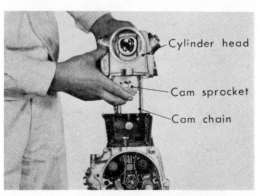

Cylinder head

Cam sprocket

Cam chain

Installing the cylinder head

2. Make sure the valve timing is correct by rotating the engine until the key of the left crankshaft is pointing toward the cylinder head, and so the "O" mark on the cam sprocket is at its topmost position.

3. Position the cylinder head nuts as illustrated and torque them down in the order shown at 6.5–9.0 ft lbs.

Cylinder head torquing sequence

Cylinder and Piston Assembly

DISASSEMBLY

1. Remove the cylinder head as described in the cylinder head "Removal and Disassembly" section.

2. Remove the cam chain guide roller pin and roller.

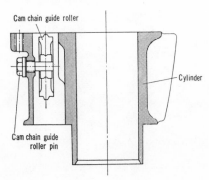

Cam chain guide roller

Cylinder

Cam chain guide roller pin

Cylinder cross-section

3. Remove the cylinder mounting bolts and lift the cylinder off the piston. This is best done with the piston at top dead center (TDC), and, as soon as there is enough room between the cylinder and the crankcase, an oil-soaked, clean rag should be inserted and wrapped around the connecting rod. This is to keep dirt and possible broken ring parts from falling into the crankcase.

Cylinder

Cylinder

4. Remove the piston pin circlip, then push the piston pin out from the opposite side with a suitable instrument. If the pin won't come free, remove the remaining circlip and drift the pin out while securely holding the connecting rod and piston steady. The piston crown may be heated with hot towels or an iron to aid in the pin removal.

5. Remove the piston from the connecting rod, and remove the piston rings if so desired by using a ring expander or by hand, taking care not to score the piston.

INSPECTION AND REPAIR

1. Consult the decarbonization section in the cylinder head "Inspection and Repair" section.

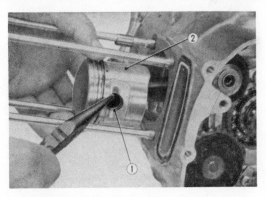

Removing the piston pin circlip

1. Piston pin circlip   2. Piston

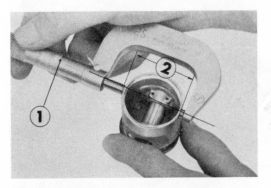

Removing the piston rings

1. Piston ring   3. Ring removing tool
2. Piston

2. Inspect the piston pin for a worn, scored, pitted, or otherwise damaged condition, and replace it as necessary. Oversize pins may be used if there is excessive clearance in the piston, but replacing the piston and pin is the better method.

3. Inspect the piston for a scored, burned, or damaged condition and replace as necessary. Measure the piston with a

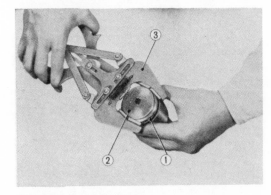

Measuring the piston

1. Micrometer   2. Piston diameter

micrometer at a right angle to the piston pin, and near the bottom of the piston skirt. The piston must be replaced if worn beyond the limit listed in the specifications chart.

4. Inspect the condition of the cylinder walls for a scored condition. The cylinder may be bored out or reamed to a serviceable condition if this will not make the cylinder walls too thin. Measure the cylinder bore at several places and replace the cylinder if worn beyond its serviceable limit.

Measuring the cylinder bore

5. Measure the piston ring end-gap to determine the necessary size of ring. Do this with a feeler gauge at the bottom of the cylinder. Oversize rings are available for standard and oversize pistons.

Measuring ring end-gap

1. Piston ring   2. Feeler gauge

6. Measure the ring side clearance with a feeler gauge, using the appropriately sized ring. The piston will have to be replaced if there is too much clearance in the ring grooves.

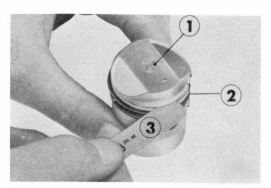

Measuring ring side clearance

1. Piston   3. Feeler gauge
2. Piston rings

7. At this time you may want to consider the bottom end. If there is excessive side-play, or up-and-down play on the connecting rod, the lower end bearing may be in need of replacement. Consult the crankcase "Disassembly" section.

ASSEMBLY

1. Assembly is basically in the reverse order of disassembly. Use new circlips and gaskets, make sure that all the components are perfectly clean, and lubricate each part with clean engine oil before assembling them.

2. Mount the rings on the piston with a ring expander if possible, or by hand, taking care not to damage the piston or break the rings. The rings should be mounted with the ring mark up. Stagger the ring gaps every 120°, and check to make sure they can rotate freely by rolling them externally in the ring groove.

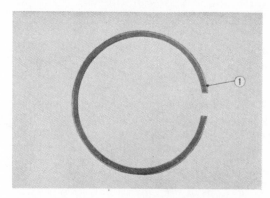

Piston ring mark

1. Ring mark

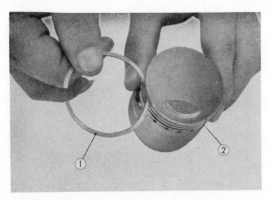

Checking piston ring contact

1. Piston ring   2. Ring grooves

3. Install the new cylinder gasket at this time.

4. Install the piston on the connecting rod so the arrow on the piston crown is pointing down. Install one circlip, position the piston on the connecting rod, slip in the piston pin, and install the remaining circlip. Lightly oil the piston pin with clean engine oil, and heat the piston crown with an iron or hot towels if necessary.

The correct position for mounting the piston

1. Arrow mark

5. Compress the rings with a hose clamp, or hold them closed by hand while slipping the cylinder down over the piston. Liberally coat the cylinder walls with clean engine oil before installing it. There should be a clean, oil-soaked rag over the crankcase hole until just before the cylinder meets the crankcase.

6. Secure the cylinder mounting bolts evenly to avoid damaging the gasket.

90 CC MODELS

Cylinder Head

REMOVAL AND DISASSEMBLY

1. Run the machine until normal operating temperature is reached, then drain the oil.

2. Remove the point cover and the left-side crankcase cover. Be prepared to catch some oil as the crankcase cover is removed.

3. Remove the stator assembly, then pull the rotor, using either the Honda rotor puller (tool no. 07011-20001) or a suitable substitute. Avoid excessive force which may damage the crankshaft.

Removing the stator assembly

1. Stator assembly

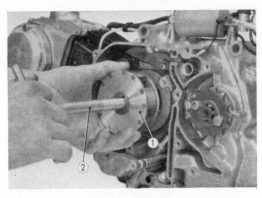

Removing the rotor

1. Rotor   2. Rotor puller

4. Remove the rocker arm side-cover.

5. Disconnect the contact breaker lead wire, remove the breaker base assembly, remove the hex bolt and the 3 x 5.2 dowel pin, then remove the breaker advance

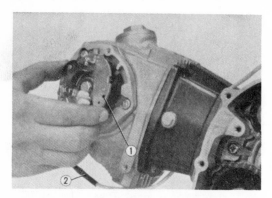

Removing the contact breaker assembly

1. Breaker assembly   2. Lead wire

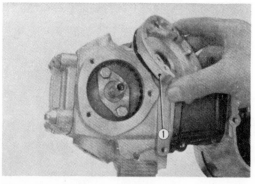

Removing the point base

1. Point base

mechanism. Remove the point base which is mounted with three screws.

6. Rotate the engine until the left crankcase woodruff key is aligned with the camshaft dowel pin hole, then remove the cam sprocket. The camshaft is now free to be removed along with the rocker arms. This

Removing the camshaft

1. Woodruff key   2. Dowel pin hole

must be done with the head still secure. Keep the rockers separate so they can be assembled as they were removed.

7. Remove the cylinder head cover and the head assembly. If the head is reluctant to separate, tap it gently with a wood block and hammer.

Cylinder head assembly

8. Disassemble the valves by compressing them with a valve spring compressor until the keepers can be removed. The keepers can be easily handled with a screwdriver with a daub of grease on its tip. Keep the assemblies separate for reassembly in their original locations.

Disassembling the valves

1. Valve spring compressor

INSPECTION AND REPAIR

1. Consult the "50, 65, and 70 cc models" cylinder head "Inspection and Repair" section.

2. A good valve seat for these engines is 0.028–0.048 in (0.7–1.2 mm), and the serviceable limit is 0.08 in (2.0 mm).

REASSEMBLY

1. Apply engine oil to the valve stems, rocker arm shafts, and cam before assembling them.

2. Assemble the valve assemblies using new keepers, install the rocker assemblies in the cylinder head, and install the rocker arm cover.

3. Position the cylinder head gaskets and slip the head into place, taking care to keep the chain free so it can be drawn up into the head.

4. Torque the head to 14.5–18.1 ft lbs in the order shown in the illustration.

Cylinder head torquing sequence

5. Rotate the engine so the woodruff key on the crankshaft cam sprocket is aligned as previously illustrated, then align the "O" mark on the sprocket and secure the sprocket. The chain must be placed on the sprocket before it is installed.

6. Slip the camshaft into position so the pin hole is toward the head cover. The valve and piston should be in the TDC position on the compression stroke (no clearance at the tappets).

7. Mount the point base on the camshaft extension using an oil seal guide such as the Honda guide (tool no. 07057-03301) or a suitable substitute. If this operation is performed without some sort of guide, the oil seal will probably leak.

Installing the point base

1. Point base

8. Insert the 3 x 5.2 guide pin in its hole and mount the spark advancer unit.

9. Install the contact breaker assembly and connect the leads.

10. Mount the rotor and stator assemblies onto the crankshaft.

11. Tune the engine, replenish the oil supply, and complete the assembly process.

Cylinder and Piston Assembly

DISASSEMBLY

1. Consult the 50, 65, and 70 cc models "Cylinder and Piston" assembly and disassembly section.

2. The cam chain and cylinder should be removed together once the chain is free of the timing sprocket.

INSPECTION AND REPAIR

1. Consult the 50, 65, and 70 cc models "Inspection and Repair" section.

ASSEMBLY

1. Consult the 50, 65, and 70 cc models "Assembly" section. The only difference in the procedures is that the piston is marked with "in" on its crown. Make sure the marking is toward the top of the engine.

Installing the camshaft

1. Camshaft   2. Cam sprocket

Mounting the piston in the correct position

1. "IN" mark   2. Piston

Aligning the cam sprocket for disassembly

1. Cam chain   4. "T" aligning mark
2. 6 mm bolts   5. Camshaft
3. Cam sprocket

100 AND 125 CC MODELS

Cylinder Head

REMOVAL AND DISASSEMBLY

1. Run the machine until its normal operating temperature is reached, then drain the oil. Remove the engine from the frame as directed in the engine "Removal and Installation" section.

2. Remove the points and dynamo covers, then remove the contact breaker baseplate.

3. Remove the hex nut securing the advance mechanism, then remove the advance unit.

4. Remove the point base, thereby revealing the cam sprocket.

Point base mounting positions

1. 5 mm screws   3. 6 mm screws
2. 6 mm bolt

5. Rotate the engine until the piston is at TDC, then remove the cam sprocket. Lift the chain over the sprocket in the direction of the cam itself. It is a good idea to attach a thin piece of mechanic's

wire to the chain so that if it falls into the crankcase, you can pull it up without going through a lot of fishing hassles. Do not loosen the cylinder head bolts until this has been accomplished.

6. Remove the four cylinder head cap nuts, align the cam lobes to the cutout on the cylinder head, and slip the camshaft from the head. It should not require undue pressure to remove the cam so if it seems hard to get it out, you probably don't have things lined up right.

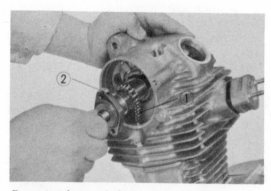

Removing the camshaft

1. Cam chain   2. Camshaft

7. Remove the tensioner stopper bolt and position the tensioner so the head can be removed. Lift off the head. If necessary, gently tap on the head with a hammer and wood block to free it.

8. Remove the rocker arms and shaft, keeping them separate so that they may be replaced in their original positions, then compress the valve springs with a suitable compressor or the Honda compressor (tool

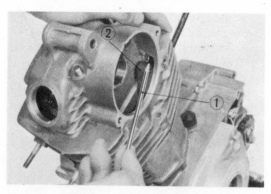

Positioning the cam chain guide for cylinder removal

1. Screwdriver   2. Cam chain guide

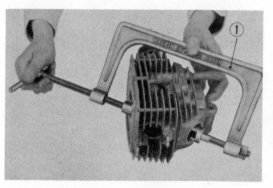

Compressing the valve springs for disassembly

1. Valve spring compressor

no. 07031-10701), until the keepers can be removed, and separate the assemblies for reassembly in their original positions.

INSPECTION AND REPAIR

1. Consult the 50, 65, and 70 cc models cylinder head "Inspection and Repair" section.

ASSEMBLY

1. Install the cam chain guide if it has been removed, then position the O-ring and dowel pins on the head.

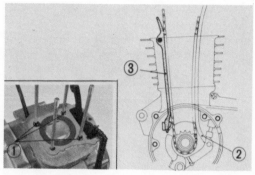

Installing the chain guide, O-rings, and dowel pins

1. Dowel pins   3. Cam chain guide
2. Cam chain tensioner

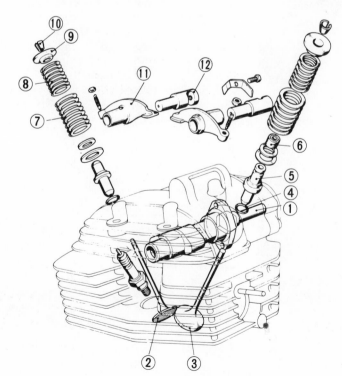

1. Camshaft
2. Inlet valve
3. Exhaust valve
4. O-ring
5. Valve guide
6. Valve stem seal
7. Valve outer spring
8. Valve inner spring
9. Valve spring retainer
10. Valve keepers
11. Rocker arm
12. Rocker arm shaft

Valve mechanism assembly

2. Assemble the valves using new keepers. The keepers are easy to handle if you place a daub of grease on the tip of a screwdriver. Lubricate all the parts as you install them.

3. Install the rockers in the head, taking care to position them in their original locations if they have not been replaced. Lubricate all parts as you install them, using clean engine oil.

4. Position the cam sprocket on the cam chain, and install the assembly in the head by using the cam chain tensioner to support them. Use a new head gasket between the head and cylinder.

5. Slip the head into place on its studs, and torque the head cap nuts to 5.8–8.7 ft lbs (tighten the cap nuts down finger-tight and then torque them in diagonal pairs) while supporting the cam sprocket and chain with a screwdriver. You should still have a wire on the chain to guard against dropping it into the crankcase.

6. Remove the cam chain from the sprocket and install the camshaft. Make sure the cam lobe is aligned with the cut-out on the cylinder head before inserting it. Rotate the cam one full revolution to bring it to a TDC position. This is assured by the cam sprocket mounting holes which won't be properly positioned unless perpendicular to the crankshaft.

Installing the cam sprocket

1. "T" mark   3. Cam sprocket
2. Mounting holes

7. Check the valve timing by aligning the "T" mark on the crankshaft with the timing mark scribed on the crankcase. Place enough tension on the cam chain to make it taut, then install and secure the cam sprocket with its mounting holes perpendicular to the crankshaft.

8. Use an oil seal guide when replacing the breaker point base assembly or the seal will probably leak.

Installing the cylinder head

1. Cam chain   3. 8 mm cap nuts
2. Screwdriver

Installing the camshaft

1. Camshaft   2. Cam lobe

Installing the automatic advance mechanism

1. Pin   2. Pin hole

9. Complete the assembly in the reverse order of disassembly, then tune the engine and replenish the oil supply.

Cylinder and Piston Assembly

DISASSEMBLY

1. Consult the 50, 65, and 70 cc models "Cylinder and Piston" assembly and disassembly section.

2. Keep a wire on the chain when you lift the cylinder over the piston.

INSPECTION AND REPAIR

1. Consult the 50, 65, and 70 cc models "Inspection and Repair" section.

2. The "in" mark on the piston crown should be toward the rear.

ASSEMBLY

1. Consult the 50, 65, and 70 cc models "Assembly" section.

2. Make sure you install the two dowel pins in the mounting base.

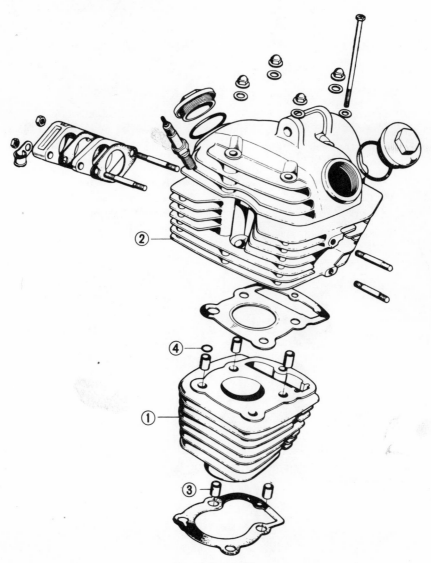

Top-end assembly

1. Cylinder   3. Dowel pins
2. Cylinder head   4. O-ring

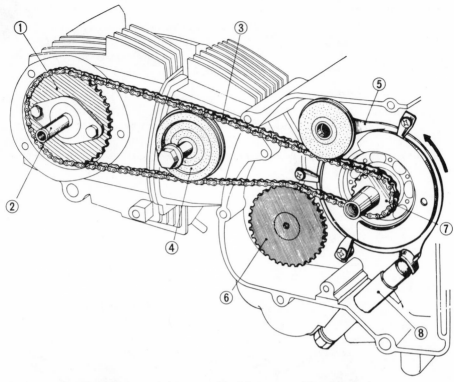

Cam chain tensioner assembly (shown is a 90 cc engine)

1. Cam sprocket
2. Camshaft
3. Cam chain
4. Cam chain guide roller tensioner
5. Cam chain tensioner
6. Cam chain guide sprocket
7. Timing sprocket
8. Tensioner push rod

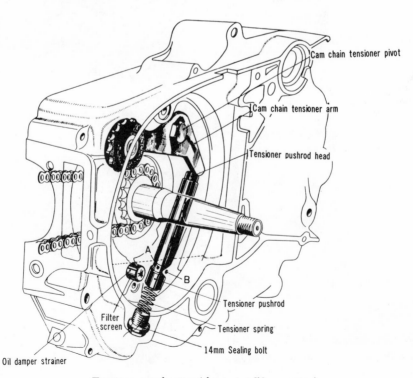

Tensioner mechanism (shown is a 50 cc engine)

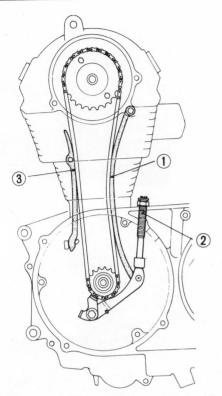

Manually adjustable tensioner mechanism (shown is a 100 cc engine)

1. Tensioner
2. Adjusting bolt
3. Tensioner guide

Bottom-End Service

CAM CHAIN TENSIONER

Disassembly

1. Remove the left-side crankcase cover, then remove the rotor and stator assemblies (all models).

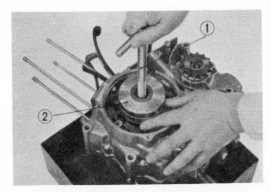

Removing the rotor assembly (shown is a 100 cc engine)

1. Dynamo rotor puller   2. Dynamo rotor

2. Remove the camshaft, then remove the cam chain from the timing and guide sprockets. Remove the tensioner from the tensioner setting plate (90 cc models).

Removing the tensioner (shown is a 90 cc engine)

1. Cam chain tensioner   3. Tensioner setting plate
2. 5 mm cross point screw

3. Remove the sealing plug from the crankcase, and remove the tensioner assembly (50, 65, and 70 cc models).

Removing the tensioner push rod

1. Sealing plug   3. Push rod
2. Spring

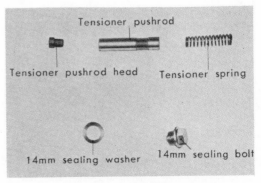

Tensioner components from a 50 cc engine

4. Remove the tensioner pivot bolt, then disassemble the cam chain tensioner and tensioner arm. Remove the push rod assembly, then pull out the tensioner adjusting bolt (100 and 125 cc models).

Tensioner and pivot assembly

    1. Pivot bolt   **3. Adjusting bolt**
    2. Tensioner arm

Inspection and Repair

1. Clean all parts in a suitable solvent and blow them dry, taking care to blow clear all of the oil passages.

2. Inspect the components for a worn or damaged condition, and replace them as necessary.

3. Inspect the tensioner spring for a worn or collapsed condition, and replace it if damaged or if it is shorter than 2.89 in. (73.5 mm) for 50, 65, or 70 cc models, and if shorter than 2.65 in. (67.4 mm) for 90 cc models.

Assembly

1. Assembly for the 50, 65, 70, and 90 cc models is in the reverse order of disassembly.

2. Reassemble the tensioner mechanism on 100 and 125 cc models in the following manner:

    a. Insert the tensioner adjusting bolt from the outside of the case, then install the case and tensioner arm rubber.

    b. Mount the tensioner on the tensioner arm pin, connect the spring to the arm, and install the tensioner arm adjusting bolt.

    c. Install the rotor assembly, and torque it to 19.0–23.0 ft lbs.

    d. Mount the AC generator by installing the cord grommet, mounting the generator, and then aligning the screw mounting holes. Secure the O-ring.

    e. Install the left crankcase cover.

Tensioner installation

    1. Spring   **2. Screwdriver**

Installing the generator

    1. Stator   **3. O-ring**
    2. Cord grommet

CLUTCH

50, 65, and 70 cc Models

DISASSEMBLY

1. Remove the right-side crankcase cover, then remove the clutch lever and outer cover.

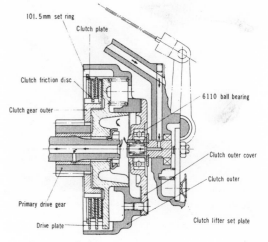

Hand-operated clutch diagram

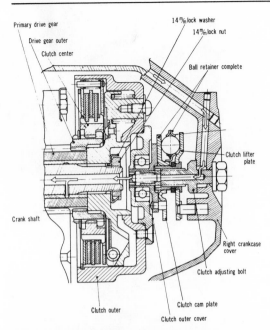

Centrifugal clutch diagram

Clutch lever, cover, and ball retainer assemblies

2. Bend back the tab on the lockwasher, remove the locknut, and lift out the clutch assembly. Removing these parts is made simpler by the use of the Honda clutch

Removing the clutch assembly

outer holder (tool no. 07024-03501) and the locknut wrench (tool no. 07086-00102), but substitutes may be used without too much trouble.

3. Disassemble the clutch assembly using either the Honda clutch assembly tool (tool no. 07038-01101) or a suitable substitute.

INSPECTION AND REPAIR

1. Clean all parts other than the clutch friction plates in a suitable solvent and blow them dry.

2. Inspect the clutch plates and discs for a worn, damaged, scored, or burned condition, and replace them as necessary. A good indication of whether or not a friction disc is worn past its useable limits is if it holds the imprint of a thumb nail pressed against it, or the disc may be measured with a vernier caliper. The specifications may be checked at the end of the chapter. Clutch plates should be replaced as a full set.

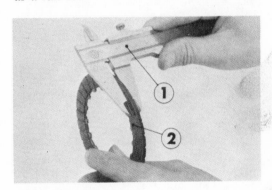

Measuring a friction disc

1. Vernier caliper   2. Friction disc

3. Inspect the clutch springs for a worn, damaged, or collapsed condition, and replace them as necessary. The springs may

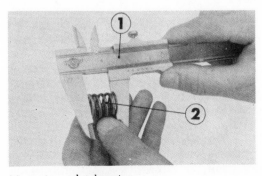

Measuring a clutch spring

1. Vernier caliper   2. Clutch spring

be measured with a vernier caliper or compared to new ones. The springs must be replaced if collapsed beyond their serviceable limit, and must be replaced as a full set.

4. Inspect the clutch center guide and the primary drive gear for a worn or damaged condition and replace them if necessary.

5. Measure the clearance between the clutch outer and the drive plate or clutch plate in the direction of normal rotation. If the clearance exceeds 0.012–0.02 in (0.3–0.5 mm), the worn parts must be replaced.

ASSEMBLY

1. Assembly is in the reverse order of disassembly.

2. Make sure the tab of the lockwasher is seated flat against the side of the locknut.

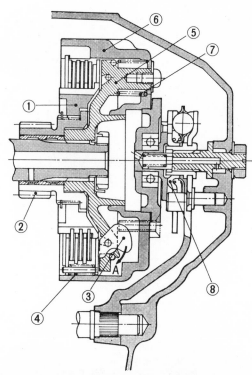

Hand-operated type clutch components

1. Clutch center	5. Drive plate
2. Drive gear	6. Clutch outer
3. Clutch weight	7. Clutch spring
4. Clutch release spring	8. Clutch cam plate

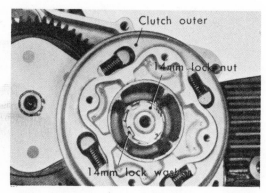

Make sure the tabs of the lockwasher seat against flats of the locknut

90 cc Models

DISASSEMBLY

1. Remove the clutch cover, the right-side crankcase cover, and the clutch outer cover.

2. Bend back the tab on the clutch lockwasher and remove the locknut. The clutch is now free to be removed as a complete assembly. The job is made simpler by using the Honda clutch outer holder (tool no. 07024-01101), but substitutes may be used without too much trouble.

3. Disassemble the clutch using the Honda clutch tool (tool no. 07038-03001) or a suitable substitute. Avoid pressing on the drive plate and damper spring retainer

Removing the clutch outer cover

1. Clutch outer cover   2. Clutch outer

if the Honda tool is to be used, or the drive plate won't be able to be compressed.

INSPECTION AND REPAIR

1. Consult the 50, 65, and 70 cc models "Inspection and Repair" section.

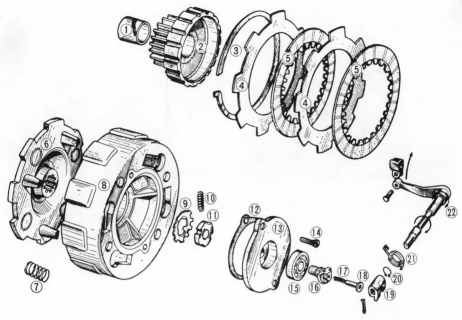

Centrifugal clutch diagram

1. Clutch center guide	9. 16 mm lockwasher	17. Oil through spring
2. Drive gear	10. Clutch damper spring	18. Oil through
3. 102.5 mm set ring	11. 16 mm locknut	19. Clutch lifter arm
4. Clutch plate	12. Clutch outer cover gasket	20. 10 mm snap-ring
5. Friction disc	13. Clutch outer cover	21. Clutch lever spring
6. Drive plate	14. 5 mm cross-screw	22. Clutch lever
7. Clutch spring	15. 6000 ball bearing	
8. Clutch outer	16. Clutch lifter	

Removing the clutch assembly

1. Clutch outer
2. 16 mm locknut "T" spanner
3. 16 mm locknut
4. Clutch outer holder

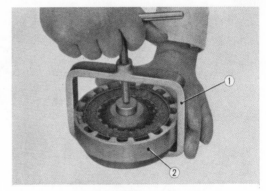

Disassembling the clutch

1. Clutch disassembling and assembling tool
2. Clutch assembly

ASSEMBLY

1. Assemble the clutch spring, drive plate, friction discs, and clutch plates into the clutch outer, then compress the drive plate and install the set ring and damper spring.

2. Mount the clutch assembly, clutch drive gear, and the center guide onto the crankshaft and torque the locknut to 54–64 ft lbs.

3. Secure the lockwasher by bending the tab up. If the tab does not seat against the

Secure the locknut by bending up the tabs of the lockwasher

1. Lockwasher

side of the nut, tighten the nut until it will. Do not loosen the nut to make the tab align properly.

4. Complete the assembly in the reverse order of disassembly by installing the outer cover, crankcase cover, and then the clutch cover together with the clutch lifter and oil guide.

100 and 125 cc Models

DISASSEMBLY

1. Remove the right-side crankcase cover, then remove the oil filter rotor as

described in the "Lubrication" chapter.

2. Remove the four bolts which secure the clutch lifter plate and remove the plate.

Clutch lifter plate securing bolts

1. 6 mm bolts

3. Remove the set ring and slip out the clutch center and the clutch discs and plates, then remove the spline washer and the clutch outer assembly.

INSPECTION AND REPAIR

1. Consult the 50, 65, and 70 cc models "Inspection and Repair" section.

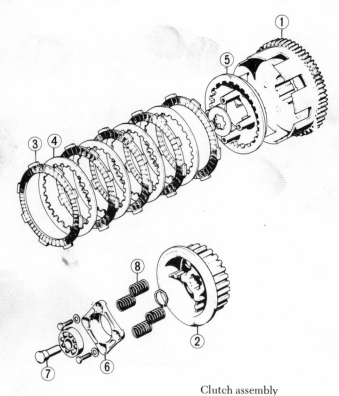

1. Clutch hub
2. Clutch center
3. Friction disc
4. Clutch plate
5. Clutch pressure plate
6. Clutch lifter plate
7. Clutch lifter guide pin
8. Clutch spring

Clutch assembly

Removing the clutch outer assembly

1. Snap-ring pliers   3. Clutch center
2. 20 mm set ring

ASSEMBLY

1. Insert the outer assembly and pressure plate, then slip the splined washer into place.

Installing the spline washer

1. 20 mm spline washer   2. Clutch outer assembly

2. Assemble the clutch discs and plates on the clutch center, then position the center on the mainshaft while rotating each plate and disc into position in their splined passageways.

Installing the clutch assembly

1. Clutch center   3. Splines
2. Clutch friction discs

3. Position the set ring, then assemble and secure the springs and lifter plate. The bolts should be tightened down evenly, then torqued diagonally to 5.8–8.7 ft lbs. Make sure you install the clutch lifter guide pin.

4. Complete the assembly in the reverse order of disassembly.

Installing the clutch lifter guide pin

1. Clutch lifter guide pin

SPLITTING THE CRANKCASES

50, 65, and 70 cc Models

1. Remove the engine from the frame, clean it off thoroughly, and place it on the work bench.

2. Remove the cylinder head, the cylinder, and the piston assemblies.

3. Remove the clutch assembly.

4. Remove the primary driven gear and the kick-starter spring.

5. Remove the oil pump assembly.

6. Remove the gearshift stopper and shifter plate.

7. Remove the left-side crankcase cover, flywheel, stator, and cam chain assembly.

8. Remove the rubber plug and gearshift drum stopper bolt.

9. Remove the final drive sprocket.

10. Separate the right crankcase from the left by tapping on the cases with a hammer and wooden block.

11. Remove the crankshaft assembly.

90 cc Models

1. Remove the engine from the frame, clean it thoroughly, and place it on the work bench.

2. Remove the clutch and gearshift spindle assemblies.

3. Remove the left crankcase cover.

4. Remove the cylinder head, cylinder, and piston assemblies.

5. Remove the 6 x 16 hex bolt and separate the left crankcase from the right side by tapping on it with a hammer and wood block.

6. Remove the crankshaft assembly.

Removing the crankshaft assembly

1. Crankshaft   2. Left crankcase

100 and 125 cc Models

1. Remove the engine from the frame, clean it thoroughly, and place it on the work bench.

2. Remove the cylinder head, cylinder, and piston assemblies.

3. Remove the right-side crankcase cover, the oil filter, and the oil pump.

4. Remove the clutch, shifter, and AC generator assemblies.

5. Remove the drive sprocket, the 11 left-side crankcase securing bolts, and the right-side crankcase securing screw.

6. Separate the crankcase halves by tapping on them with a soft mallet or a hammer and wood block.

Splitting the cases

1. Left crankcase   2. Right crankcase

7. Gently tap out the crankshaft by tapping on its right side to loosen it, while supporting the crankcase, and then carefully pulling it free.

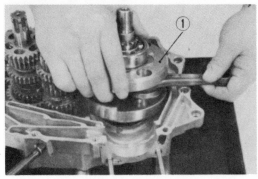

Removing the crankshaft assembly

1. Crankshaft assembly

CRANKSHAFT

INSPECTION AND REPAIR
(ALL MODELS)

Honda recommends the replacement of the crankshaft assembly whenever any of

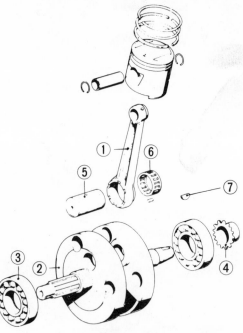

Crankshaft assembly (shown is a 100 cc engine)

1. Connecting rod
2. Crankshaft
3. Main bearing
4. Timing sprocket
5. Crankpin
6. Connecting rod bearing retainer
7. Woodruff key

its components fail, wear beyond their serviceable limit, or appear ready to fail. The crankshaft must be right in all respects or it could cause damage to the piston, cylinder walls, timing gear, and clutch, and besides that, the machine simply won't perform as it should. Perform the following tests and replace the assembly if your results indicate that the components are past their serviceable limit. Consult your dealer if you are in doubt about anything.

1. Support the crankshaft on a pair of V-blocks, or so it can be rotated smoothly and evenly, then measure the crankshaft run-out with a dial indicator.

Measuring crankshaft runout

    1. Dial indicators   2. "V" block

2. Support the crankshaft on centers or so the bearings can be moved without disturbing the crankshaft itself. Measure the play in the bearing with a dial indicator or with feeler gauges. Measure the play at various positions on the bearings. Make sure you measure both the axial and vertical play.

Measuring axial clearance

    1. Crankshaft   3. "V" block
    2. Feeler gauge

3. Measure the connecting rod side- and radial play. Use a feeler gauge for measuring the side-play, and a dial indicator for measuring the radial play.

Measuring connecting rod side-play

    1. Crankshaft   3. Feeler gauge
    2. Connecting rod

Measuring connecting rod radial-play

    1. Dial indicator   2. Connecting rod

4. Measure the dimensions of the connecting rod small-end for wear or damage. If it is worn past the point at which the clearance can be taken up by oversize piston pins, the crankshaft will have to be replaced.

5. Inspect the condition of the timing sprocket for cracked, chipped, or worn teeth, and replace it if necessary. If the rest of the crankshaft is in good condition, it may be worth your while to purchase a new sprocket and take the assembly to a machine shop. The sprocket can be pressed off and replaced with an arbor press. Use a new woodruff key if you do this. If it looks like you'll need a new crankshaft soon, however, you'd be better off buying one at this time.

CRANKCASE ASSEMBLY (ALL MODELS)

1. Assembly is basically the reverse order of disassembly. Make sure you use new gaskets wherever applicable, and install the dowel pins in their correct location when putting the cases together. A light coat of gasket sealer may be used at your own discretion.

Installing the right crankcase (shown is a 50 cc engine)

2. Assemble the crankshaft into the left crankcase on the 90 cc and smaller models, and into the right crankcase on the 100 and 125 cc models. Take care in fitting the crankshaft into the case as rough handling

or undue pressure may damage the assembly, the case itself, or the bearings.

3. Install the cam chain guide sprocket at this time on 90 cc models.

4. Assemble the cylinder, cylinder head, gearshift, and clutch assemblies in that order.

SHIFTER MECHANISM

50, 65, and 70 cc Models

DISASSEMBLY

1. Complete the procedures listed in the "Splitting the Crankcases" section.

2. The gearshift drum and fork assembly can be removed along with the transmission assembly after the kick-starter spindle is disengaged.

INSPECTION AND REPAIR

1. Clean all parts in a suitable solvent and blow them dry.

2. Inspect the components for obvious wear or damage and replace them as necessary.

3. Measure the thickness of the ends of the shifter fork to determine if they have been worn past their serviceable limits. Use a micrometer and measure both ends. It is a good idea to compare the fork to a new one if possible to determine wear.

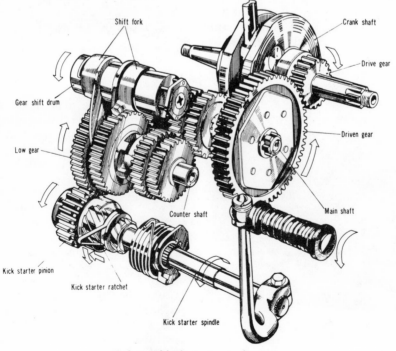

Shifter and kick-starter mechanisms

4. Measure the inside diameter of the shifter fork with an inside micrometer to determine if it has worn past its serviceable limit.

5. Measure the outside diameter of the shifter drum using a micrometer, and replace it if worn past its serviceable limit. You don't want a lot of play between the drum and forks.

ASSEMBLY

1. Assembly is basically in the reverse order of disassembly. Make sure all components are perfectly clean, and lubricate them with clean engine oil before installation.

2. Assemble the shifter forks to the drum and position the assembly on the countershaft in the manner shown in the accompanying illustration. Make sure the guide pin and guide pin clip are in good condition, and that they are installed securely.

3. Apply a daub of a strong screw and bolt sealer to the stopper plate mounting screw so the screw can't work its way loose.

4. Make sure the transmission engages smoothly and positively in all gears before you complete the assembly. It is recommended that you thoroughly check over the transmission at this time for wear or damage that might cause sloppy gear engagements.

90 cc Models

DISASSEMBLY

1. Remove the clutch assembly as described in the "Clutch" section.

2. Remove the 20 mm circlip which secures the primary driven gear, and remove the gear.

3. Remove the shifter drum stopper, then pull the shifter spindle free while holding the shifter arm down so that it is not engaging the shifter drum stopper plate.

Removing the shifter spindle

1. Shifter arm

4. If you wish to work on the shifter drum and forks, the crankcases will have to be split as described in the "Splitting the Crankcases" section.

5. Remove the kick-starter spindle, then remove the mainshaft, countershaft, and shifter drum assemblies from the left crankcase.

Removing the kick-starter spindle

1. Kick-starter spindle   3. Transmission countershaft
2. Transmission mainshaft   4. Shifter drum

6. Disassemble the shifter forks from the shifter drum by removing the gearshifter guide pin clip and pin, then slide the forks from the drum.

Removing the primary driven gear retaining ring

1. Primary driven gear   2. 20 mm circlip

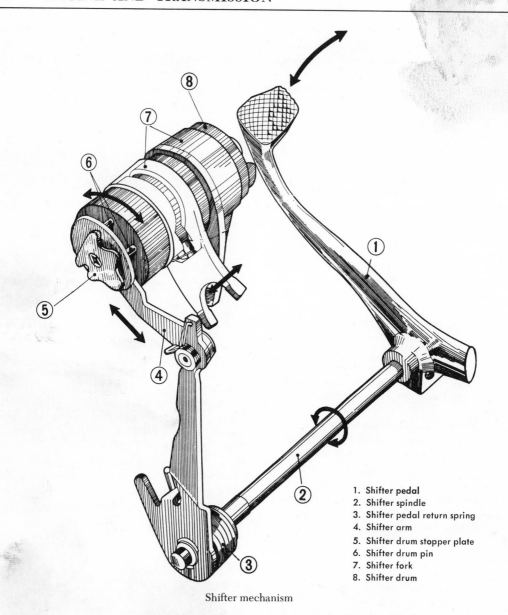

1. Shifter pedal
2. Shifter spindle
3. Shifter pedal return spring
4. Shifter arm
5. Shifter drum stopper plate
6. Shifter drum pin
7. Shifter fork
8. Shifter drum

Shifter mechanism

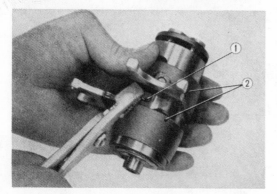

Removing the shifter forks

1. Shifter guide pin clip   2. Shifter fork

INSPECTION AND REPAIR

1. Consult the 50, 65, and 70 cc models "Inspection and Repair" section.

2. In addition to the other measurements, measure the shifter drum groove with feeler gauges or a small inside micrometer if one is available, and replace the drum if the grooves are worn past their serviceable limits.

ASSEMBLY

1. Slip the shifter forks onto the shifter drum and secure them with the guide pins and clips. Use new pins and clips if the

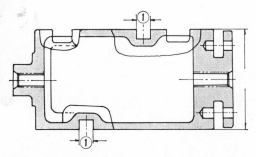

Shifter drum groove

1. Shifter drum groove

Assembling the shifter drum stopper

1. Shifter drum stopper   2. Shifter drum stopper plate

old ones don't look perfect. Make sure that the forks are in their correct position. There is a "R" mark on the right-side fork. Check the operation of the forks for smoothness.

2. Remove the circlip with a set of snap-ring pliers (if not available, you'll have to pry it out with a screwdriver), and remove the gearshift plate and spring.

Location of the "R" mark on the right-side shifter fork

1. "R" mark   3. Shifter drum
2. Shifter fork

Removing the circlip

1. Snap-ring pliers   2. Circlip

2. Install the transmission assemblies in the left crankcase half and check the action of the forks and gears for smooth and positive action.

3. Install the kick-starter spindle, then assemble the crankcase halves.

4. Complete the assembly in the reverse order of disassembly. Carefully check the operation of all the components as you install them. Make sure the return springs snap the components back into position, and carefully check the operation of the shifter arm on the drum stopper plate.

100 and 125 cc Models

DISASSEMBLY

1. Remove the right-side crankcase cover, then remove the oil filter rotor and clutch assemblies.

3. Remove the shifter drum stopper and shifter cam.

4. Remove the shifter pedal, then pull the shifter spindle out.

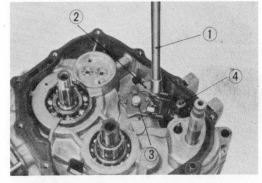

Location of the shifter components

1. 6 mm box wrench   3. Gearshift cam
2. Gearshift drum stopper   4. Gearshift spindle

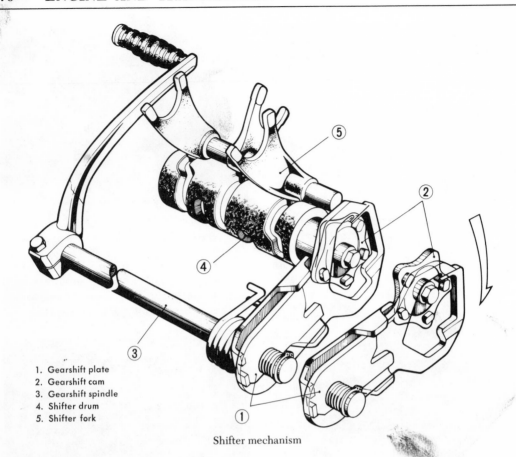

1. Gearshift plate
2. Gearshift cam
3. Gearshift spindle
4. Shifter drum
5. Shifter fork

Shifter mechanism

5. If you wish to work on the shifter forks or drum, the crankcases will have to be split as described in the "Splitting the Crankcases" section.

6. Remove the kick-starter spindle, then lift out the mainshaft, countershaft, and shifter drum all at the same time.

7. Remove the shifter fork guide shaft to remove the shifter forks.

INSPECTION AND REPAIR

1. Consult the 90 cc models "Inspection and Repair" section.

ASSEMBLY

1. Slip the left-side gearshifter fork onto the guide shaft. Use a thin screwdriver or some other suitable instrument to install the spring and 4 x 10 rollers on the guide shaft.

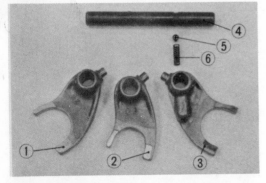

Shifter fork assembly

1. Right-side shifter fork
2. Center shifter fork
3. Left-side shifter fork
4. Shifter fork guide shaft
5. 4 X 10 roller
6. Spring

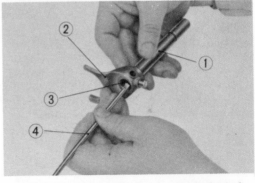

Installing the spring and rollers on the guide shaft

1. Shifter fork guide shaft
2. Left-side shifter fork
3. 4 X 10 roller
4. Screwdriver

2. Assemble the kick-starter (if necessary) spindle into the right-side crankcase. Secure the spring by inserting one end into the hole in the case, and then hook the other end of the spring onto the case boss.

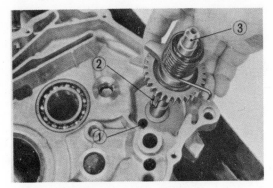

Installing the kick-starter spindle

1. Hole   3. Kick-starter spindle
2. Spring

3. Mount the countershaft and mainshaft assemblies into the right-side crankcase, then install the gearshifter drum. Position the neutral switch rotor so it faces the cylinder assembly. This will make the installation of the shifter forks much easier.

Proper direction for installing the shifter drum

1. Shifter drum   3. Countershaft
2. Mainshaft

4. Position the right-side shifter fork on the countershaft high gear, then raise the gear until the cam guide pin can be assembled into the guide groove on the drum, and install the center shifter fork in the same manner. Work from the countershaft end.

5. Position the left-side gearshifter fork, align the holes in the three forks, then insert the shaft from the top.

Installing the right-side shifter fork

1. Right-side shifter fork

Aligning the cam pin

1. Cam pin   2. Pin hole

Positioning the center shifter fork

1. Center shifter fork

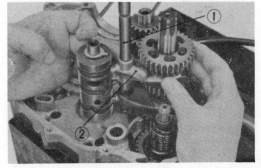

Positioning the left-side shifter fork

1. Shifter fork guide shaft   2. Left-side shifter fork

6. Install the gearshift assembly, then mount the left-side crankcase. Make sure the kick-starter spindle shaft is perfectly perpendicular to the hole in the left crankcase.

7. Assemble the shifter cam so the cam pin is inserted into the hole in the drum.

Installing the spindle

1. Boss   2. Return spring

8. Assemble the gearshifter assembly, making sure that the end of the return spring is hooked onto the crankcase boss.

9. Install the shifter drum stopper and the gearshifter plate, then mount the spring and secure the assembly with the circlip.

10. Complete the assembly in the reverse order of disassembly.

KICK-STARTER MECHANISM (ALL MODELS)

All of the models covered in this guide use the same basic kick-starter system. Honda has produced some models in this class which depend on dog-gear engagement rather than the traditional vertical method, but all this means is that the same parts will wear out differently, but will wear out just the same.

When you step down on the kick-starter lever, the kick-starter spindle rotates and the ratchet, which is held against the spindle in the direction of rotation, runs along the spindle groove to mesh with low gear on the countershaft. The torque produced by the kick-starter is transmitted to the engine crankshaft by the mainshaft which is engaged with the clutch center, and this causes the engine to turn over and hopefully start. As the engine starts, the speed of the pinion becomes greater than the

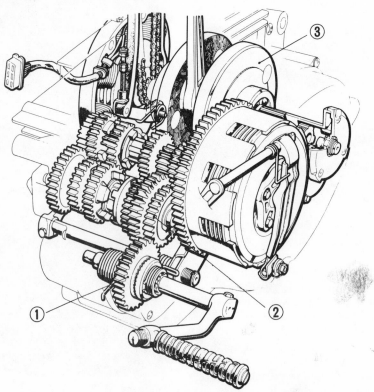

Kick-starter and transmission assemblies (shown is a 100 cc engine)

1. Kick-starter pinion   2. Primary starter idle gear

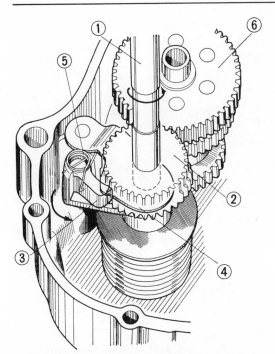

Kick-starter assembly

1. Starter spindle
2. Starter pinion
3. Starter ratchet flange
4. Starter guide
5. Starter pawl spring
6. Countershaft low gear

Removing the kick-starter (shown is a 50 cc engine)

speed of the spindle, and the ratchet is forced back by the return spring and the change in velocity of the spindle. The kick-starter spring returns the spindle to its original position, and the ratchet fully disengages the pinion and returns to its original position.

Follow the following instructions and don't worry about minor variations. Put everything back the way you found it and you can't go wrong. Kick-starters are pretty hard to mess up.

Disassembly

1. Remove the clutch, flywheel and stator assemblies, the primary driven gear, the gearshifter spindle, and the 16 mm circlip from the kick-starter spindle.

2. Remove the kick-starter spring retainer and the kick-starter spring.

3. Separate the crankcases and lift out the kick-starter spindle which seats in the left-side crankcase.

Inspection and Repair

1. Clean all parts in a suitable solvent and blow them dry.

2. Inspect all the parts for a worn or damaged condition and replace them as necessary. Replace the spring if the lever does not return immediately after being depressed.

3. Inspect the ratchet pawl and the kick-starter pinion teeth for a worn, chipped, or otherwise damaged condition, and replace them as necessary.

Assembly

1. Assembly is basically the reverse order of disassembly.

2. Make sure the spring will return the kick-starter lever properly before you complete the assembly procedures.

3. Use new circlips and gaskets wherever applicable.

TRANSMISSION

The transmissions used on the single-cylinder Hondas can usually be rebuilt unless the shaft is damaged. There is often one gear which is an integral part of the shaft, and of course the splines are a part of the shaft, so if either of these items, or if the shaft itself, is damaged or worn, the shaft will have to be replaced. If one of the gears is damaged, it can be removed and replaced by removing the snap-rings which secure it to the shaft. It is a good practice to replace all of the parts which make up an individual gear system, since when one goes it either takes the rest with it or is an indication that the associated parts haven't long to go. This means that if the bike keeps jumping out of third gear, for instance, you should examine and replace the idler gear, the dog gear, the driven gear, the shifter fork, and possibly even the shifter drum.

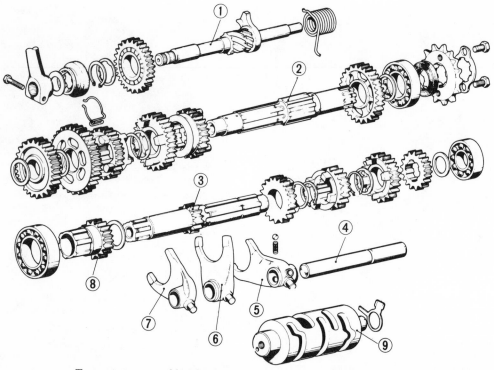

Transmission assembly (shown is the gearbox from a 100 cc engine)

1. Kick-starter spindle
2. Countershaft
3. Mainshaft
4. Shifter fork guide shaft
5. Left-side shifter fork
6. Center shifter fork
7. Right-side shifter fork
8. Primary starter gear
9. Shifter drum

Now that you've got the whole engine taken down, you should go over everything. This means that if you see a chipped gear you should consider replacing it now rather than in a few months when it gets really bad or maybe even fails and seizes the entire gearbox. If something is getting dangerously close to being in need of replacement, do it now. Make sure that all parts have been cleaned thoroughly before you begin to put it back together, and liberally douse the entire assembly with oil so there is a protective film between the metal surfaces. For longer transmission life on five-speed models, install the locating circlips with the smooth edge against the thrust washer. Always use new circlips whenever you remove one.

POSI-TORQUE MECHANISM

CT90 models from frame no. 122551 and engine no. 000001A come equipped with the posi-torque mechanism which allows you to select a high- or low-speed range of gearing by a simple manual adjustment.

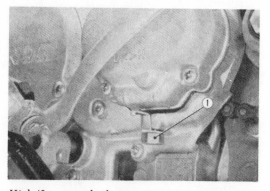

High / Low-speed selector

1. Speed selector

This is a great saving in time and energy over the traditional system of mounting a larger rear sprocket and an additional length of chain.

Disassembly

1. Remove the posi-torque cover which is located on the left-side crankcase. It may be necessary to remove the gear-shifter lever depending on how it has been mounted.

2. Remove the posi-torque low gear and the counter gear assembly along with the countershaft assembly.

3. Remove the posi-torque high gear by removing the 20 mm circlip and the splined washer.

4. To remove the drive sprocket, the left-side crankcase cover will have to be removed, and the chain will have to be removed or at least unhooked from the sprocket.

Inspection and Repair

1. Clean all parts in a suitable solvent and blow them dry.

2. Inspect all parts for a worn or damaged condition and replace them as necessary. Pay careful attention to the gear teeth and the dogs which are the first parts to go.

3. If any gears have chipped teeth, or if any of the dogs or dog holes are worn or damaged, the gears should be replaced along with any gears with which they mesh.

Assembly

1. Assembly is the reverse order of disassembly. Use new gaskets and circlips wherever applicable.

Torque Specifications

Although it is not absolutely essential that you torque every bolt to the manufacturer's specifications, it certainly helps to provide the uniform pressure required for certain operations (i.e., torquing down the cylinder head). If you use a torque wrench, you'll all but eliminate the possibility of snaping off the heads of bolts, or breaking studs off so they become next to impossible to remove. A torque wrench isn't very expensive and will provide assurance and accuracy. Make sure the wrench you select is marked in foot pounds or kilograms centemeter as these are the values used by Honda.

In 1970 Honda started using ISO nuts and bolts instead of the JIS hardware they had been using up to that time. The main difference is in the number of threads per millimeter, and the two can be differentiated by the small figure-eight on the heads of the ISO bolts. ISO hardware will stand up to greater torque values than the JIS type, so know what kind you are torquing before you start. Incidentally, the two types are not interchangeable, so if you start to turn something in and it seems like it's going to fit and then all of a sudden it doesn't want to turn anymore, don't force it because you may be using the wrong type and this will strip the threads for sure.

As a general rule you may use the following torque values:

(ft lbs)	JIS	ISO
6 mm	5	6
8 mm	10	16
10 mm	19	31
12 mm	34	54

Some useful torque specifications follow.

50, 65, 70, and 90 cc Models

Bolts And Nuts	Tightening Torque ft lbs	kg-cm	Bolts And Nuts	Tightening Torque ft lbs	kg-cm
R and L Crankcase	5.8– 8.0	(80–110)	Shift drum stopper plate	6.5– 9.4	(90–130)
Cam chain guide roller pin	5.1– 9.4	(70–130)	Shift drum stopper	7.2–11.6	(100–160)
Cylinder head stud nut	6.5– 8.7	(90–120)	Clutch nut	27.5–32.5	(380–450)
Cylinder side bolt	5.8– 8.0	(80–110)	R Crankcase cover	5.8– 8.7	(80–120)
Cylinder head side bolt	7.2–10.8	(100–150)	Stater	5.8– 8.7	(80–120)
Cam sprocket	3.6– 6.5	(50– 90)	Fly wheel	23.9–27.5	(330–380)
Cylinder head R side cover	5.1– 6.5	(70– 90)	Rotor	15.9–21.7	(220–300)
Cylinder head L side cover	5.8– 8.7	(80–120)	Drive sprocket	6.5–10.8	(90–150)
Tappet adjustment	5.1– 7.2	(70–100)	L Crankcase cover	5.8– 8.0	(80–110)
Cam chain tensioner push rod	10.8–18.1	(150–250)	Drain cock bolt	18.1–25.3	(250–350)
Oil pump	5.8– 8.7	(80–120)	Spark plug	8.0–10.8	(110–150)
Shift drum side bolt	6.5–10.8	(90–150)	Carburetor	6.5–10.1	(90–140)

100 and 125 cc Models

UNIT: kg-m (ft-lb)

Engine Item	Torque values	Frame Item	Torque values
Cylinder head	1.8– 2.0 (11.5–14.5)	Front axle nut	4.0– 5.0 (29.0–36.0)
Spark advance	0.8– 1.2 (5.8– 8.7)	Rear axle nut	4.0– 5.0) (29.0–36.0)
Cam sprocket	0.8– 1.2 (5.8– 8.7)	Rear fork pivot bolt	3.0– 4.0 (21.7–29.0)
Cylinder mount bolt, 6 mm	1.2– 1.8 (8.7–13.0)	Engine mounting bolt	2.0– 2.5 (14.5–18.8)
Left crankcase cover	0.8– 1.2 (5.8– 8.7)	Handle mounting bolt	0.9– 1.1 (6.50–7.95)
AC rotor	2.6– 3.2 (18.8–23.2)	Steering stem nut	6.0– 8.0 (43.3–57.8)
AC generator mounting screw	0.8– 1.2 (5.8– 8.7)	Front cushion mounting bolt	4.0– 5.0 (29.0–36.0)
Cam chain tensioner arm	0.8– 1.2 (5.8– 8.7)	Rear cushion mounting nut	3.0– 4.0 (21.7–29.0)
Right crankcase cover screw	0.8– 1.2 (5.8– 8.7)	Torque link mounting bolt	2.0– 2.5 (14.5–18.0)
Oil filter cover screw	0.8– 0.4 (2.2– 2.9)	Top bridge locknut	4.0– 4.8 (29.0–34.7)
Oil filter (locknut, 16 mm)	4.0– 5.0 (29.0–36.0)	Final driven sprocket	2.0– 2.5 (14.5–18.0)
Oil pump gear cover bolt	0.4– 0.6 (2.9– 4.4)	Seat mounting bolt	2.0– 2.5 (14.5–18.0)
Clutch mounting bolt	0.8– 1.2 (5.6– 8.7)		
Gearshift drum stopper bolt	0.8– 1.2 (5.6– 8.7)		
Gearshift drum cam bolt	0.8– 1.2 (5.6– 8.7)		

Engine, Clutch, and Transmission Specifications

Model	C50 C50M S50 Standard Value	Serviceable Limit
CYLINDER HEAD		
Valve guides:		
outside diameter (in./mm)	0.394/10.0	——
interference fit (in./mm)	0.002–0.006/0.40–0.065	——
inside diameter (in./mm)	0.217/5.5	0.199/5.53
Intake valve:		
valve seat (in./mm)	0.040–0.051/1–1.3	0.080/2.0
total length (in./mm)	2.600/66.0	2.530/65.6
stem diameter (in./mm)	0.217/5.5	0.214/5.44
head thickness (in./mm)	0.020/0.5	0.008/0.2
stem-to-guide clearance (in./mm)	0.0004–0.0012/0.010–0.030	0.0023/0.06
Exhaust valve:		
valve seat (in./mm)	0.040–0.051/1–1.3	——
total length (in./mm)	2.573/65.3	2.557/64.9
stem diameter (in./mm)	0.217/5.5	0.213/5.4
head thickness (in./mm)	0.026/0.7	0.016/0.4
stem-to-guide clearance (in./mm)	0.0012–0.0020/0.030–0.050	0.0032/0.08
Outer valve spring:		
free-length (in./mm)	1.110/28.1	1.060/26.9
compressed pressure (lbs/in.)	16.0 ± 1.2/0.980	14.0/0.980
(kg/mm)	7.2 ± 55/24.9	6.4/24.9
tilt	1°30′	2°
Inner valve spring:		
free-length (in./mm)	0.990/25.1	0.940/23.9
compressed pressure (lbs/in.)	18.0 ± 0.88/0.690	15.8/0.690
(kg/mm)	8.2 ± 4/17.5	7.2/17.5
tilt	1°30′	2°
Camshaft:		
left-end diameter (in./mm)	1.140–1.110/29.00–28.927	1.135/28.8
right-end diameter (in./mm)	1.140–1.110/29.00–28.927	1.135/28.8
shaft run-out (in./mm)	NA	0.0020/0.05
cam height (in./mm)	0.200/5.076	0.190/4.9
left-end bearing diameter (in./mm)	1.140/29.00	1.145/29.06
right-end bearing diameter (in./mm)	1.140/29.00	1.145/29.06
cam sprocket root diameter (in./mm)	2.104 ± 0.001/53.41 ± 0.025	2.09/53.00
Rocker arm:		
wear slipper (in./mm)	NA	NA
shaft bore (in./mm)	NA	NA
Rocker arm shaft:		
shaft diameter (in./mm)	NA	NA
shaft clearance (in./mm)	NA	NA
CYLINDER AND PISTON ASSEMBLY		
Cylinder:		
cylinder taper (in./mm)	NA	NA
cylinder bore (in./mm)	1.54/39.0	1.74/44.1
surface roughness (micron)	1.5	——

Engine, Clutch, and Transmission Specifications (cont.)

Model	C50 C50M S50 Standard Value	Serviceable Limit
CYLINDER AND PISTON ASSEMBLY		
Piston:		
piston diameter (in./mm)	1.5346–1.5354/38.98–39.00	1.73/33.88
ring side clearance (in./mm)	0.0006–0.00177/0.015–0.045	0.0047/0.12
oil ring side clearance (in./mm)	0.0004–0.0017/0.005–0.12	0.005/0.12
piston-to-piston pin clearance (in./mm)	0.00008–0.00055/0.002–0.014	0.0020/0.05
Piston rings:		
ring thickness (in./mm)	$0.079 \pm 0.04/2.0 \pm 0.1$	0.07/1.8
oil ring thickness (in./mm)	$0.071 \pm 0.0004/1.8 \pm 0.1$	0.063/1.6
ring end gap (in./mm)	0.004–0.0118/0.1–0.3	0.0197/0.5
oil ring end gap (in./mm)	0.12/0.30	0.020/0.50
CAM CHAIN TENSIONER		
Tensioner spring:		
spring free-length (in./mm)	3.04/77.2	2.89/73.5
spring tension (in./lbs)	$0.874/0.99 \pm 0.08$	0.87/0.79
(mm/kg)	$22.2/0.45 \pm 0.04$	22.2/0.36
roller diameter	0.391/35.3	1.359/34.5
CLUTCH		
Friction disc and clutch plate:		
thickness of disc (in./mm)	0.138/3.5	0.122/3.1
thickness of plate (in./mm)	$0.063 \pm 0.0020/1.6 \pm 0.05$	0.059/1.5
warpage of plate (in./mm)	NA	0.006/0.15
backlash of plate (in./mm)	NA	NA
backlash of disc (in./mm)	NA	NA
Clutch center guide:		
inside diameter (in./mm)	0.670/17.00	0.674/17.1
outside diameter (in./mm)	0.827/21.00	0.787/19.98
length (in./mm)	0.812/20.6	0.8/20.4
run-out (in./mm)	0.0012/0.03	0.006/0.15
crankshaft to guide clearance (in./mm)	NA	NA
Primary drive gear:		
inside diameter (in./mm)	0.830/21.00	0.833/21.15
chordal distance across three teeth (in./mm)	0.551/14.001	0.540/13.7
Clutch spring:		
free-length (in./mm)	①	②
spring tension (lb/in.)	③	④
(kg/mm)		
CRANKSHAFT		
Crankshaft:		
run-out at the bearings (in./mm)	0.0006/0.015	0.0020/0.05
axial clearance (in./mm)	0.0002–0.001/0.004–0.036	0.004/0.1
clearance normal to axis (in./mm)	0.0004–0.001/0.010–0.025	0.002/0.05
sprocket root diameter (in./mm)	$0.994 \pm 0.001/25.24 \pm 0.025$	0.991/25.19
right-side spline play (in./mm)	0.0004–0.0020/0.010–0.040	0.0032/0.08
maximum shaft run-out (in./mm)	0.002 TIR/0.05 TIR	0.008/0.2
Crankpin:		
outside diameter (in./mm)	0.91/23.1	0.908/23.045
interference fit (in./mm)	0.0020–0.0034/0.052–0.087	——

Engine, Clutch, and Transmission Specifications (cont.)

Model	C50 C50M S50 Standard Value	Serviceable Limit

CRANKSHAFT

Connecting rod:

	C50 C50M S50 Standard Value	Serviceable Limit
small-end-to-piston pin clearance (in./mm)	0.001–0.002/0.016–0.043	0.0032/0.08
small-end deflection (in./mm)	0.060/1.5	0.120/3.0
large-end end-play (in./mm)	0.004–0.014/0.10/0.35	0.024/0.6
bearing clearance (in./mm)	0–0.0005/0–0.012	0.002/0.05
small-end bore (in./mm)	0.512/13.00	0.52/13.1

① S65	0.756/19.2	③ S65	(lb/in.)	(kg/mm)
S50	0.744/18.9	S50	29.0 ± 1.75/0.504	13.2 ± 0.8/12.8
C50, C50M, C65, C65M	0.772/19.6	C50, C50M,	29.0 ± 1.75/0.504	13.2 ± 0.8/12.8
CL70, SL70	0.787/20.0	C65, C65M	12.8 ± 0.66/0.532	5.85 ± 0.3/13.5
C70, C70M	0.843/21.4	CL70, SL70	17.4–19.6/0.504	7.9–8.9/12.8
② S65	0.717/18.2	C70, C70M	13.3–14.7/0.532	6.05–6.65/13.5
S50	0.717/18.2	④ S65	14.3/0.504	6.5/12.8
C50, C50M, C65, C65M	0.720/18.2	S50	14.3/0.504	6.5/12.8
CL70, SL70	0.748/19.0	C50, C50M,		
C70, C70M	0.830/20.4	C65, C65M	11.0/0.532	5.0/13.5
		CL70, SL70	16.3/0.504	7.4/12.8
		C70, C70M	11.8/0.532	5.35/13.5

Model	C65 C65M S65 Standard Value	Serviceable Limit

CYLINDER HEAD

Valve guides:

	C65 C65M S65 Standard Value	Serviceable Limit
outside diameter (in./mm)	0.394/10.0	——
interference fit (in./mm)	0.002–0.006/0.040–0.065	——
inside diameter (in./mm)	0.217/5.5	0.199/5.53

Intake valve:

valve seat (in./mm)	0.040–0.051/1–1.3	0.080/2.0
total length (in./mm)	2.540/64.5	2.580/64.1
stem diameter (in./mm)	0.217/5.5	0.214/5.44
head thickness (in./mm)	0.020/0.5	0.008/0.2
stem-to-guide clearance (in./mm)	0.0004–0.0012/0.010–0.030	0.0023/0.06

Exhaust valve:

valve seat (in./mm)	0.040–0.051/1–1.3	——
total length (in./mm)	2.483/63.9	2.502/63.5
stem diameter (in./mm)	0.217/5.5	0.213/5.4
head thickness (in./mm)	0.026/0.7	0.016/0.4
stem-to-guide clearance (in./mm)	0.0012–0.0020/0.030–0.050	0.0032/0.08

Outer valve spring:

free-length (in./mm)	1.080/27.4	1.030/26.2
compressed pressure (lbs/in.)	16.0 ± 1.2/0.980	14.0/0.98
(kg/mm)	7.2 ± 0.55/24.9	6.4/24.9
tilt	1°30′	2°

Inner valve spring:

free-length (in./mm)	0.990/25.1	0.940/23.9
compressed pressure (lbs/in.)	18.0 ± 0.88/0.690	15.8/0.690
(kg/mm)	8.2 ± 0.4/17.5	7.2/17.5
tilt	1°30′	2°

Engine, Clutch, and Transmission Specifications (cont.)

Model	C65 C65M S65 Standard Value	Serviceable Limit
CYLINDER HEAD		
Camshaft:		
left-end diameter (in./mm)	1.140–1.110/29.00–28.927	1.135/28.8
right-end diameter (in./mm)	1.140–1.110/29.00–28.927	1.135/28.8
shaft run-out (in./mm)	NA	0.0020/0.05
cam height (in./mm)	0.200/5.076	0.190/4.9
left-end bearing diameter (in./mm)	1.140/29.00	1.145/29.06
right-end bearing diameter (in./mm)	1.140/29.00	1.145/29.06
cam sprocket root diameter (in./mm)	2.10 ± 0.001/53.41 ± 0.025	2.09/53.00
Rocker arm:		
wear slipper (in./mm)	NA	NA
shaft bore (in./mm)	NA	NA
Rocker arm shaft:		
shaft diameter (in./mm)	NA	NA
shaft clearance (in./mm)	NA	NA
CYLINDER AND PISTON ASSEMBLY		
Cylinder:		
cylinder taper (in./mm)	NA	NA
cylinder bore (in./mm)	1.750/44.0	NA
surface roughness (micron)	1.5	——
Piston:		
piston diameter (in./mm)	1.734/43.5	1.708/42.45
ring side clearance (in./mm)	0.0006–0.00177/0.015–0.045	0.0047/0.12
oil ring side clearance (in./mm)	0.0004–0.0017/0.010–0.045	0.005/0.12
piston-to-piston pin clearance (in./mm)	0.00008–0.00055/0.002–0.014	0.0020/0.05
Piston rings:		
ring thickness (in./mm)	0.079 ± 0.04/2.0 ± 0.1	0.07/1.8
oil ring thickness (in./mm)	0.099 ± 0.004/2 ± 0.1	0.071/1.8
ring end gap (in./mm)	0.0059–0.0138/0.15–0.35	0.0197/0.5
oil ring end gap (in./mm)	0.004–0.014/0.1–0.35	0.020/0.50
CAM CHAIN TENSIONER		
Tensioner spring:		
spring free-length (in./mm)	3.04/77.2	2.89/73.5
spring tension (in./lbs)	0.87/0.99 ± 0.08	0.87/0.79
(mm/kg)	22.2/0.45 ± 0.04	22.2/0.36
roller diameter	0.391/35.3	1.359/34.5
CLUTCH		
Friction disc and clutch plate:		
thickness of disc (in./mm)	0.138/3.5	0.122/3.1
thickness of plate (in./mm)	0.063 ± 0.0020/1.6 ± 0.05	0.59/1.5
warpage of plate (in./mm)	NA	0.006/0.15
backlash of plate (in./mm)	NA	NA
backlash of disc (in./mm)	NA	NA
Clutch center guide:		
inside diameter (in./mm)	0.670/17.00	0.674/17.1
outside diameter (in./mm)	0.827/21.00	0.787/19.98
length (in./mm)	0.812/21.06	0.8/20.4
run-out (in./mm)	0.0012/0.03	0.006/0.15
crankshaft to guide clearance (in./mm)	NA	NA

Engine, Clutch, and Transmission Specifications (cont.)

Model	C65 C65M S65		
		Standard Value	Serviceable Limit

CLUTCH

Primary drive gear:
inside diameter (in./mm)		0.830/21.00	0.833/21.15
chordal distance across three teeth (in./mm)		0.541/13.723	0.540/13.7

Clutch spring:
free-length (in./mm)		①	②
spring tension (lb/in.)		③	④
(kg/mm)			

CRANKSHAFT

Crankshaft:
run-out at the bearings (in./mm)		0.0006/0.015	0.0020/0.05
axial clearance (in./mm)		0.0002–0.001/0.004–0.036	0.004/0.1
clearance normal to axis (in./mm)		0.0004–0.001/0.010–0.025	0.002/0.05
sprocket root diameter (in./mm)		0.994 ± 0.001/25.24 ± 0.025	0.991/25.19
right-side spline play (in./mm)		0.0004–0.0020/0.010–0.040	0.0032/0.08
maximum shaft run-out (in./mm)		0.002 TIR/0.05 TIR	0.008/0.2

Crankpin:
outside diameter (in./mm)		0.91/23.1	0.908/23.045
interference fit (in./mm)		0.0020–0.0034/0.052–0.087	———

Connecting rod:
small-end-to-piston pin clearance (in./mm)		0.001–0.002/0.016–0.043	0.0032/0.08
small-end deflection (in./mm)		0.060/1.5	0.120/3.0
large-end end-play (in./mm)		0.004–0.014/0.10/0.35	0.024/0.6
bearing clearance (in./mm)		0–0.0005/0–0.012	0.002/0.05
small-end bore (in./mm)		0.512/13.00	0.52/13.1

① S65	0.756/19.2	③ S65	(lb/in.)	(kg/mm)
S50	0.744/18.9	S50	29.0 ± 1.75/0.504	13.2 ± 0.8/12.8
C50, C50M, C65, C65M	0.772/19.6	C50, C50M,	29.0 ± 1.75/0.504	13.2 ± 0.8/12.8
CL70, SL70	0.787/20.0	C65, C65M	12.8 ± 0.66/0.532	5.85 ± 0.3/13.5
C70, C70M	0.843/21.4	CL70, SL70	17.4–19.6/0.504	7.9–8.9/12.8
② S65	0.717/18.2	C70, C70M	13.3–14.7/0.532	6.05–6.65/13.5
S50	0.717/18.2	④ S65	14.3/0.504	6.5/12.8
C50, C50M, C65, C65M	0.720/18.2	S50	14.3/0.504	6.5/12.8
CL70, SL70	0.748/19.0	C50, C50M,		
C70, C70M	0.830/20.4	C65, C65M	11.0/0.532	5.0/13.5
		CL70, SL70	16.3/0.504	7.4/12.8
		C70, C70M	11.8/0.532	5.35/13.5

Engine, Clutch, and Transmission Specifications (cont.)

Model	CL70 C70 C70M SL70 Standard Value	Serviceable Limit
CYLINDER HEAD		
Valve guides:		
outside diameter (in./mm)	NA	——
interference fit (in./mm)	NA	——
inside diameter (in./mm)	0.2156–0.2159/5.475–5.485	NA
Intake valve:		
valve seat (in./mm)	0.040–0.051/1.0–1.3	0.080/2.0
total length (in./mm)	2.600/66.0	2.530/65.6
stem diameter (in./mm)	0.2148–0.2187/5.455–5.465	0.2126/5.40
head thickness (in./mm)	0.020/0.5	0.008/0.2
stem-to-guide clearance (in./mm)	0.004–0.0012/0.01–0.03	0.0032/0.08
Exhaust valve:		
valve seat (in./mm)	0.040–0.051/1.0–1.3	0.080/2.0
total length (in./mm)	2.573/65.3	2.577/64.9
stem diameter (in./mm)	0.2070–0.2109/5.435–5.445	0.2048/5.38
head thickness (in./mm)	0.020/0.5	0.008/0.2
stem-to-guide clearance (in./mm)	0.0012–0.002/0.03–0.05	0.004/0.10
Outer valve spring:		
free-length (in./mm)	1.106/28.1	1.059/26.9
compressed pressure (lbs/in.)	14.66–17.09/0.980	10.14/0.980
(kg/mm)	6.65–7.75/24.9	4.6/24.9
tilt	NA	NA
Inner valve spring:		
free-length (in./mm)	①	②
compressed pressure (lbs/in.)		
(kg/mm)	③	④
tilt	NA	NA
Camshaft:		
left-end diameter (in./mm)	NA	NA
right-end diameter (in./mm)	NA	NA
shaft run-out (in./mm)	NA	NA
cam height (in./mm)	1.0266/26.076	1.012/25.8
left-end bearing diameter (in./mm)	NA	NA
right-end bearing diameter (in./mm)	NA	NA
cam sprocket root diameter (in./mm)	NA	NA
Rocker arm:		
wear slipper (in./mm)	NA	NA
shaft bore (in./mm)	NA	NA
Rocker arm shaft:		
shaft diameter (in./mm)	NA	NA
shaft clearance (in./mm)	NA	NA

① CL70, SL70
    1.004/25.5
C70, C70M
    0.988/25.1
② CL70, SL70
    0.957/24.3
C70, C70M
    0.941/23.9

③ CL70, SL70
    7.87–8.55/0.894
    3.55–3.85/22.7
C70, C70M
    5.37–6.03/0.894
    2.45–2.75/22.7

④ CL70, SL70
    6.84/0.894
    3.1/22.7
C70, C70M
    4.41/0.894
    2.0/22.7

Engine, Clutch, and Transmission Specifications (cont.)

Model	CL70 C70 C70M SL70 Standard Value	Serviceable Limit
CYLINDER AND PISTON ASSEMBLY		
Cylinder:		
cylinder taper (in./mm)	NA	NA
cylinder bore (in./mm)	⑤	⑥
surface roughness (micron)	1.5	——
Piston:		
piston diameter (in./mm)	1.8492–1.8500/46.98–47.00	1.847/46.9
ring side clearance (in./mm)	0.0006–0.0018/0.015–0.045	0.0047/0.12
oil ring side clearance (in./mm)	0.0004–0.0018/0.010–0.045	0.0047/0.12
piston-to-piston pin clearance (in./mm)	NA	NA
Piston rings:		
ring thickness (in./mm)	NA	NA
oil ring thickness (in./mm)	NA	NA
ring end gap (in./mm)	0.0059–0.0138/0.15–0.35	0.0197/0.5
oil ring end gap (in./mm)	0.0059–0.01575/0.15–0.40	0.0197/0.5
CAM CHAIN TENSIONER		
Tensioner spring:		
spring free-length (in./mm)	3.04/77.2	2.89/73.5
spring tension (in./lbs)	0.874/0.99 ± 0.08	0.87/0.79
(mm/kg)	22.2/0.45 ± 0.04	22.2/0.36
roller diameter	0.391/35.3	1.359/34.5
CLUTCH		
Friction disc and clutch plate:		
thickness of disc (in./mm)	0.138/3.5	0.122/3.1
thickness of plate (in./mm)	0.063 ± 0.0020/1.6 ± 0.05	0.059/1.5
warpage of plate (in./mm)	NA	0.006/0.15
backlash of plate (in./mm)	NA	NA
backlash of disc (in./mm)	NA	NA
Clutch center guide:		
inside diameter (in./mm)	0.670/17.00	0.674/17.1
outside diameter (in./mm)	0.827/21.00	0.787/19.98
length (in./mm)	0.812/20.6	0.8/20.4
run-out (in./mm)	0.0012/0.03	0.006/0.15
crankshaft to guide clearance (in./mm)	NA	NA
Primary drive gear:		
inside diameter (in./mm)	NA	NA
chordal distance across three teeth (in./mm)	NA	NA

⑤ CL70, SL70
    1.8510–1.8514/47.015–47.025
C70, C70M
    1.8506–1.8510/47.005–47.015

⑥ CL70, SL70
    1.854/47.1
C70, C70M
    1.854/47.1

Engine, Clutch, and Transmission Specifications (cont.)

Model	CL70 C70 C70M SL70 Standard Value	Serviceable Limit
CLUTCH		
Clutch spring:		
free-length (in./mm)	①	②
spring tension (lb/in.)	③	④
(kg/mm)		
CRANKSHAFT		
Crankshaft:		
run-out at the bearings (in./mm)	0.0006/0.015	0.0020/0.05
axial clearance (in./mm)	0.0002–0.001/0.004–0.036	0.004/0.1
clearance normal to axis (in./mm)	0.0004–0.001/0.010–0.025	0.002/0.05
sprocket root diameter (in./mm)	0.994 ± 0.001/25.24 ± 0.025	0.991/25.19
right-side spline play (in./mm)	0.0004–0.0020/0.010–0.040	0.0032/0.08
maximum shaft run-out (in./mm)	0.002 TIR/0.05 TIR	0.008/0.2
Crankpin:		
outside diameter (in./mm)	0.91/23.1	0.908/23.045
interference fit (in./mm)	0.0020–0.0034/0.052–0.087	——
Connecting rod:		
small-end-to-piston pin clearance (in./mm)	0.001–0.002/0.016–0.043	0.0032/0.08
small-end deflection (in./mm)	0.060/1.5	0.120/3.0
large-end end-play (in./mm)	0.004–0.014/0.10/0.35	0.024/0.6
bearing clearance (in./mm)	0–0.0005/0–0.012	0.002/0.05
small-end bore (in./mm)	0.512/13.00	0.52/13.1

①			③		(lb/in.)	(kg/mm)
	S65	0.756/19.2		S65		
	S50	0.744/18.9		S50	29.0 ± 1.75/0.504	13.2 ± 0.8/12.8
	C50, C50M, C65, C65M	0.772/19.6		C50, C50M,	29.0 ± 1.75/0.504	13.2 ± 0.8/12.8
	CL70, SL70	0.787/20.0		C65, C65M	12.8 ± 0.66/0.532	5.85 ± 0.3/13.5
	C70, C70M	0.843/21.4		CL70, SL70	17.4–19.6/0.504	7.9–8.9/12.8
②	S65	0.717/18.2		C70, C70M	13.3–14.7/0.532	6.05–6.65/13.5
	S50	0.717/18.2	④	S65	14.3/0.504	6.5/12.8
	C50, C50M, C65, C65M	0.720/18.2		S50	14.3/0.504	6.5/12.8
	CL70, SL70	0.748/19.0		C50, C50M,		
	C70, C70M	0.830/20.4		C65, C65M	11.0/0.532	5.0/13.5
				CL70, SL70	16.3/0.504	7.4/12.8
				C70, C70M	11.8/0.532	5.35/13.5

Model	S90 SL90 CL90 CL90L CD90 C90 CT90 Standard Value	Serviceable Limit
CYLINDER HEAD		
Valve guides:		
outside diameter (in./mm)	0.396–0.3966/10.055–0.1065	——
interference fit (in./mm)	0.002–0.003/0.640–0.065	——
inside diameter (in./mm)	0.215–0.216/5.475–5.485	0.217/5.525
Intake valve:		
valve seat (in./mm)	0.028–0.048/0.7–1.2	0.08/2.0
total length (in./mm)	2.648–2.153/67.2–67.4	2.632/66.8
stem diameter (in./mm)	0.2149–0.2153/5.455–5.465	0.2141/5.435
head thickness (in./mm)	0.024–0.032/0.6–0.8	0.012/0.3
stem-to-guide clearance (in./mm)	0.0004–0.0012/0.01–0.03	0.0028/0.08

Engine, Clutch, and Transmission Specifications (cont.)

Model	S90 SL90 CL90 CL90L CD90 C90 CT90 Standard Value	Serviceable Limit
CYLINDER HEAD		
Exhaust valve:		
valve seat (in./mm)	0.028–0.048/0.7–1.2	0.08/2.0
total length (in./mm)	2.593–2.600/65.8–66.0	2.577/65.4
stem diameter (in./mm)	0.214–0.215/5.455–5.465	0.214/5.435
head thickness (in./mm)	0.024–0.032/0.6–0.8	0.012/0.3
stem-to-guide clearance (in./mm)	0.0012–0.0020/0.03–0.05	0.0032/0.1
Outer valve spring:		
free-length (in./mm)	1.253/31.8	1.207/30.6
compressed pressure (lbs/in.)	17.38–19.58/1.095	NA
(kg/mm)	7.9–8.9/27.8	NA
tilt	NA	1.5°
Inner valve spring:		
free-length (in./mm)	1.044/26.5	1.005/25.5
compressed pressure (lbs/in.)	20.90–23.10/1.73	NA
(kg/mm)	9.5–10.5/18.4	NA
tilt	NA	1.5°
Camshaft:		
left-end diameter (in./mm)	1.0208–1.025/25.917–25.930	0.9913/25.180
right-end diameter (in./mm)	0.7060–0.6730/17.927–17.938	0.7147/17.900
shaft run-out (in./mm)	0.0004/0.01	0.0020/0.05
cam height (in./mm)	0.9792–0.98396/24.90–24.98	0.9684/24.6
left-end bearing diameter (in./mm)	1.0236–1.0244/26.00–26.020	1.0256/26.05
right-end bearing diameter (in./mm)	0.7086–0.7093/18000–18018	0.7106/18.05
cam sprocket root diameter (in./mm)	2.103–2.105/53.435–53.385	2.09/53.00
Rocker arm:		
wear slipper (in./mm)	NA	6.0012/0.3
shaft bore (in./mm)	0.3937–0.3943/10.00–10.015	0.40–10.1
Rocker arm shaft:		
shaft diameter (in./mm)	0.3926–0.3933/9.972–9.987	0.3934/9.920
shaft clearance (in./mm)	0.0005–0.0017/0.013–0.043	0.0031/0.08
CYLINDER AND PISTON ASSEMBLY		
Cylinder:		
cylinder taper (in./mm)	0.0004/0.01	0.002/0.05
cylinder bore (in./mm)	1.9685–1.9688/50.00–50.01	1.9739/50.10
surface roughness (micron)	1.5	——
Piston:		
piston diameter (in./mm)	1.9673–1.9681/49.97–49.99	NA
ring side clearance (in./mm)	0.0004–0.018/0.01–0.1	0.004/0.1
oil ring side clearance (in./mm)	NA	NA
piston-to-piston pin clearance (in./mm)	NA	NA
Piston rings:		
ring thickness (in./mm)	0.0808–0.0812/1.175–1.190	0.0445/1.13
oil ring thickness (in./mm)	0.9743–0.9802/2.475–2.490	0.0953/2.43
ring end gap (in./mm)	0.006–0.014/0.15–0.35	0.02/0.5
oil ring end gap (in./mm)	0.0059–0.157/0.15–0.40	0.020/0.5
CAM CHAIN TENSIONER		
Tensioner spring:		
spring free-length (in./mm)	2.772/70.4	2.654/67.4
spring tension (in./oz)	1.931/2.275–2.285	1.931/1.400
(mm/g)	49.00/65.00–81.00	49.00/40.00
roller diameter	NA	NA

Engine, Clutch, and Transmission Specifications (cont.)

Model	S90 SL90 CL90 CL90L CD90 C90 CT90 Standard Value	Serviceable Limit
CLUTCH		
Friction disc and clutch plate:		
thickness of disc (in./mm)	0.1102–0.1141/2.8–2.9	0.0944/2.4
thickness of plate (in./mm)	0.0760–0.0815/1.93–2.07	0.073/1.85
warpage of plate (in./mm)	0.0079/0.2	0.0196/0.5
backlash of plate (in./mm)	0.008/0.2	0.036/0.7
backlash of disc (in./mm)	0.008/0.2	0.0196/0.7
Clutch center guide:		
inside diameter (in./mm)	NA	NA
outside diameter (in./mm)	NA	NA
length (in./mm)	NA	NA
run-out (in./mm)	NA	NA
crankshaft to guide clearance (in./mm)	0.0002–0.0019/0.005–0.047	0.060/0.15
Primary drive gear:		
inside diameter (in./mm)	0.945–0.946/24.00–24.02	0.951/24.15
chordal distance across three teeth (in./mm)	0.5496–0.5504/13.96–13.98	0.5484/13.93
Clutch spring:		
free-length (in./mm)	①	1.0236/26.0
spring tension (lb/in.)	②	NA
(kg/mm)		
CRANKSHAFT		
Crankshaft:		
run-out at the bearings (in./mm)	0.0006/0.015	0.004/0.1
axial clearance (in./mm)	0.004–0.019/0.10–0.35	0.032/0.8
clearance normal to axis (in./mm)	0–0.004/0–0.01	0.002/0.05
sprocket root diameter (in./mm)	NA	NA
right-side spline play (in./mm)	NA	NA
maximum shaft run-out (in./mm)	NA	NA
Crankpin:		
outside diameter (in./mm)	NA	NA
interference fit (in./mm)	NA	NA
Connecting rod:		
small-end-to-piston pin clearance (in./mm)	NA	NA
small-end deflection (in./mm)	NA	NA
large-end end-play (in./mm)	NA	NA
bearing clearance (in./mm)	NA	NA
small-end bore (in./mm)	0.5517–0.5523/14.012–14.028	0.5531/14.05

① S90, SL90, CL90,
   CL90L, CD90   1.0551/26.8
   C90, CT90   1.0630/27.0
② S90, SL90, CL90,   (lb/in.)   (kg/mm)
   CL90L, CD90   44.453–48.863/0.6890   20.16–22.16/17.5
   C90, CT90   22.0–22.9/0.591   10.0–10.4/15.0

Engine, Clutch, and Transmission Specifications (cont.)

Model	CB100 CL100 SL100 CB125S CD125S SL125 Standard Value	Serviceable Limit
CYLINDER HEAD		
Valve guides:		
outside diameter (in./mm)	NA	——
interference fit (in./mm)	NA	——
inside diameter (in./mm)	NA	NA
Intake valve:		
valve seat (in./mm)	0.028/0.7	0.059/1.5
total length (in./mm)	NA	NA
stem diameter (in./mm)	0.214–0.215/5.450–5.565	0.2130/5.420
head thickness (in./mm)	NA	NA
stem-to-guide clearance (in./mm)	NA	NA
Exhaust valve:		
valve seat (in./mm)	0.028/0.7	0.059/1.5
total length (in./mm)	NA	NA
stem diameter (in./mm)	0.214–0.215/5.430–5.445	0.2126/5.400
head thickness (in./mm)	NA	NA
stem-to-guide clearance (in./mm)	NA	NA
Outer valve spring:		
free-length (in./mm)	①	②
compressed pressure (lbs/in.)	NA	NA
(kg/mm)		
tilt	NA	NA
Inner valve spring:		
free-length (in./mm)	③	④
compressed pressure (lbs/in.)	NA	NA
(kg/mm)		
tilt	NA	NA
Camshaft:		
left-end diameter (in./mm)	NA	NA
right-end diameter (in./mm)	NA	NA
shaft run-out (in./mm)	NA	NA
cam height (in./mm)	NA	NA
left-end bearing diameter (in./mm)	NA	NA
right-end bearing diameter (in./mm)	NA	NA
cam sprocket root diameter (in./mm)	NA	NA
Rocker arm:		
wear slipper (in./mm)	NA	NA
shaft bore (in./mm)	NA	NA
Rocker arm shaft:		
shaft diameter (in./mm)	NA	NA
shaft clearance (in./mm)	NA	NA
CYLINDER AND PISTON ASSEMBLY		
Cylinder:		
cylinder taper (in./mm)	NA	NA
cylinder bore (in./mm)	⑤	⑥
surface roughness (micron)	1.5	——

Engine, Clutch, and Transmission Specifications (cont.)

Model	CB100 CL100 SL100 CB125S CD125S SL125 Standard Value	Serviceable Limit
CYLINDER AND PISTON ASSEMBLY		
Piston:		
piston diameter (in./mm)	⑦	⑧
ring side clearance (in./mm)	0.0008–0.0011/0.025–0.030	0.0275/0.7
oil ring side clearance (in./mm)	NA	NA
piston-to-cylinder clearance (in./mm)	0.0004–0.0020/0.01–0.05	NA
Piston rings:		
ring thickness (in./mm)	NA	NA
oil ring thickness (in./mm)	NA	NA
ring end gap (in./mm)	0.0059–0.0138/0.15–0.35	0.0197/0.5
oil ring end gap (in./mm)	0.0059–0.0158/0.15–0.04	0.0197/0.5
CAM CHAIN TENSIONER		
Tensioner spring:		
spring free-length (in./mm)	NA	NA
spring tension (in./oz)	NA	NA
(mm/g)	NA	NA
roller diameter	NA	NA
CLUTCH		
Friction disc and clutch plate:		
thickness of disc (in./mm)	0.114/2.9	0.102/26.00
thickness of plate (in./mm)	NA	NA
warpage of plate (in./mm)	NA	NA
backlash of plate (in./mm)	NA	NA
backlash of disc (in./mm)	NA	NA
Clutch center guide:		
inside diameter (in./mm)	NA	NA
outside diameter (in./mm)	NA	NA
length (in./mm)	NA	NA
run-out (in./mm)	NA	NA
crankshaft to guide clearance (in./mm)	NA	NA
Primary drive gear:		
inside diameter (in./mm)	NA	NA
chordal distance across three teeth (in./mm)	NA	NA
Clutch spring:		
free-length (in./mm)	NA	NA
spring tension (lb/in.)	NA	NA
CRANKSHAFT		
Crankshaft:		
run-out at the bearings (in./mm)	0.001/0.03	0.004/0.1
axial clearance (in./mm)	NA	NA
clearance normal to axis (in./mm)	NA	NA
sprocket root diameter (in./mm)	NA	NA
right-side spline play (in./mm)	NA	NA
maximum shaft run-out (in./mm)	NA	NA
Crankpin:		
outside diameter (in./mm)	NA	NA
interference fit (in./mm)	NA	NA

Engine, Clutch, and Transmission Specifications (cont.)

Model	CB100 CL100 SL100 CB125S CD125S SL125 Standard Value	Serviceable Limit

CRANKSHAFT

Connecting rod:

small-end-to-piston pin clearance (in./mm)	NA	NA
small-end deflection (in./mm)	NA	NA
large-end end-play (in./mm)	0.004–0.014/0.10–0.35	0.0032/0.8
bearing clearance (in./mm)	0–0.0004/0–0.01	0.0020/0.05
small-end bore (in./mm)	NA	NA

① CB100, CL100, SL100	1.591/40.4	
CB125S, CD125S, SL125	1.610/40.9	
② CB100, CL100, SL100	1.535/39.0	
CB125S, CD125S, SL125	1.555/39.5	
③ CB100, CL100, SL100	1.406/35.7	
CB125S, CD125S, SL125	1.318/33.5	
④ CB100, CL100, SL100	1.358/34.5	
CB125S, CD125S, SL125	1.259/32.0	
⑤ CB100, CL100, SL100	1.9881–1.9885/50.50–50.51	
CB125S, CD125S, SL125	2.2047–2.2051/56.00–56.01	
⑥ CB100, CL100, SL100	1.992/50.6	
CB125S, CD125S, SL125	2.2086/56.1	
⑦ CB100, CL100, SL100	1.987–1.988/50.47–50.49	
CB125S, CD125S, SL125	2.2035–2.2043/55.97–53.99	
⑧ CB100, CL100, SL100	1.980/50.3	
CB125S, CD125S, SL125	2.1968/55.80	

Valve Timing

S50 S65 CL70 SL70

Valve timing

inlet valve opens	5° BTDC
inlet valve closes	30° ABDC
exhaust valve opens	40° BBDC
exhaust valve closes	5° ATDC

S90 CL90 SL90

Valve timing

inlet valve opens	5° BTDC
inlet valve closes	35° ABDC
exhaust valve opens	25° BBDC
exhaust valve closes	5° ATDC

C50 C50M C65 C65M

Valve timing

inlet valve opens	0° BTDC
inlet valve closes	20° ABDC
exhaust valve opens	25° BBDC
exhaust valve closes	5° BTDC

CL90L CD90 C90 CT90

Valve timing

inlet valve opens	5° BTDC
inlet valve closes	20° ABDC
exhaust valve opens	25° BBDC
exhaust valve closes	5° ATDC

C70 C70M

Valve timing

inlet valve opens	5° BTDC
inlet valve closes	20° ATDC
exhaust valve opens	25° BBDC
exhaust valve closes	5° BTDC

CB100 CL100 SL100 CB125S CD125S SL125

Valve timing

inlet valve opens	
inlet valve closes	NA
exhaust valve opens	
exhause valve closes	

BTDC.................before top dead center
ABDC..............after bottom dead center
BBDC.............before bottom dead center
ATDC.................after top dead center

5 · Lubrication System

All of the Honda single-cylinder engines are lubricated by a mechanical oil pump. Some of the older models (50 and 90 cc models mostly) used a two-gear pump at one time, but now they all use a trochoid pump. The advantage of the trochoid type is that it is more compact, one gear rotating inside another rather than two gears

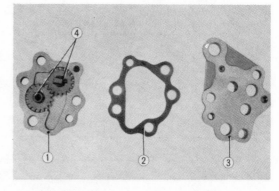

Gear type oil pump

1. Oil pump cover   3. Oil pump body
2. Oil pump cover gasket   4. Oil pump gear

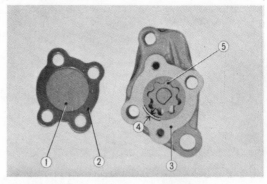

Trochoid type oil pump

1. Oil pump cover
2. Oil pump cover gasket
3. Oil pump body
4. Outer rotor-to-pump body clearance
5. Inner rotor

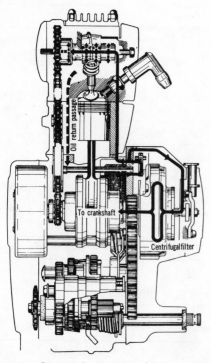

Lubrication diagram for 50, 65, and 70 cc engines

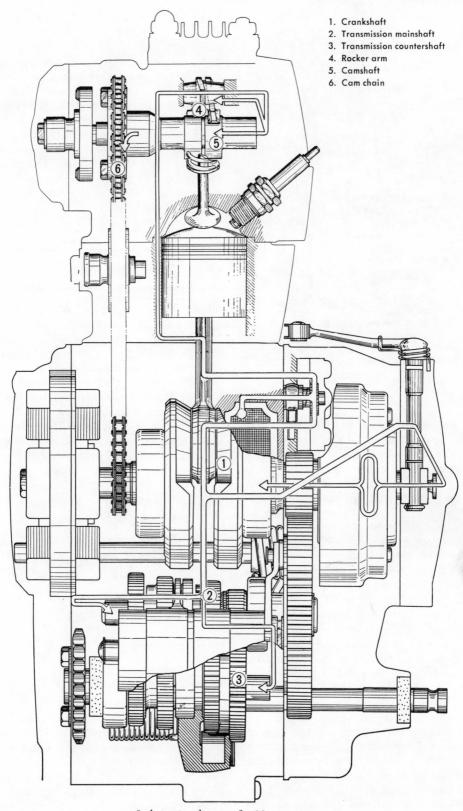

1. Crankshaft
2. Transmission mainshaft
3. Transmission countershaft
4. Rocker arm
5. Camshaft
6. Cam chain

Lubrication diagram for 90 cc engines

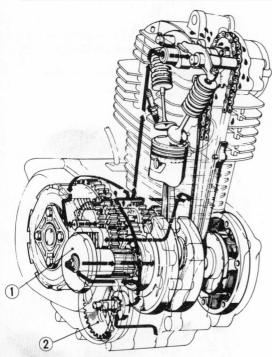

Lubrication diagram for 100 and 125 cc engines

1. Oil filter   2. Oil pump

side-by-side, and it is more efficient and reliable since it doesn't depend on springs and balls and other such things which tend to get stuck and fail relatively easily.

The trochoid pump consists of an inner and outer rotor, both equipped with a different number of teeth. The difference in the shape and number of teeth causes the pumping action, and the output of the pump is also determined by these factors.

The oil sits in the bottom of the crankcase until drawn into the oil strainer and routed through the engine. The oil travels through the right crankcase, through a passageway in the right crankcase cover, to the centrifugal oil filter, and then to the crankshaft and transmission assemblies. The transmission is splash-lubricated in the 50, 65, and 70 cc models, and is lubricated through passages in the mainshaft and countershaft in the larger models.

The other pumping route takes care of the top end, and the oil which passes through the camshaft also lubricates the cam chain on its way to the sump. Eventually all the oil returns to the sump from which it is again routed through the engine.

The oil pump should require little if no

attention for many miles unless it is abused. Oil pump components will wear prematurely if the oil is not changed regularly, and if the filters are not kept clean. Provide the pump with these little courtesies and you can be pretty sure that you'll rebuild the engine a few times before the pump itself ever requires attention. It is a good practice however, to check the pumping pressure periodically (every 12 months or 10,000 miles). This service should be carried out by your dealer as it requires special tools that are not worth your while to buy.

Oil Pump

50, 65, 70, AND 90 CC MODELS

Disassembly

1. Remove the right-side crankcase cover and clutch assemblies.

2. Remove the oil pump assembly by removing the 6 mm bolts and the hex bolt which secure it to the crankcase.

3. The pump may be further disassembled or replaced as a unit. The disassembly procedures are quite straightforward.

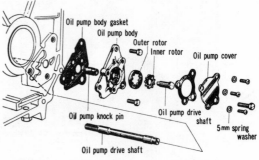

Oil pump assembly

Inspection and Repair

1. Clean all components other than the gaskets in a suitable solvent and blow them dry. Replace any obviously damaged parts, and use new gaskets when reassembling the assembly.

2. Rotate the pump driveshaft by hand, check it for smooth motion, and replace it as necessary.

3. Measure the clearance between the outer rotor and the pump body using

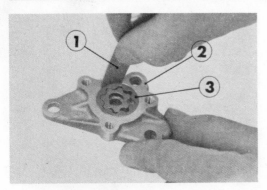

Measuring rotor-to-pump body clearance

    1. Feeler gauge   3. Outer rotor
    2. Pump body

feeler gauges, and replace the necessary parts if worn beyond their serviceable limits.

4. Measure the rotor-to-rotor clearance using feeler gauges, and replace them as necessary.

5. Measure the end-play of the rotor by placing a straightedge over the pump body, and measuring the clearance between the top of the rotor and the straightedge with feeler gauges. Replace the rotor if necessary.

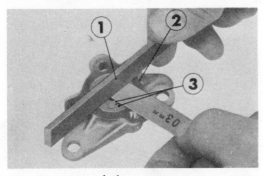

Measuring rotor end-play

    1. Straightedge   3. Rotor
    2. Pump body

6. On gear and rotor type pumps, check for gear backlash. If the backlash is excessive, the gears should be replaced as a pair. You'll probably know that there is excessive play there because the pump operation will be noisy. Backlash, unless extreme, will probably not affect the pumping pressure.

Assembly

1. Assembly is basically the reverse order of disassembly.

2. Place the inner rotor and outer rotor together, then install the assembly in the right crankcase. Use new gaskets whenever applicable.

100 AND 125 CC MODELS

Disassembly

1. Remove the right-side crankcase and oil filter rotor covers, then remove the 6 mm locknut and remove the oil filter rotor.

Removing the oil filter rotor

    1. 16 mm wrench   2. Oil filter rotor

2. Remove the oil pump gear cover.

3. Remove the tachometer pinion gear on the CB and SL 125 cc models.

Removing the oil pump drive gear

    1. Oil pump drive gear   2. Shaft

4. Remove the oil pump drive gear, then remove the pump assembly.

5. Remove the oil pump shaft, then remove the outer rotor.

Inspection and Repair

1. Clean all parts other than gaskets in a suitable solvent and blow them dry.

2. Inspect all parts for obvious damage

Removing the oil pump body

1. 6 mm bolts   2. Oil pump body

Installing the O-rings

1. O-ring

and replace them as necessary. The two rotors must be replaced as a pair.

3. The general practice, if the pump is not putting out, is to replace either the entire assembly, or try to replace individual parts. Since there are no available specifications for these models, the best bet is to replace the assembly.

Assembly

1. Assembly is basically in the reverse order of disassembly.

2. Install the pump with the concave portion of the pump on the convex portion of the oil pump plate.

3. Install the pump body, taking care to replace the two O-rings.

4. Bring the oil pump shaft into alignment with the cutout on the inner rotor gear, then assemble the unit.

5. Install the tachometer pinion gear on CB and SL 125 cc models.

6. Assemble the oil pump drive gears, then mount and secure the pump gear cover.

7. Mount the oil filter rotor and torque the locknut to 29–36 ft lbs. Make sure you use the lockwasher.

8. Install the remaining covers.

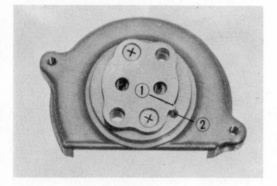

Aligning the cover on the plate

1. Cover mark   2. Plate mark

Installing the pump shaft

1. Pump shaft

Oil Pump Specifications

90 cc and Under, Trochoid Type Pump	Standard Value	Serviceable Limit
Clearance between rotor and housing	0.004–0.006 in. (0.10–0.15 mm)	Replace if over 0.0079 in. (0.20 mm)
Clearance between rotor and top of housing	0.008–0.027 in. (0.02–0.07 mm)	Replace if over 0.0047 in. (0.12 mm)
Clearance between rotors	0.008–0.028 in. (0.02–0.07 mm)	Replace if over 0.0047 in. (0.12 mm)
Rotor backlash	0.006 in. (0.15 mm)	Replace if over 0.008 in. (0.2 mm)
Gear Type Pump		
Clearance between gear and housing	0.0020–0.0035 in. (0.05–0.09 mm)	Replace if over 0.0059 in. (0.15 mm)
Gear backlash	0.0037–0.0014 in. (0.0940–0.188 mm)	Replace if over 0.0118 in. (0.30 mm)

Oil Pump Pressure

50, 65, and 70 cc models	NA
90 cc models (trochoid type)	1400 cc (85.43 cu in.)/min @ 8000 rpm
(gear type)	1200 cc (73.22 cu in.)/min @ 4000 rpm
100 and 125 cc models	2.4 l/min @ 10,000 rpm

6 · Fuel System

Carburetor

All of the carburetors used on the single-cylinder Hondas are of the traditional, direct-control type, and are manufactured by Keihin. These carburetors are designed to provide excellent performance throughout a wide range of atmospheric conditions without modifications becoming necessary in even the most extreme conditions.

OPERATIONAL DESCRIPTION

The throttle twist-grip is connected to, and directly controls, the throttle slide; the amount which the throttle is opened directly corresponds to the slide position, which in turn determines the venturi size. After air is drawn into the carburetor and past the slide, it enters a relatively low-pressure area, and in so doing, draws fuel up past the jet needle. In this way, the proper air/fuel mixture is created, due to the relationship between the intake manifold vacuum and air velocity through the carburetor. The size of the jet and the taper of the jet needle determine how much fuel is drawn for a given amount of vacuum and air velocity.

It can be seen here that if the throttle is opened suddenly (yanking the slide up just as quickly) at low rpm, air velocity through the venturi will be low because of the low intake vacuum and large throttle (venturi) opening, and an insufficient amount of fuel will be drawn for the volume of air inducted. This creates a momentary lean mixture condition and causes a hesitation before the engine accelerates smoothly. It also can be seen that lowering or raising the jet needle position relative to the slide, or changing the size of the main jet, will have an effect on the mixture strength. Changing the position of the needle taper will affect running at mid-range throttle openings (from about 1/4–3/4 throttle) and changing the main jet will affect the full throttle operation. This is so because, at small throttle openings, the needle effectively plugs the jet tube completely and the low-speed system takes over, while at full throttle, the needle is withdrawn from the jet tube enough so that the main jet is virtually unrestricted.

Low-Speed System

At small throttle openings (approximately 1/4–1/8 throttle), the carburetor low-speed system is in operation. Air entering the carburetor is regulated by the air screw, after which it enters the low-speed jet bleed hole. The air then mixes with the fuel entering the low-speed jet and the mixture is then discharged from the pilot outlet under the slide. The mixture is then carried into the engine along with the small amount of air allowed to pass through the slight opening or cutaway of

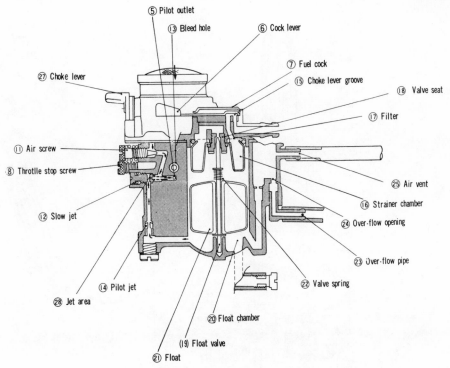

⑤ Pilot outlet
⑬ Bleed hole
⑥ Cock lever
⑦ Fuel cock
⑰ Choke lever
⑮ Choke lever groove
⑱ Valve seat
⑰ Filter
⑪ Air screw
⑧ Throttle stop screw
㉕ Air vent
⑯ Strainer chamber
⑫ Slow jet
㉔ Over-flow opening
㉓ Over-flow pipe
⑭ Pilot jet
㉒ Valve spring
㉘ Jet area
⑳ Float chamber
⑲ Float valve
㉑ Float

Carburetor used on the C series 50, 65, and 70 cc engines

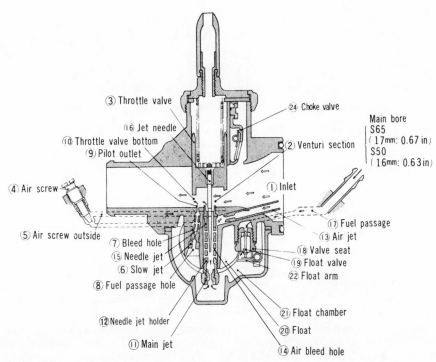

③ Throttle valve
㉔ Choke valve
⑯ Jet needle
⑩ Throttle valve bottom
② Venturi section
⑨ Pilot outlet
④ Air screw
① Inlet
⑤ Air screw outside
⑰ Fuel passage
⑦ Bleed hole
⑬ Air jet
⑮ Needle jet
⑱ Valve seat
⑥ Slow jet
⑲ Float valve
⑧ Fuel passage hole
㉒ Float arm
⑫ Needle jet holder
㉑ Float chamber
⑪ Main jet
⑳ Float
⑭ Air bleed hole

Main bore
S65
(17mm: 0.67 in)
S50
(16mm: 0.63 in)

Carburetor used on the S series 50, 65, and 70 cc engines

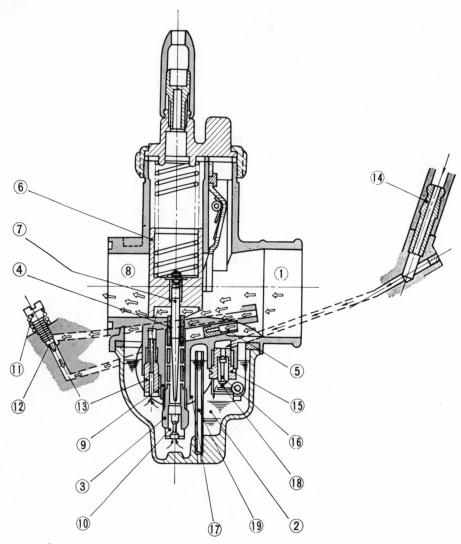

Carburetor used on 90 cc models (except for CT90 models from frame no. 000001A)

1. Inlet side of carburetor	8. Outlet side of carburetor	14. Fuel passage
2. Float chamber	9. Air bleed holes	15. Valve seat
3. Needle jet holder	10. Main jet	16. Float valve
4. Needle jet	11. Air screw	17. Float
5. Air jet	12. Opening of the air screw	18. Float arm
6. Throttle valve	13. Slow jet	19. Overflow pipe
7. Jet needle		

the slide. As the slide is raised past ¼ throttle opening, the relatively small amount of mixture discharged by the low-speed jet is overshadowed by the volume of air now being allowed to enter, and, of course, the main jet system is coming into play as the needle is withdrawn from the jet tube. At the same time, increased air flow and vacuum (bypassing the air screw), and increased pressure through the venturi (over the low-speed jet discharge outlet) effectively closes off the low-speed system and the transition to the main system is complete.

Float Chamber

In order to maintain the correct flow of fuel to the carburetor jets at all engine speeds and throttle openings, a sufficient amount of fuel under relatively constant delivery pressure must be available. The float chamber serves to accomplish this.

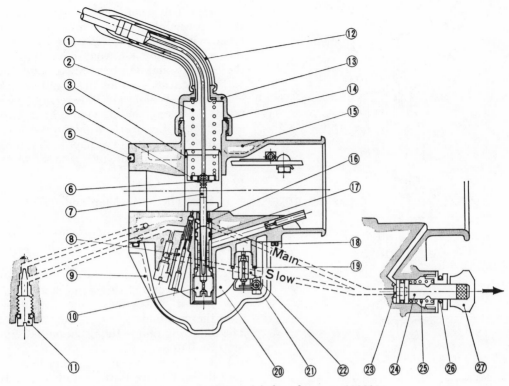

Carburetor used on CT90 models from frame no. 000001A

1. Throttle cable adjuster	8. Slow jet	15. Body	22. Float valve
2. Throttle spring	9. Float chamber body	16. Needle jet	23. Rubber cap
3. Throttle valve	10. Main jet	17. O-ring	24. Check valve
4. Needle clip plate	11. Air screw	18. O-ring	25. Coil spring
5. O-ring	12. Rubber cap	19. Washer	26. Special clip
6. Bar clip	13. Top	20. Float	27. Knob
7. Jet needle	14. Top washer	21. Float arm pin	

Fuel entering the float chamber from the fuel tank must pass between the float needle and seat valve. As fuel fills the chamber, the float rises with the fuel level and when a preset level is reached, the float shuts off flow by pressing the needle against the seat, closing the valve. As fuel is consumed and the level drops, the float will have followed the level, allowing more fuel to enter so that a constant level will be maintained.

It is very important that the float level be correctly set so that the proper mixture strength is maintained. An adjustable float level gauge, suitable for most motorcycle carburetors, is available from Honda dealers (tool no. 07144–99998). An improperly set float level can cause poor or erratic performance in both the low- and high-speed ranges.

Adjusting the float level

1. Float level gauge

CARBURETOR OVERHAUL

When working on any of these carburetors, keep in mind that the components are

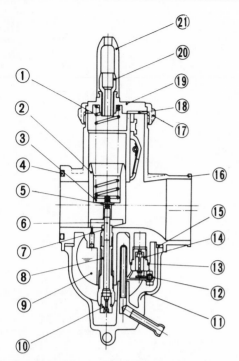

Carburetor used on 100 and 125 cc engines

1. Coil spring	12. Arm pin
2. Throttle valve	13. Valve seat
3. Needle clip plate	14. Slow jet
4. O-ring	15. Float chamber washer
5. Bar clip	16. Body
6. Jet needle	17. Cap
7. Needle jet	18. Top washer
8. Needle jet holder	19. Top
9. Float	20. Cable adjuster
10. Main jet	21. Rubber cap
11. Float chamber body	

machined to exacting specifications and must not be treated roughly. It is possible to purchase a rebuilding kit for any of these units, and it is suggested that you use all the parts which come in the kit. Clean all the parts in a suitable solvent such as gasoline, and blow them dry, if possible, with compressed air.

Look for blunted adjusters which indicate that the screws have been forced into their seats, and may have even done damage to them. A situation like this could call for replacing the carburetor body. Carefully examine all passages as they can become blocked partially and cause erratic performance. Check for burrs or score marks on the slide, jet, or jet needle which could cause the carb to hang-up. Inspect the float for a gas-logged condition which would make replacement necessary. Gas-

kets, especially float bowl gaskets, lose all their crushability after they have been toyed with a few times. Even if you don't buy a rebuilding kit, you should replace the gaskets and O-rings. Make sure the carburetor seats well on the manifold. Air leaks will make your machine seem like it's on its last legs, and if you ride it long enough with the overlean mixture a situation like this causes, you'll probably do a lot of damage to the piston and valves.

Removal and Installation

1. Turn off the fuel tap and disconnect the fuel line.

2. Unscrew the carburetor cap, carefully withdraw the slide, and place the assembly out of the way.

3. Loosen and slide back the air cleaner connecting clamp at the carburetor.

4. Unbolt and remove the carburetor from the manifold.

The following points should be noted during installation:

1. Tighten the mounting bolts that secure the carburetor to the manifold evenly to avoid crushing the manifold spacer gasket.

2. When installing the slide in the carburetor, take special care not to damage the needle when dropping it into the jet tube. Make sure the needle starts into the tube, and check to make sure that the tab in the slide bore engages the slot in the slide. Lightly coating the slide with clean engine oil is a good idea as it will help lubricate the slide in the bore. Make sure there is no chance that dirt has gotten into the bore before you install the slide, as dirt will chew up the surface of a slide in short order, thereby causing air leaks.

3. Tighten down the carburetor cap firmly, then check the operation of the throttle linkage. If it binds check the cable for kinks, then check the slide to make sure it is in correctly and that it will slide down the bore of its own weight. The slide may be lightly sanded with fine sandpaper if it is burred or has a high spot.

4. Reset the adjustments after the carburetor is mounted, then run a plug check to make sure your mixture is correct.

Disassembly

1. Disconnect the carburetor slide from the throttle cable by compressing the spring and feeding the inner cable into the

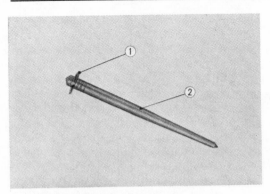

Jet needle and needle clip

1. Needle clip   2. Jet needle

slide so that the cable end can be disengaged from the retaining slot. The needle and clip will have to be removed.

2. Release the float bowl by swiveling back the retaining clip. Either try to hold the bowl in its normal position so you don't spill the gas all over the engine, or drain the bowl by removing the drain plug and allowing the gas to drain off into a suitable receptacle.

3. Tap out the float pin from the float tang using a small diameter rod or drift. Remove the float and lift the float valve needle out of the valve seat. Unscrew the valve seat from the carburetor body.

4. Using a small screwdriver, remove the main jet, low-speed jet, throttle stop-screw, and the air screw.

5. Unscrew the main jet tube using a suitably sized wrench.

Inspection and Repair

1. Clean all parts, other than the gaskets, in a suitable solvent and blow them dry. If you use an acid type carburetor cleaner, do not clean the float or any other rubber or plastic parts in it as they will be damaged by it.

2. Make sure that the surface of the throttle slide is clean and smooth. Light scoring can be smoothed with fine emery cloth.

3. Examine the jet needle for wear as indicated by bright spots or an uneven taper. If wear is noticeable, replace both the needle and the needle jet tube.

4. Examine the float valve needle for wear. If replacement is necessary, replace the needle and seat as a unit.

5. Inspect the carburetor body for cracks, and replace it as necessary.

Assembly

1. Assembly is basically in the reverse order of disassembly. Use new gaskets and O-rings.

2. The float level must be checked and adjusted if necessary. The float should be positioned so that when the float arm just touches the tip of the float needle, the distance from the top of the float to the float bowl mating surface on the carburetor is as close as possible to the specification given at the end of the chapter for your carburetor.

3. Do not overtighten the jets when installing them in the carburetor body.

4. Make sure that the jet needle is installed in the same position as when removed. Changing the needle position in the slide will affect the mid-throttle range operation.

5. After installing the carburetor, check for smooth operation of the choke. If the choke hasn't been properly reassembled, the bike will run excessively lean.

Fuel Tap

REMOVAL, CLEANING, AND INSPECTION

1. Turn the tap to the "stop" position and disconnect the fuel lines. Be prepared to catch the run-off from the fuel lines in a suitable receptacle.

2. Raise the seat and either remove the tank or raise the rear of it up and support it (if applicable). On step-through type frames, the fuel tap is located at the carburetor and can be reached without removing anything.

3. Drain the strainer cup by removing the drain plug at the bottom of the cup, or just unscrew the cup and hold it in such a way as not to allow the fuel to drip on everything.

4. Remove the O-ring and fuel strainer from the cup.

5. Remove the two mounting screws and remove the fuel tap.

6. Remove the two screws from the lever retaining plate and remove the plate, O-ring, and gasket.

7. Clean all the components in a suitable solvent and blow them dry. Inspect

all the parts for wear, cracks, or any other damage which could contribute to a fuel leak.

8. Assemble the tap in the reverse order of disassembly using all new gaskets and O-rings. If there have been leaks at the fittings where the lines meet the tap, either replace the lines if they are worn or punctured, or secure them with a hose clamp or a piece of mechanic's wire wrapped around the line and fitting. If these don't work try using a silicone-based sealant.

9. Install the tap on the tank and check for proper fuel flow by turning on the tap and allowing the gas to run out into a suitable receptacle. Make sure you don't have the reserve and normal supply lines reversed.

10. Lower the tank (if applicable), install the fuel lines, and check the system for leaks. If the system doesn't work, check to make sure that the gas cap vent hole is not plugged.

Fuel Tank

Honda uses steel fuel tanks on all of the models covered in this guide. If a tank should begin to leak along a seam, it can be repaired by welding, or at least temporarily by silicone unless the leak is on the bottom of the tank and is under pressure when the tank is full.

Welding a tank is a dangerous business for those who don't really know what they're doing, so it is suggested you consult your dealer. If he isn't equipped to do work such as this, he can probably direct you to a qualified welder. If you are good with a torch and wish to do the work yourself, make sure there are no gas fumes left in the tank before you get started or you are liable to blow the tank up.

If a tank becomes rusted inside due to an improper storage procedure, it probably can still be salvaged unless really rusted out. If you use a tank with rust in it you should thoroughly clean out the fuel filter regularly. Most of the flaky rust can be removed by placing some small, loose bearings in the tank and shaking them around. The bearings will knock the rust loose and it can then be flushed out. Use small bearings so as not to dent the tank, and repeat the process several times to get out as much rust as possible. If a sand blaster is available you can clean the tank out in no time at all. When you are finished, flush the tank out several times with kerosine or gas to keep the grit out of the fuel filter.

Carburetor Specifications

Setting Specifications

Model / Carburetor type		C65 1000-112 (1000-113)	C65M 1000-115	C50 1000-110 (1000-145)	C50M 1000-111	S65 PW16FA6 (CF130) PW16FA10 (CYFF130)	S50 PW16FA11
Setting mark		65H (Y65H)	65MB	C50C	50MB	17-B	K
Throttle bore		13φ (0.512 in.)	13φ	13φ	13φ	16 mm (0.630 in.)	16 mm (0.630 in.)
Venturi bore		14φ (0.551)	14φ	13φ	13φ	17 mm (0.670 in.) equiv	16 mm (0.630 in.) equiv
Main jet		no. 72	no. 72	no. 70	no. 72	no. 85	no. 78
Air jet		no. 150	no. 150	no. 150	no. 150	no. 150	no. 120
Main air bleed	AB1	0.4φ × 2 (0.0157 in.)	0.5φ × 2	0.5φ × 2	0.5φ × 2	0.5 mm (0.0197 in.) × 4	0.9 mm (0.0354 in.) × 4
	1.5	0.4φ × 2	0.4φ × 2		0.4φ × 2		
	2	0.4φ × 2	0.4φ × 2	0.4φ × 2	0.4φ × 2	0.9 mm (0.0354 in.) × 2	0.6 mm (0.0236 in.) × 2
	3	0.4φ × 2	0.4φ × 2	0.4φ × 2	0.4φ × 2		0.6 mm (0.0236 in.) × 2
	4	0.4φ × 2	0.4φ × 2	0.4φ × 2	0.4φ × 2	0.5 mm (0.0197 in.) × 2	0.6 mm (0.0236 in.) × 2
	5	0.4φ × 2	0.4φ × 2				
	6	0.4φ × 2	0.4φ × 2	0.4φ × 2	0.4φ × 2	0.5 mm (0.0197 in.) × 2	0.6 mm (0.0236 in.) × 2
Needle jet		3.0 × 2.8 mm (0.118 × 0.110 in.) 3φ × 2.8 recess	3φ × 2.8	3φ × 2.5	3φ × 2.5	2.6 mm (0.1023 in.) [3.4 (0.134 in.) recess]	2.6 mm (0.1023 in.) [3.4 (0.134 in.) recess]
Jet needle		13243 3 stage	13243 3 stage	13239 3 stage	13239 3 stage	16305 3 stage	16232 3 stage
Cutaway (throttle valve)		no. 2.0 [1.2 × 0.15] (0.047 × 0.006 in.) 2.0 (1.2φ × 0.15)	no. 2.0 (1.2 × 0.15)	no. 2.0 (1.2φ × 0.15)	no. 2.0 (1.2 × 0.15)	no. 1.5 [1.2 × 0.3] (0.047 × 0.012 in.)	no. 1.5 [1.2 × 0.3] (0.047 × 0.012 in.)
Air screw		1¼ ~ ⅛	1¼ ~ ⅛	1¼ ± ⅛	1¼ ± ⅛	1½ ~ ⅛	1½ ~ ⅛
Slow jet		no. 35	no. 35	no. 35	no. 35	no. 38	no. 35
Slow air bleed	1	0.8 mm (0.315 in.) × 2 0.8φ × 2	0.9φ × 2	0.8φ × 2	0.9φ × 2	0.7 mm (0.0276 in.) × 2	0.8 mm (0.0315 in.) × 2
	2	0.8 mm (0.315 in.) × 2 0.8φ × 2	0.8φ × 2	0.8φ × 2	0.8φ × 2	0.7 mm (0.0276 in.) × 2	0.8 mm (0.0315 in.) × 2
	3	0.8 mm (0.315 in.) × 2 0.8φ × 2	0.9φ × 2	0.8φ × 2	0.9φ × 2	0.7 mm (0.0276 in.) × 2	0.7 mm (0.0276 in.) × 2
	4	0.8 mm (0.315 in.) × 2 0.8φ × 2	0.8φ × 2	0.8φ × 2	0.8φ × 2	0.7 mm (0.0276 in.) × 2	0.7 mm (0.0276 in.) × 2
Valve seat		1.2 mm (0.0473 in.) 1.2φ	1.2φ	1.2φ	1.2φ	1.0 mm (0.0394 in.)	1.0 mm (0.0394 in.)
Pilot jet		no. 35	no. 35	no. 35	no. 35		
Pilot outlet		0.9 mm (0.0354 in.) P = 5.0	0.9φ P = 5.0	0.9φ P = 5.0	0.9φ P = 5.0	1.0 mm (0.0394 in.) P = 5.5	1.0 mm (0.0394 in.) P = 5.5
Fuel level (actual fuel height)		17.5 mm (0.689 in.) 17.5	17.5	15.5	15.5	19.5 mm (0.768 in.) Height of float	19.5 mm / 0.768 in. Height of float

Carburetor Specifications (cont.)

		Model	CL70	C70	C70M
	Carburetor type		——	DP 13 N 14 AI	DP 13N 14 AI
	Setting mark		AL 70 B	C 70 C	C 70 MA
	Main jet		no. 72	no. 75	no. 75
	Air jet		no. 90	no. 150	no. 150
		AB 1	0.6 mm (0.024 in.) × 4	0.4 mm (0.016 in.) × 2	0.4 mm (0.016 in.) × 2
		1.5	——	0.4 mm (0.016 in.) × 2	0.4 mm (0.016 in.) × 2
		2	0.6 mm (0.024 in.) × 2	0.4 mm (0.016 in.) × 2	0.4 mm (0.016 in.) × 2
	Main air 3		——	0.4 mm (0.016 in.) × 2	0.4 mm (0.016 in.) × 2
	bleed 4		0.7 mm (0.028 in.) × 2	0.4 mm (0.016 in.) × 2	0.4 mm (0.016 in.) × 2
		5	0.7 mm (0.028 in.) × 2	0.4 mm (0.016 in.) × 2	0.4 mm (0.016 in.) × 2
		6	——	0.4 mm (0.016 in.) × 2	0.4 mm (0.016 in.) × 2
Setting Specifications	Needle jet		2.6 mm (0.102) × 3.7R	2.1 mm (0.083) × 3.0R	2.1 mm (0.083 in.) × 3.0R
	Jet needle		2°30" 2 steps 2.535 mm (0.0998 in.)	2°30" 2.5 steps 2.04 mm (0.0803 in.)	3°00" 3 steps 2.05 mm (0.0807 in.)
	Cutaway		no. 2.5 width 1.2 mm (0.047 in.) depth 0.2 mm (0.008 in.)	no. 2.5 width 1.2 mm (0.047 in.) depth 0.2 mm (0.008 in.)	no. 2.5
	Air screw		1⅛ ± ⅛	1½ ± ⅛	1⅛ ± ⅛
	Slow jet		no. 38	no. 35	no. 35
		1	0.9 mm (0.0354 in.) × 2	0.8 mm (0.031 in.) × 2	0.8 mm (0.031 in.) × 2
	Slow air 2		0.9 mm (0.0354 in.) × 2	0.8 mm (0.031 in.) × 2	0.8 mm (0.031 in.) × 2
	bleed 3		0.9 mm (0.0354 in.) × 2	0.8 mm (0.031 in.) × 2	0.8 mm (0.031 in.) × 2
		4	0.9 mm (0.0354 in.) × 2	0.8 mm (0.031 in.) × 2	0.8 mm (0.031 in.) × 2
	Pilot jet		——	no. 35	no. 35
	Valve seat		1.0 mm (0.039 in.)	1.2 mm (0.047 in.)	1.2 mm (0.047 in.) × 2
	By-pass		0.9 mm (0.035 in.) P = 5.4 mm (0.213 in.)	0.92 mm (0.036 in.) P = 50 mm (0.197 in.)	0.92 mm (0.036 in.) P = 50 mm (0.197 in.)
	Main bore		15 mm (0.591 in.)	14 mm (0.551 in.)	14 mm (0.551 in.)
	Fuel level		7.0 mm (0.276 in.)	13.5 mm (0.531 in.)	15.5 mm (0.610 in.)

Model	CB100, CL100, SL100	CB125S, SL125S
Main jet	no. 110	no. 105
Air jet	no. 100	no. 100
Needle jet	2.6φ × 3.8φ length 10	2.6φ × 3.8φ length 10
Needle jet holder	5.0φ	5.0φ
Jet needle	2°30" × 3 step 2.495φ	2°30" × 5 step 2.495φ
Air screw	1½ ± ⅛	1½ ± ⅛
Throttle valve	no. 2.5 cutaway width 1.2 depth 0.2	no. 2.5 cutaway width 1.8 depth 0.2
Slow jet	no. 38 1 0.8φ × 2 2 0.8φ × 2 3 0.8φ × 2	no. 38 0.9φ × 2 × 4
Fuel level	24 mm (0.9449 in.)	24 mm (0.9449 in.)

Carburetor Specifications (cont.)

Model		*S90*	*CL90, CL90L*	*CD90*	*C90*	*CT90*	*CT90 (from F. No. 000001A)*
Carburetor type		1000–133–00	1000–152–00	1000–131–00	1000–109–00	1000–108–00	1000–108–00
Main jet		no. 85	no. 85	no. 90	no. 75	no. 72	no. 80
Air jet		no. 150	no. 150	no. 150	no. 120	no. 120	no. 120
Main air bleed	AB 0	—	—	—	—	—	—
	1	0.7 × 4	0.7 × 2	0.7 × 2	0.5 × 2	0.4 × 2	1.3 × 2
	2	0.6 × 2	0.7 × 2	0.7 × 2	—	0.4 × 2	0.6 × 4
	3	0.6 × 2	0.7 × 2	0.7 × 2	0.4 × 2	0.4 × 2	0.4 × 2
	4	0.6 × 2	0.7 × 2	0.7 × 2	0.4 × 2	0.4 × 2	—
	5	0.6 × 2	0.7 × 4	0.7 × 2	0.4 × 2	0.4 × 2	0.4 × 2
Needle jet		2.60 × 3.7	2.60 × 3.7	2.60 × 3.5	2.60 × 3.7	2.60 × 3.5	2.60 × 3.4
Jet needle		18241 2 stage	18241 2 stage	183011 3 stage	16332 2 stage	16332 3 stage	3 stage
Cutaway (throttle valve)		no. 2.5 width: 1.2, depth: 0.3 cutout provided	no. 2.5 width: 1.2, depth: 0.3 cutout provided	no. 2.5 cutout not provided	no. 2.0 width: 1.2, depth: 0.3 cutout provided	no. 2.0 width: 1.4, depth: 0.3	no. 2.5 width: 1.2, depth: 0.2
Air screw		1¼ ± ⅛	1⅜ ± ⅛	1¼ ± ⅛	1.0 ± ⅛	1⅜ ± ⅛	1⅛ ± ⅛
Slow jet	1	0.9 × 2	0.9 × 2	0.9 × 2	0.8 × 2	0.9 × 2	0.8 × 2
	2 no. 38	0.9 × 2 no. 35	0.9 × 2 no. 40	0.9 × 2 no. 40	0.8 × 2 no. 40	0.9 × 2 no. 38	0.8 × 2
	3	0.9 × 2	0.9 × 2	0.9 × 2	0.8 × 2	0.9 × 2	0.8 × 2
	4	—	0.9 × 2	0.9 × 2	—	0.9 × 2	—
Valve seat		1.5	1.5	1.5	1.2	1.2	1.5
By-pass		1 2	1 1.0 2	1 2	1 2	1 2	—
Pilot outlet		1 1.0 pitch 7.0	1 pitch 7.0	1 1.1 pitch 6.3	1 1.2 pitch 5.1	2 1.0 pitch 5.1	1 0.9 pitch 5.5
Pilot air jet		—	—	—	no. 60	—	—
P.W.J.		—	—	—	—	—	—
P.W.A.J.		—	—	—	—	—	—
Fuel level		16.5	19.5	19.5	19.5	19.5	27 (adjustment height 23.5)
Setting mark		S 90 C	L 90 A	B	D	B	T 90 KA

7 · Electrical System

Charging System

Honda uses two types of electrical system on the models covered in this guide. The simpler method of generating power, and that which is used on all of the 50, 65, and 70 cc models, is the magneto system which uses AC current produced by a permanently magnetized flywheel, an ignition coil, and a lighting coil. The flywheel is secured to the end of the crankshaft and the coils are mounted in a fixed position within the flywheel circumference. The flywheel's rotating magnetic field cuts across the coil windings and, due to the constantly reversing magnetic field, induces an AC current through the coils.

The ignition coil current then travels through the condenser, points, secondary ignition coil (which boosts the voltage to a point where the spark will jump the gap of the spark plug), and spark plug. The lighting coil current is connected to a load with the proper inductance, so that when current rises with the engine speed, resistance to the AC current increases. This serves to regulate voltage. The lighting coil is also connected to a selenium rectifier which converts the AC current to DC for charging the battery. Of the models equipped with this system, only the C50M, C65M, and the C70M come equipped with electric starting.

The other system which is used on all of the other models is an alternator system which produces AC current through a rotor and stator assembly. It operates in basically the same way as the magneto system, but in this case the permanent magnet (rotor) revolves within the fixed coils (stator). The current passes from the stator to a selenium rectifier where it is converted into DC and is used for ignition and lighting.

If a charging system fault is suspected, the first thing to do is check the overload

Flywheel   Stator assembly

Flywheel generator

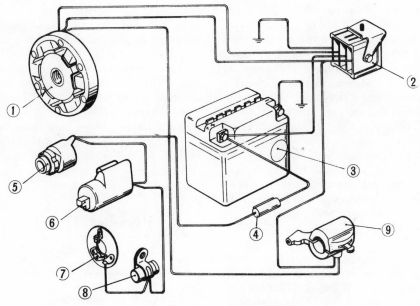

Alternator generating system

1. Alternator
2. Selenium rectifier
3. Battery
4. Fuse
5. Combination switch
6. Ignition coil
7. Breaker points
8. Condenser
9. Lighting switch

fuse located near the battery. If it is not burned out, inspect the wires and connections at the battery, alternator, rectifier, and regulator (if applicable). Make sure that the rectifier is securely mounted to the frame. If any defects are found, alternator output should be checked (after the fault is corrected) to ensure that the alternator and rectifier have not been damaged by being inadvertently disconnected from the circuit. If no obvious fault can be found in the charging system, refer to the following sections for testing and repair procedures.

Component Testing

TESTING THE IGNITION SYSTEM

The first things to check, and this applies to any and all electrical problems, are the fuse, battery, and the wiring connectors. The fuse is located in a tubular plastic case near the battery, and is checked visually for continuity of the filament. The battery can be checked with a jumper wire or by turning on the lights. If the lights go on, there should be enough juice left to at least start the bike. The

connectors are not so easily checked since the connectors often look like they are making contact while they are not. At least make a visual inspection of the connectors involved by getting out the old wiring diagram and tracing the current. A test light can be used to tell you whether or not you are getting continuity from one end of a wire to the other, but this might be better saved to later.

The next thing to check for is spark to the plug. This is easily done by inserting a spark plug into the high-tension lead and grounding it against the cylinder head. If, upon rotating the engine, there is a spark to the plug, you know that the problem is not in the ignition system and you should go on to the fuel system. If there was no spark, you'll have to begin tracing the system starting at the contact points. Check for continuity through the points, condenser, coil, and the associated wiring. If this doesn't locate the problem, you'll have to go back to the generating source and then to the ignition switch.

TESTING THE RECTIFIER

If alternator output is satisfactory but the battery discharges as the engine is running, it is quite possible that the rectifier is not functioning properly (assuming that the battery is in good condition and is capable of taking on a charge). Before removing and testing the rectifier, make sure that it is mounted solidly on the frame. The rectifier is grounded through its mounting and will not operate without a good ground. Never loosen or tighten the nut that holds the rectifier unit together, as this will adversely affect the operation of the rectifier.

To test the rectifier, first pull apart the plastic connector, unscrew the mounting nut, and remove the rectifier unit. There are four diodes inside the rectifier, which, if functioning properly, will allow electricity to pass in only one direction. To check the diodes you can use either a multimeter or a test light and the motorcycle battery. If the test light and battery are to be used, simply run a length of wire off one battery terminal and connect one of the test light leads to the other terminal. The two free wire ends will be used to check electrical continuity of the diodes.

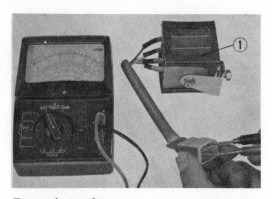

Testing the rectifier
1. Selenium rectifier

Connect the positive lead to the yellow wire and the negative lead to the red-white wire, as shown in test one of the accompanying table. Reverse the leads so that the negative lead is connected to the red/white wire. The test light should light (or the gauge needle should respond) in one direction only. Repeat in the same manner for test steps two, three, and four in the table. Continuity in both directions (when reversing the leads) indicates a defective diode, in which case the rectifier unit must be replaced.

Rectifier Test Table

	Connection		
Test Leads		Rectifier Terminal	Resistance Value
1. $+ \left(- \right)$ $- \left(+ \right)$		Yellow Red/white	
2. $+ \left(- \right)$ $- \left(+ \right)$		Pink Red/white	Satisfactory if between 5–40Ω
3. $+ \left(- \right)$ $- \left(+ \right)$		Green Yellow	
4. $+ \left(- \right)$ $- \left(+ \right)$		Green Pink	

The diodes are quite susceptible to failure from excessive heat and electrical overload. Observe the following precautions to avoid rectifier failure.

1. Do not reverse battery polarity when installing or reconnecting the battery. The electrical system is negative ground.

2. Do not use high-voltage test equipment to test the rectifier diodes.

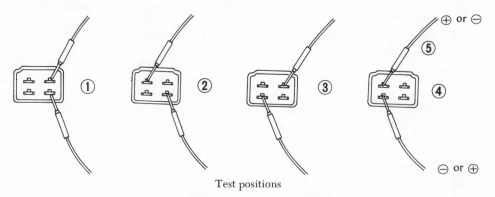

Test positions
1. Green and pink leads
2. Pink and red/white leads
3. Green and yellow leads
4. Red/white and yellow leads
5. Tester leads

3. Do not run the engine with the rectifier disconnected.

4. Do not charge the battery without first disconnecting, and isolating, one of the battery cables.

ALTERNATOR SERVICE

Uncouple the alternator leads at the connector block and check continuity between the three stator coil leads (yellow, pink, and white) using a multimeter or a test light and battery. Connect one of the test leads to the pink wire and the other to first the yellow and then the white wire. If there is continuity in both cases, the stator coil is satisfactory. Standard stator coil resistance is 1.1 ohms (pink to yellow wire) and 0.55 ohms (pink to white wire). The stator coil assembly can be taken off after the left side cover is removed.

Starter motor for a 50 cc engine

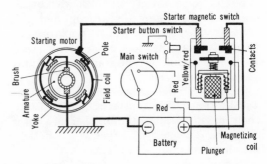

Starter wiring diagram

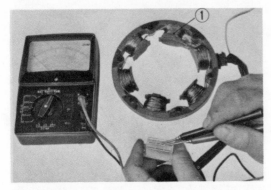

Testing the stator coil

1. Stator coil

Starting System

The starting system consists of the starter motor and clutch, the solenoid, and the handlebar-mounted starter switch. When the button is pressed, the electrical circuit to the solenoid is closed and the solenoid is activated, sending the battery current directly to the starter motor. The starting system is quite reliable and it is unlikely that you will experience any major problems.

TESTING

1. If the starter will not operate, switch on the headlight and observe its intensity. If it is dim when the starter is not being operated, check the battery connections and recharge the battery. If the headlight doesn't light, check the fuse, and the battery connections, and check the electrical continuity of the wire between the ignition switch and the battery.

If the headlight is bright, press the starter button momentarily and watch the light. If it remains bright, touch a screwdriver blade between the two starter solenoid terminals. If the starter operates, connect a test light between the small yellow/red wire on the solenoid and ground. If the test light comes on as the button is pushed, the solenoid is faulty. If it does not light, look for defective wiring between the starter button and the ignition switch, or simply a burned out starter button switch. If the starter does not operate and the headlight dims as the main solenoid terminals are bridged, the starter motor is faulty. If the headlight does not dim, look for a bad connection at the starter.

If the starter motor operates freely but will not turn the engine over, the starter clutch is not operating (a rare occurrence). To remove the clutch it will be necessary to first take off the left-side crankcase cover and remove the alternator rotor. If the overrunning clutch is defective and the starter keeps spinning after the engine starts, it must be repaired immediately to prevent serious damage to the starter assembly.

STARTER MOTOR SERVICE

1. Check for electrical continuity between the commutator and armature core using a multimeter or test light and battery. If continuity exists, the armature coil is grounded and the armature or complete starter motor should be replaced.

2. Check continuity between the brush wired to the stator (field) coil and the starter motor cable terminal. Lack of continuity indicates that an open circuit exists in the stator coil and the starter motor unit should be replaced.

3. Examine the carbon brushes for damage to the contact surfaces and measure their length. Replace the brushes as a set if they are damaged in any way or if they measure less than 0.3 in. (7.5 mm).

4. Brush spring tension should be determined with a small pull-scale which your dealer can probably supply. Replace the springs if they exert less than 0.8 lbs of tension.

5. Polish the commutator with fine emery cloth and blow it off thoroughly before installing it. Check the following components for excessive wear and damage: clutch spring and rollers; bearings; bushings; oil seal; reduction gears; and the sprockets. Replace all parts as necessary if worn or damaged. When reassembling the starter clutch, apply a thin coat of silicone grease to the rollers.

STARTER SOLENOID SERVICE

The solenoid is an electromagnetic switch that closes and completes the circuit between the starter and the battery when activated by the starter button. The solenoid is a necessary addition to the starting circuit because the starter button switch is not capable of handling the amperage load required to operate the starter, and because mounting a heavy-duty switch on the handlebar, with the large cable needed to handle the load, is impractical.

If the solenoid does not work, check the continuity of the primary coil by connecting a multimeter or test light and battery to the two small solenoid leads. Lack of continuity indicates an open circuit and the solenoid must be replaced. If the primary coil winding is continuous, disassemble the solenoid and clean the contact points with emery paper or a small file. The points, after long use, have a tendency to become pitted or burned due to the large current passing across them. Be sure to disconnect the battery before disconnecting the cables from the solenoid when it is to be removed. Replace the solenoid if cleaning the points fails to repair it.

BATTERY

Maintenance, testing, and recharging procedures for the battery are covered in chapter two.

IGNITION SYSTEM

The servicing and adjustment of the ignition system components is covered in chapter three.

Wiring Diagrams

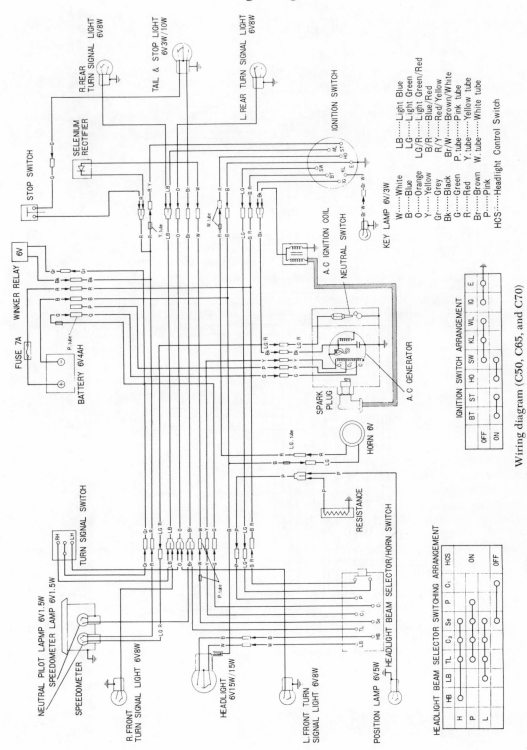

Wiring diagram (C50, C65, and C70)

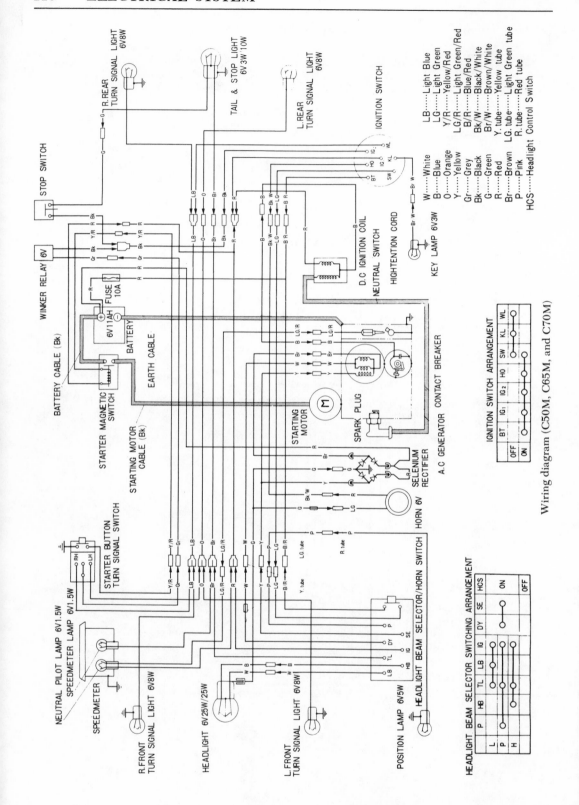

Wiring diagram (C50M, C65M, and C70M)

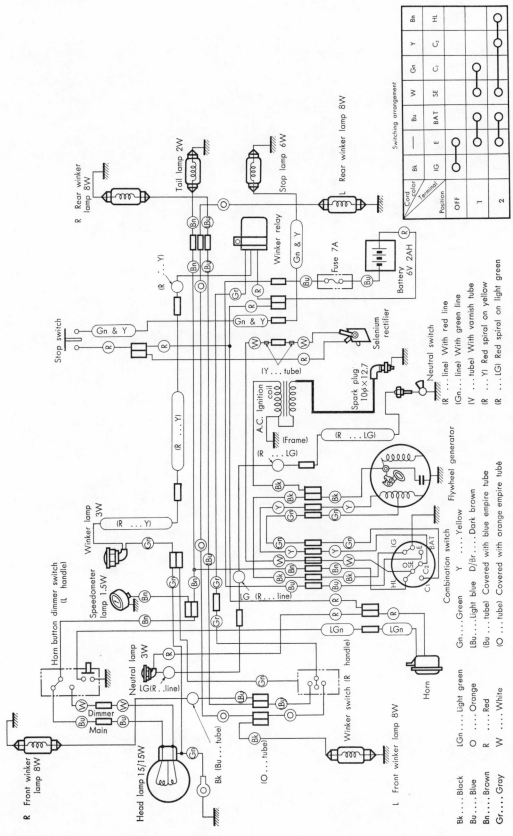

Wiring diagram (S50 and S65)

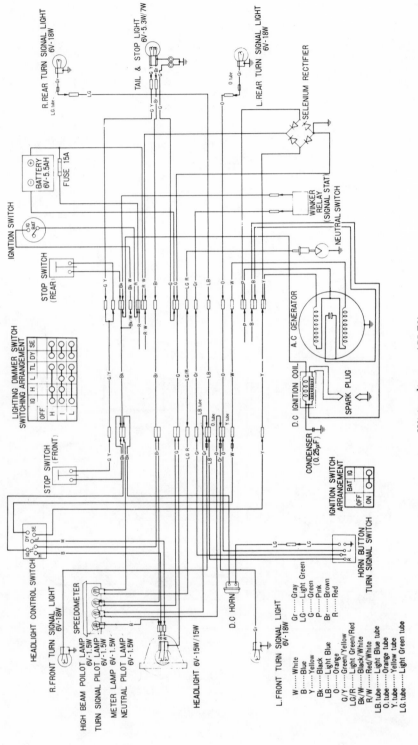

Wiring diagram (CL70)

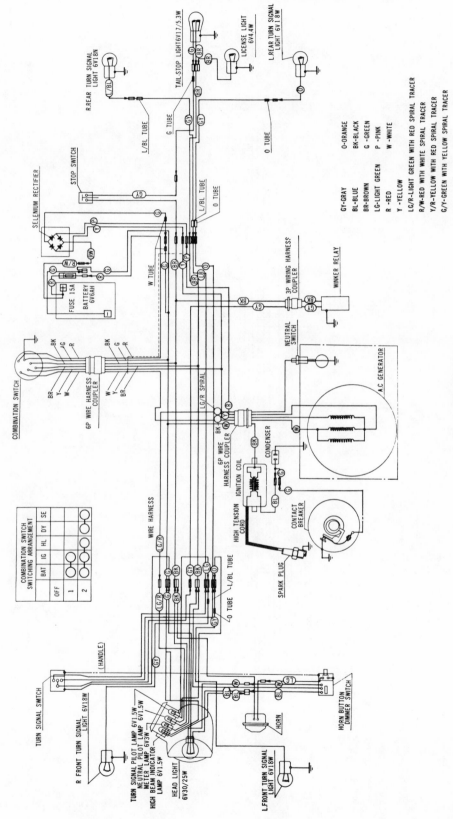

Wiring diagram (S90)

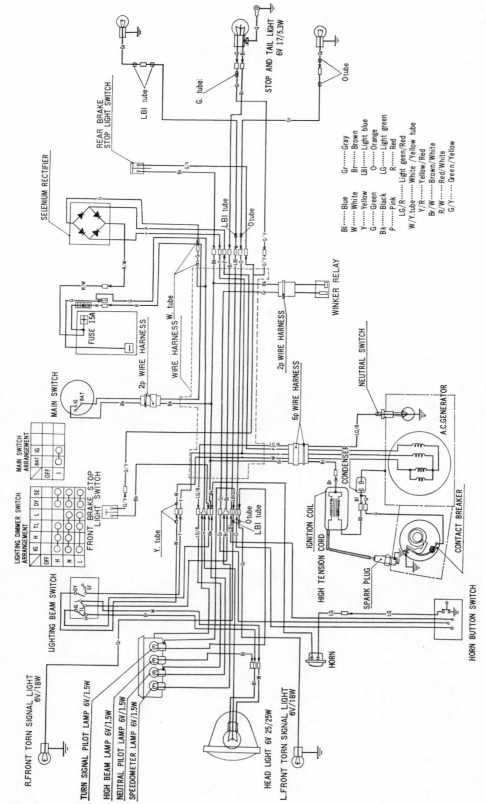

Wiring diagram (CL90 and CL90L)

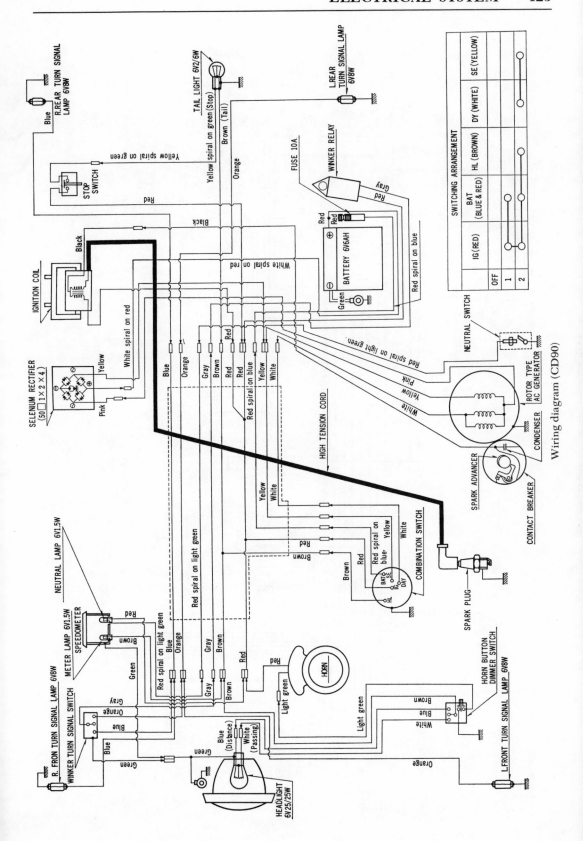

Wiring diagram (CD90)

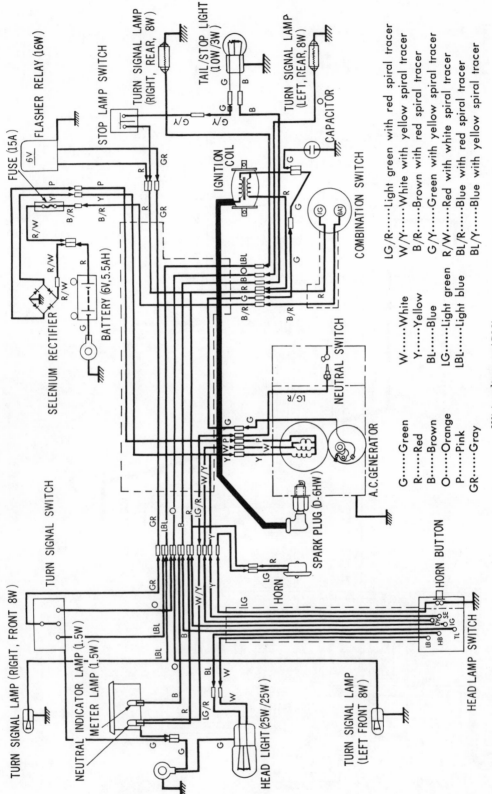

Wiring diagram (C90)

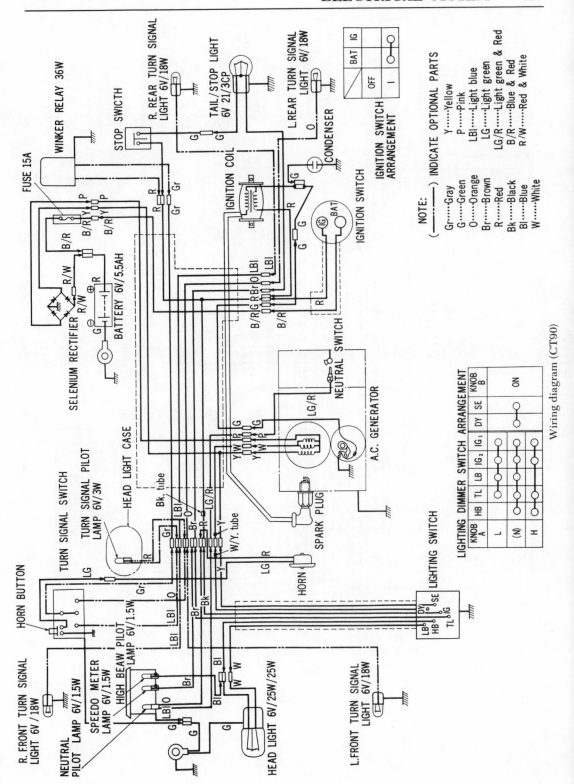

Wiring diagram (CT90)

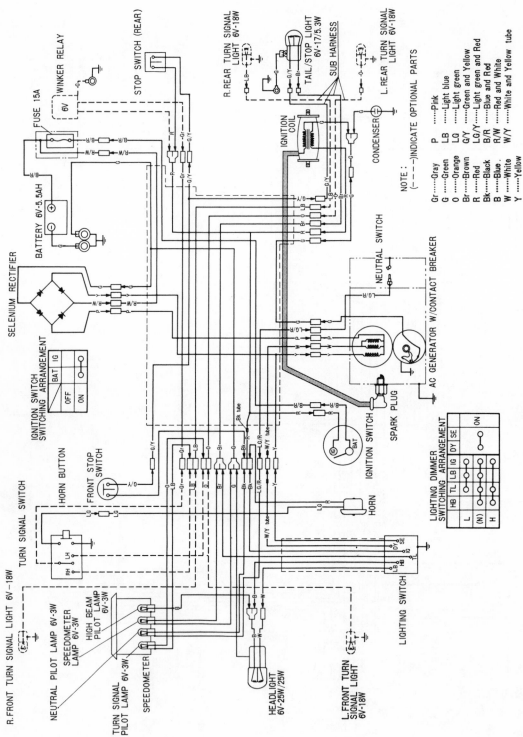

Wiring diagram (CT90 from frame no. 000001A)

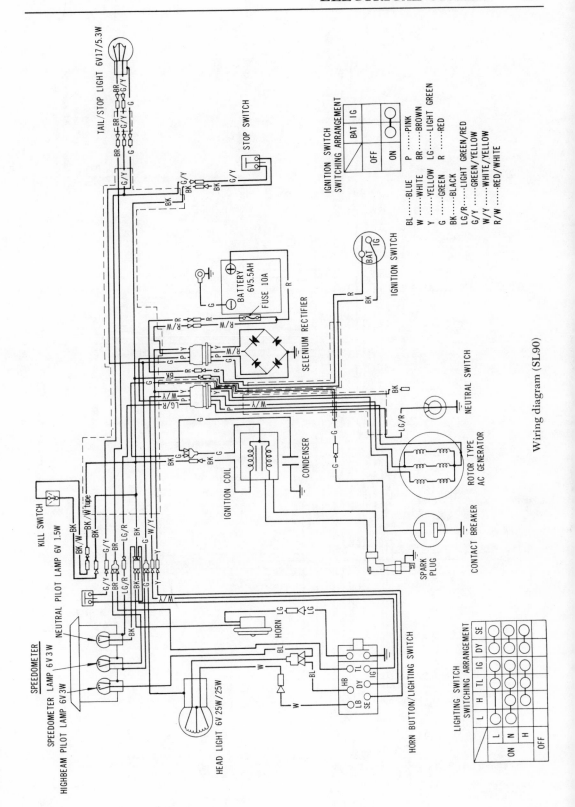

Wiring diagram (SL90)

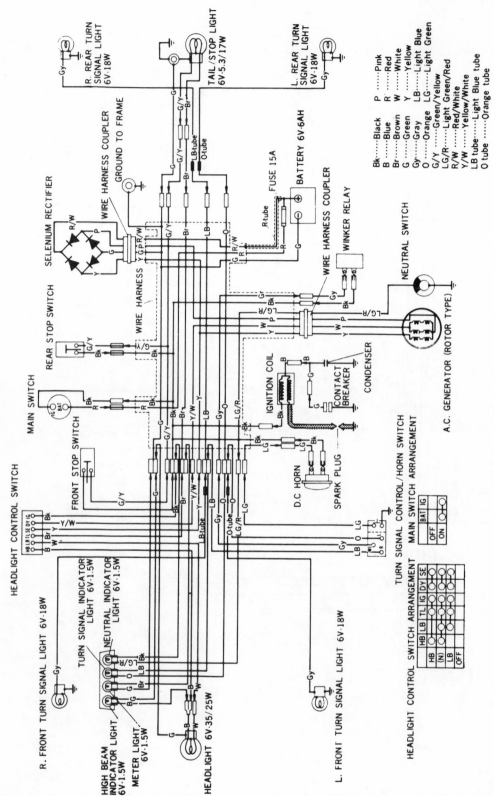

Wiring diagram (CB100)

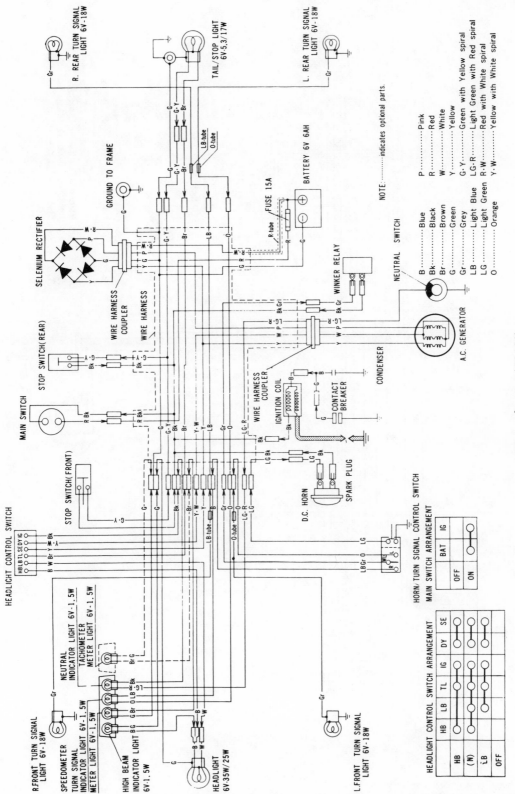

Wiring diagram (CL100)

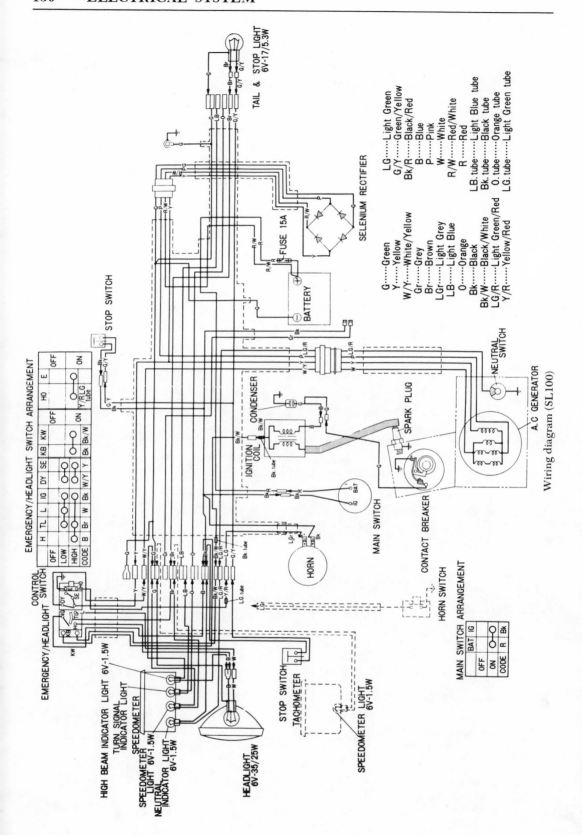

Wiring diagram (SL100)

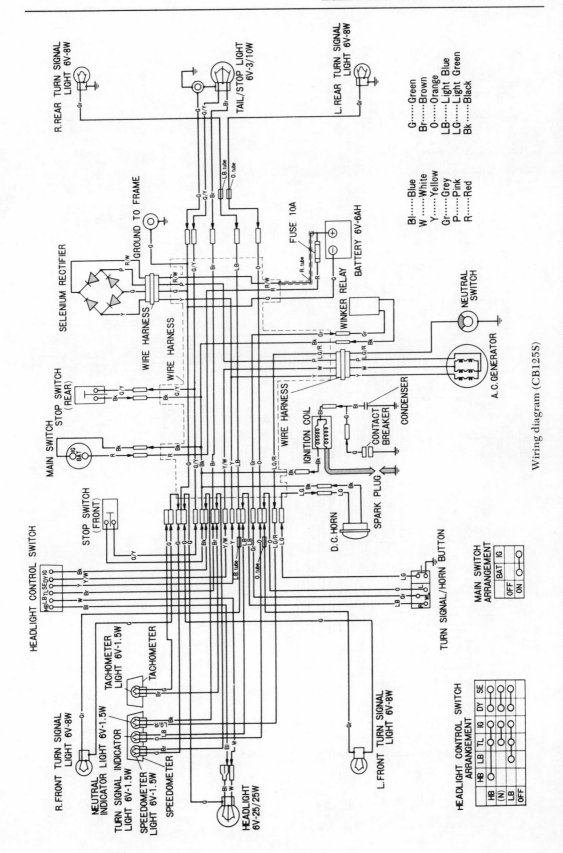

Wiring diagram (CB125S)

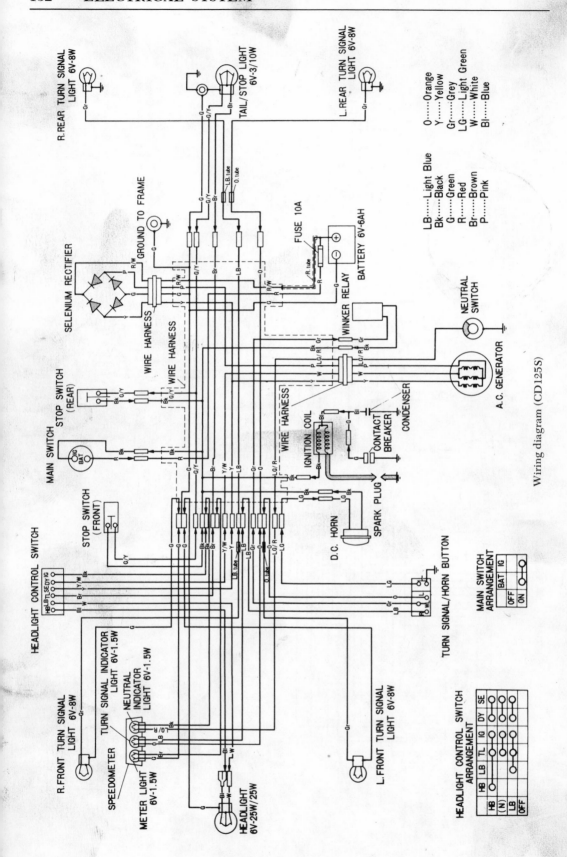

Wiring diagram (CD125S)

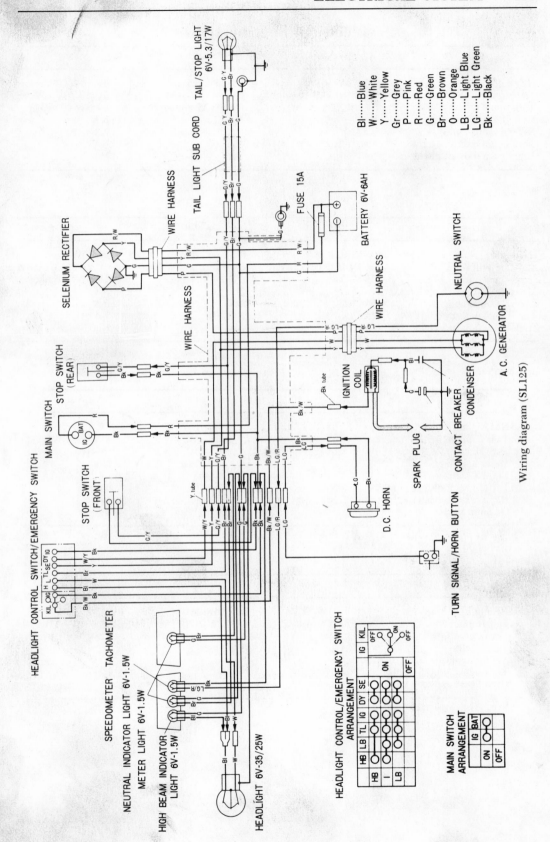

Wiring diagram (SL125)

Electrical Specifications

Model	C50	C50M	S50
Headlight	6V-15W/15W	6V-25W/25W	6V-15W/15W
Tail/stoplight	6V-3W/6V-10W red	6V-3W/6V-10W red	6V-2W/6V-6W red
Turn signal light	6V-8WX2 amber	6V-8WX2 amber	6V-8WX2 amber
Meter light	NA	NA	NA
Neutral indicator light	NA	NA	NA
Turn signal indicator light	NA	NA	NA
High-beam indicator light	NA	NA	NA

Model	C65	C65M	S65
Headlight	6V-15W/15W	6V-25W/25W	9V-15W/15W
Tail/stoplight	6V-3W/6V-10W red	6V-3W/6V-10W red	6V-2W/6V-6W red
Turn signal light	6V-8WX2 amber	6V-8WX2 amber	6V-8WX2 amber
Meter light	NA	NA	NA
Neutral indicator light	NA	NA	NA
Turn signal indicator light	NA	NA	NA
High-beam indicator light	NA	NA	NA

Model	CL70	C70	C70M
Headlight	6V-15W/15W	6V-15W/15W	6V-15W/25W
Tail/stoplight	6V-5.3W/17W	6V-3W/10W	6V-3W/10W
Turn signal light	6V-18W	6V-8W	6V-8W
Meter light	NA	NA	NA
Neutral indicator light	——	6V-5W	6V-5W
Turn signal indicator light	NA	NA	NA
High-beam indicator light	NA	NA	NA
Oil lamp light	——	6V-3W	6V-3W

Model	S90	SL90	CL90, CL90L
Headlight	6V-25W/25W	6V-25W/25W	6V-25W/25W
Tail/stoplight	6V-2W/6V-6W	6V-17W/6V-5.3W	6V-5W/6V-17W
Turn signal light	6V-8W	NA	6V-18W
Meter light	NA	NA	NA
Neutral indicator light	NA	NA	NA
Turn signal indicator light	NA	NA	NA
High-beam indicator light	NA	NA	NA

Electrical Specifications (cont.)

Model	CD90	C90	CT90
Headlight	6V-25W/25W	6V-25W/25W	6V-25W/25W
Tail/stoplight	6V-5W/6V-10W	6V-3W/6V-10W	①
Turn signal light	6V-10W	6V-8W	②
Meter light	NA	NA	NA
Neutral indicator light	NA	NA	NA
Turn signal indicator light	NA	NA	NA
High-beam indicator light	NA	NA	NA

① CT90   6V-5W/6V-18W
  CT90 (after F. no. 000001A) 6V-5W/6V-17W
② CT90   none
  CT90 (after F. no. 000001A) 6V-18W (option)

Model	CB100	CL100	SL100
Headlight	6V-35W/25W	6V-35W/25W	6V-35W/25W
Tail/stoplight	6V-5.3W/17W	6V-5.3W/17W	6V-5.3W/17W
Turn signal light	6V-18W	6V-18W	——
Meter light	6V-1.5W	6V-1.5W	6V-1.5W
Neutral indicator light	6V-1.5W	6V-1.5W	6V-1.5W
Turn signal indicator light	6V-1.5W	6V-1.5W	——
High-beam indicator light	6V-1.5W	6V-1.5W	6V-1.5W

Model	CB125S	CD125S	SL125
Headlight	6V-25W/25W	6V-25W/25W	6V-25W/35W
Tail/stoplight	6V-3W/10W	6V-3W/10W	6V-5.3W/17W
Turn signal light	6V-8W	6V-8W	——
Meter light	6V-1.5W	6V-1.5W	6V-1.5W
Neutral indicator light	6V-1.5W	6V-1.5W	6V-1.5W
Turn signal indicator light	6V-1.5W	6V-1.5W	——
High-beam indicator light	6V-1.5W	6V-1.5W	6V-1.5W

8 · Chassis

Honda uses two methods of producing frames; one is the pressed steel type common to the C and S models, and the other is the tubular steel, double down-tube type employed on the SL models. Both types are sprung in the rear by shock absorbers attached to a movable swing arm, and all are sprung in the front by either a leading link suspension (such as on all of the step-through frame models), or a more traditional telescopic oil-dampened type. Single leading shoe brakes are used front and back to provide the stopping power for all

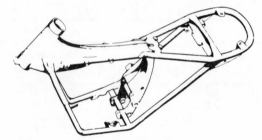

Tubular steel type frame (shown is an SL100)

of these models, and all come equipped with internally baffled mufflers.

An important thing to remember when working on the frame components is that they are all subjected to a great deal of vibration and road shock, and consequently they must be kept firmly tightened. Before you begin work you should clean the machine, and have a clean area to work in, especially if you are working on front suspension units which wear quickly when dirty. Also it helps when you can see all of the bolts, so you don't wind up pulling on something for a half hour only to discover that it's still secured by another bolt that was hidden under a glob of dirt and grease.

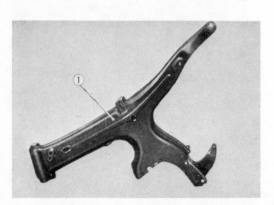

Pressed steel type frame (shown is an S90)

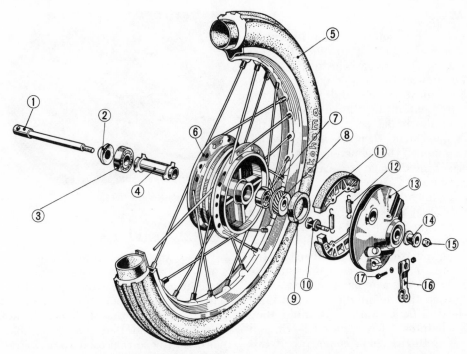

Front wheel assembly (shown is a CL90 assembly)

1. Front wheel axle
2. Oil seal
3. Ball bearing
4. Distance collar
5. Front wheel tire
6. Front wheel hub
7. Ball bearing
8. Speedometer gear
9. Oil seal
10. Front brake cam
11. Brake shoe
12. Brake shoe spring
13. Front brake panel
14. Front wheel side collar
15. Axle nut
16. Front brake arm
17. Hex bolt

Wheels and Tires

REMOVAL AND INSTALLATION

Front Wheel

1. Block up the front of the motorcycle so the front wheel can spin freely.

2. Disconnect the front brake and speedometer cables at the front wheel.

3. Remove the front axle nut and pull out the front axle. The wheel is now free to be removed.

4. Remove the front brake assembly by pulling free the front brake panel from the hub.

5. Installation is in the reverse order of disassembly.

Removing the front axle

1. Front axle

Separating the brake panel from the hub

1. Wheel hub   2. Brake panel

Rear Wheel

1. Place the motorcycle on its center stand, or find some way to block the rear wheel up so that it can spin freely.

2. Disconnect the rear brake by removing the adjusting nut and slipping the brake rod out of the brake lever. Press down on the brake pedal and block the pedal's movement, then release the pedal. In this manner the adjusting nut will be kept free from damage as it can turn without resistance. Take care not to lose the cylinder which fits in the brake lever. Remove the rear brake torque link nut and disconnect the link.

3. Remove the muffler if it will interfere in pulling the axle out. Remember that the axle comes out on the side opposite the end on which the axle nut is fitted.

4. Loosen the chain adjusters and push the wheel as far forward as possible, then lift the chain off a few sprocket teeth, and rotate it until the chain comes off. If this fails you, you can still disconnect the master link. In this case you should wire the chain ends to the frame so the chain doesn't come off the front sprocket.

5. Remove the axle nut and pull the axle out. The rear wheel is now free for removal, and the rear brake panel may be removed.

6. Installation is in the reverse order of disassembly.

Removing the rear wheel

WHEEL SERVICE

Check the wheel run-out on a truing stand or on the axle (the chain must be disconnected when working on the rear wheel), or make yourself a stand. The only requirements are that the wheel be able to spin freely, and that the stand hold the wheel steady so that oscillations caused by the stand don't confuse the measurement. Spin the wheel and check the run-out with a dial indicator. If the run-out exceeds 0.080 in. (2.0 mm), if the rim or spokes are damaged, or if the wheel is obviously out of true, you should consult your dealer. Truing a wheel is nothing more than tightening the spokes opposite the high sections of rim in order to even things out, but a certain amount of skill and experience that

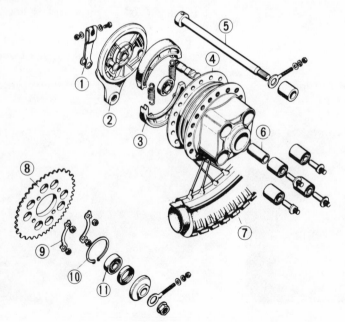

1. Brake arm
2. Brake panel
3. Brake shoe
4. Wheel hub
5. Wheel axle
6. Axle distance collar
7. Tire
8. Final driven sprocket
9. Lockwasher
10. Circlip
11. Wheel bearing

Rear wheel assembly (shown is CL90 assembly)

Tightening spokes

cannot be gained from a book is required to do the job correctly.

If you can fabricate a stand (the front forks off a bicycle will do nicely), you can attempt to true the wheel. You'll need a spoke wrench or a pair of pliers to adjust the spoke nipples. Start off by adjusting all of the nipples to a point where the same number of threads are showing, then tighten them all down evenly one turn at a time. Just tighten the spokes until firm. If it works out great. If not, you can still always take it to the shop. Keep the spokes taut, since once they loosen, the wheel will swiftly go out of true. Tap each spoke with a wrench. Those which do not have a metallic ring to them should be tightened. Be careful not to break the spokes or pull the rim out of true.

WHEEL BALANCING

1. Raise the wheel off the ground and rotate it lightly. If the wheel does not rotate freely, back off on the brake adjuster until it does. The drive chain must be disconnected from rear wheels, otherwise an accurate balance will not be obtained.

2. Observe where the wheel stops after being spun and mark it with chalk. This should be the heaviest part of the wheel. Spin the wheel and let it stop several times to make sure that you really do have the heaviest part marked.

3. Attach a weight (available in 5, 10, 15, and 20 grams) to the spoke nipple at the highest position where the wheel has stopped. Spin the wheel again and observe where it stops. The idea is to get the proper weight positioned on the wheel so that it does not end up at any particular position when it stops spinning. Different weights may have to be tried at various

positions to achieve this. Lock the weight into place with pliers after you've found the spot. Solder may be used if weights are not available. Wrap the solder wire around the spoke nipple and secure it with tape. It may prove necessary to use several weights to achieve balance. If all attempts to balance the wheel prove unsuccessful, consult your local dealer.

TIRE REMOVAL AND INSTALLATION

1. Remove the wheel from the motorcycle.

2. Lay the wheel on a cloth or a piece of cardboard to protect the hub.

3. Remove the valve core and the valve stem retaining nut.

4. Step down on the tire to break it loose from the rim, then repeat this operation on the opposite side.

Breaking the bead loose

1. Tire   2. Tire irons

5. Use two small tire irons, placed near the valve stem about 5 in. apart, to pry the tire bead over the rim while depressing the bead opposite the irons. Remove one iron and work around the rim until the bead is clear of the rim all the way around, taking care to avoid pinching the tube with the tire irons (especially if you are using screwdrivers instead of tire irons).

6. Remove the tube and, if the tire is to be replaced, lever the other bead over the rim in the same manner. If the tube has been removed to repair a puncture, be sure to check the tire casing for the cause of the flat and for damage.

Installation is accomplished in the following manner:

1. Coat the tire beads with tire mount-

ing solution or liquid detergent. If the tire has been removed from the rim, lever one side onto the rim. If the tire has a balance mark on it, the mark should be at the valve stem.

2. Install the valve core in the stem, inflate the tube slightly, and install it into the tire casing. Insert the valve stem into the valve stem hole in the rim. Partially install the valve stem retaining nut to hold the tube in position.

3. It will now be possible to slip about ¾ of the bead over the rim by hand. The remaining section can be positioned by using a rubber mallet or the tire irons. Again, if the irons are used, be careful not to pinch the tube.

4. Rotate the tire on the rim until the balance mark on the tire aligns with the valve stem.

5. Inflate the tire to about 40 psi and then deflate it completely. This will ensure that the beads are seated properly and that the tube will not be deformed when reinflated. Inflate the tire to the correct pressure and tighten the valve stem retaining nut.

Brakes

Honda uses single leading shoe, internally expanding, drum brakes on all of the models covered in this guide on both the front and rear wheels. The brakes are actuated by the brake lever which is moved whenever tension is placed on the brake lever or pedal. The actuating lever is connected to a cam which is rotated when the lever is moved, and this causes the brake shoes to be pressed against the brake hub.

Brakes most often become unserviceable due to glazing of the shoes, or because the shoes have become worn past their adjustable limit. If the shoes become glazed, they can be returned to a serviceable condition by sanding off the glazing with coarse sandpaper or with a wire wheel. It is not necessary to return the shoes to a like-new condition, but only to remove the glazed portion so the shoes will have more bite against the drum. Whenever the wheels are removed it is a good idea to examine the shoes and sand them down if necessary. At this time the brake hub

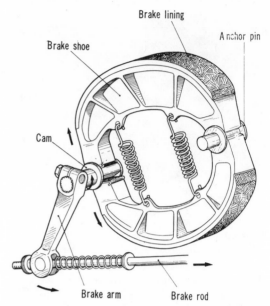

Brake operation

should also be attended to. The hub must be perfectly clean of oil, dirt, and glazing, and may be roughed up slightly with some fine sandpaper. Take care not to score the hub when roughing it up, because all you want to do is give the shoes something to grab. If the shoes are worn to the point where they won't contact the drum sufficiently to stop the bike, it is possible to increase their life span by shifting the position of the brake actuating lever. The lever is on a splined shaft and can be removed by removing the pinch bolt, prying the lever apart with a screwdriver, and pulling it off the shaft. Reposition the lever a few degrees to the rear for back brakes, and forward for front brakes, then secure it on the shaft. This will bring more shoe into contact with the drum, and can be done until the shoe itself is worn past its serviceable limit. If there is not enough pad left on the shoe, you stand the chance of scoring the drum by applying the brakes after the rivets have become exposed, so check the shoes before performing this act.

If the shoes become oil- or grease-impregnated, they must be replaced as the grease or oil will become a lubricating film, especially when hot, and keep the brakes from grabbing. If the drum itself is damaged or out of true, the brakes will not stop smoothly. This sort of trouble is best left to your dealer to take care of since it requires either a new drum or turning the

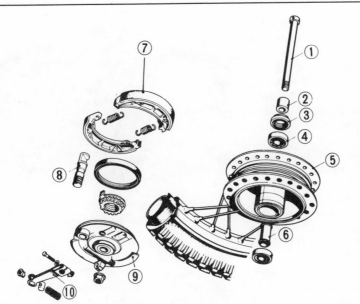

1. Front axle
2. Side collar
3. Oil seal
4. Wheel bearing
5. Hub
6. Axle distance collar
7. Brake shoe
8. Brake cam
9. Brake panel
10. Brake actuating lever

Front brake and hub assembly (shown is a CB100 assembly)

old one down on a special machine. There are many other malfunctions which can occur to the brakes that will hamper their performance. Most of these require replacing the defective component(s). Consult the "Troubleshooting" chapter for additional information.

SHOE REPLACEMENT (ALL MODELS)

1. Remove the wheel from the motorcycle as described in the "Wheels and Tires" section.

2. Remove the brake panel from the hub assembly.

3. Measure the drum inside diameter with a vernier caliper and replace it, if out of true or if worn past its serviceable limit.

4. Remove the shoes by spreading them away from the panel and lifting them off.

Removing the brake shoes
1. Brake shoes

5. Inspect the springs for a worn or damaged condition and replace them as necessary.

6. Measure the brake linings and replace them if worn past their serviceable limit.

Measuring the hub inside diameter

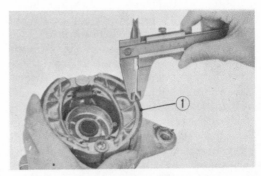

Measuring brake linings
1. Brake lining

7. Install the brakes on the panel by attaching them together with the return springs, and pressing them into position on the panel.

8. Mount the drum and check to see if the entire surface of the shoe is contacting the drum. If both ends touch the drum, file down one end of the shoe until it only touches at one end.

9. If the brake squeals, you can either wait until it wears in or you can file down the shoe slightly as illustrated. Avoid removing too much of the shoe or the braking performance will be negatively affected.

10. Complete the assembly process in the reverse order of disassembly.

11. Adjust the brakes as described in the "Maintenance" chapter. Avoid heavy braking for at least 500 miles whenever the shoes or drum have been replaced in order to allow them to seat properly.

Wheel Bearings

All of the models covered in this guide come equipped with ball bearings that do not require frequent periodic service. The bearings will probably need repacking before they need to be replaced, and their need of attention is indicated by either a rumbling noise or by excessive play. Periodically check the bearings by grasping the wheel at three o'clock and at nine o'clock, and wiggle the wheel back and forth. Then grasp the wheel at twelve o'clock and pull it back and forth. If there is noticeable axial or radial play, the bearings should be removed and inspected.

If the balls or races appear worn, pitted, or otherwise damaged, the bearing should be replaced. If the bearing's action when spinning on the axle is not smooth, the bearings should be repacked. If, after rechecking the bearing's motion, it still isn't smooth, the bearing should be replaced. Always replace bearings as sets.

Bearings are removed and replaced by drifting them out with a suitable drift (the rear sprocket will have to be removed to get at the rear wheel bearings). Make sure the spacer and bearing seals are well seated. This is also a good time to check the axle for a warped or bent condition.

Installing wheel bearings

1. Bearing driver

Spin the axle and check the run-out with a dial indicator, and replace it if the run-out exceeds 0.020 in. (0.5 mm). Always pack the bearings in fresh grease, and always replace the oil seal. Never spin an insufficiently lubricated bearing as it may be damaged. You will find that lubricating the bearing with engine oil will make installation easier.

Final Drive

CHAIN INSPECTION

The chain should be regularly inspected for wear and damage in the following manner:

1. Place the bike on the centerstand and thoroughly lubricate the chain using one of the many chain care products available. Engine oil may be used if necessary but it doesn't provide the kind of protection against friction and rust that a chain needs.

2. Measure the amount of slack at the middle of the run and adjust the chain as necessary. Consult the "Maintenance" chapter for details.

3. Slowly rotate the wheel and examine the chain for:

    a. Damaged rollers;

    b. Loose pins;

    c. Rusted or pitted links;

    d. Binding or kinked links.

Replace the chain if the rollers are damaged, if the pins are loose, or if the rusted or binding links cannot be worked free with lubrication.

4. Replace the chain if it is worn past the point where an accurate adjustment can be made. This is an extreme case, as chains are usually worn past their serviceable limit long before they get to this point. If you can pull the chain ¼ in. or more off of the rear sprocket (when the chain is properly adjusted) at the middle of the portion of the sprocket on which the chain is seated, the chain should be replaced. Another test of a worn chain is to remove the chain and stretch it out to its longest length and then measure it. Compress the links so the chain is its shortest and measure it again. If the difference is greater than ¼ in. per foot of chain, the chain should be replaced. Remember that a stretched-out or damaged chain is more apt to break than one which is kept properly adjusted and lubricated, and a flying drive chain is a dangerous situation both to the driver and the machine.

SPROCKET INSPECTION

Check the sprockets for broken or worn teeth every time you adjust and inspect the chain. Worn teeth have a hooked, assymetrical appearance. If the sides of the teeth are worn, the indication is that the sprockets are misaligned (primarily the drive sprocket provided you kept the rear wheel correctly aligned) and should be replaced and shimmed until properly aligned. In any case of wear or damage, the sprockets should be replaced, ideally as a set along with the chain. Remember that worn sprockets can ruin a good chain, and vice-versa. Do not hesitate to replace the chain and both sprockets, if need be, to avoid costly and dangerous chain failure.

CHAIN REMOVAL AND INSTALLATION

The chain is ready to be removed as soon as the master link is disconnected. Threading the chain back onto the countershaft sprocket is made considerably easier if you have either an old chain or if you are installing a new chain. All you have to do is connect the replacement chain to the chain being removed with a piece of wire or with a master link, then rotate the rear wheel until the replacement chain is on the sprockets and the old chain is off. Now all you have to do is to install the master link and adjust the chain. Use a

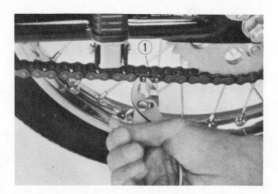

Disconnecting the drive chain

1. Drive chain

new master link spring clip whenever possible, and make sure that the closed portion of the clip is facing the direction of normal chain rotation. If the chain comes off the sprockets, it may become necessary to remove the cover over the countershaft sprocket so the chain can be threaded into place. Whenever working with the chain, your work can be made considerably easier if you keep the chain on the countershaft sprocket by wiring the ends to the frame. Always lubricate the chain after installing it and make sure that any grit from the floor has been removed.

SPROCKET REMOVAL AND INSTALLATION

To get at the countershaft sprocket the cover will have to be removed and the chain loosened or disconnected. The sprocket can be unbolted after the locktabs (if applicable) are bent back. The final drive sprocket can be removed from the rear wheel hub only after the wheel has been removed. The disassembly procedure is quite straightforward and should present no problem. Consult the accompanying illustrations if you have any trouble remembering how to put it all back together once the sprockets have been exchanged. Use new locktabs whenever possible as these become fatigued quickly from repeated bending.

On the CT90 models with frame numbers prior to CT 90-122550, both the final drive sprockets are mounted to the driven flange, and may be replaced independently of one another.

At this time it is advisable that you examine the rear hub dampers, bearings, and

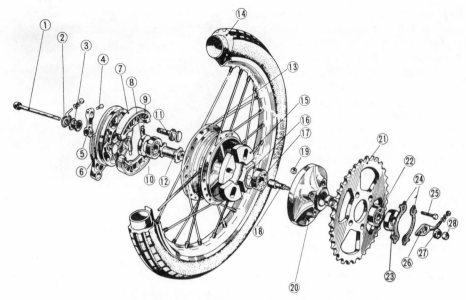

Drive sprocket and rear wheel assembly (shown is a CL90)

1. Rear wheel axle	15. Rear wheel damper
2. Right drive chain adjuster	16. O-ring
3. Rear brake panel side collar	17. Ball bearing
4. Hex bolt	18. Rear axle sleeve
5. Rear brake arm	19. Thin nut
6. Rear brake panel	20. Final driven flange
7. Brake shoe	21. Final driven sprocket
8. Oil seal	22. Ball bearing
9. Brake shoe spring	23. Oil seal
10. Ball bearing	24. Tongued washer
11. Rear brake cam	25. Driven sprocket setting bolt
12. Rear axle distance collar	26. Left drive chain adjuster
13. Rear wheel hub	27. Rear axle sleeve nut
14. Rear wheel tire	28. Axle nut

brakes since the rear wheel assembly will have to be taken down.

REAR HUB DAMPER SERVICE

The rear hub dampers serve to absorb the power pulse to the rear wheel so gear shifts feel smoother to the rider. There is no set mileage or time period at which the dampers need to be serviced, but after the machine has many thousands of miles on it, or after it has been used over a long period of time, the dampers tend to crack and deteriorate. The only service they require is replacement. This is accomplished by removing the drive sprocket and the driven flange (if applicable). The dampers are readily exchanged and the wheel can be reassembled. Use new O-rings (if applicable) and locktabs whenever possible to ensure proper functioning of the assembly.

Front Suspension

HANDLEBARS

Removal

1. Remove the fairing (if applicable) and place it out of the way.

2. Disconnect the speedometer and front brake cables. The speedometer cable can be disconnected at either the front wheel or at the point where it joins the speedometer inside the headlight shell. The brake cable should be disconnected at the handlever.

3. Unscrew the carburetor cap and carefully pull out the slide assembly. Disconnect the throttle cable at the slide. The cable can now be disconnected at the handlebar.

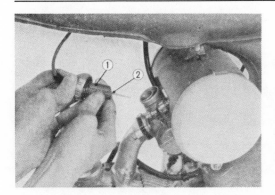

Removing the throttle slide
1. Throttle slide   2. Jet needle

Removing the handlebar
1. 6 mm mounting bolts   2. Handlebar upper holders

4. Disconnect the clutch cable at the clutch lever. It may be necessary to adjust the cable to provide more slack.

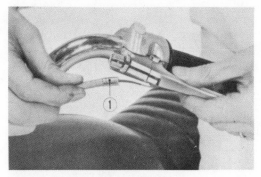

Disconnecting the clutch cable
1. Clutch cable

5. Remove the headlight unit and disconnect the leads from the switches.

6. Disconnect and remove the handlebar assembly by removing the mounting hardware. On models with the pressed steel type of handlebar, the mounting

Disconnecting the electrical leads
1. Electrical leads

points are on the bottom of the handlebar; on the steel tube type, the mounting bolts are at the center of the bars and are plainly visible.

Inspection and Repair

1. Inspect all the cables for a worn, kinked, or damaged condition and replace them as necessary. Check all cables for freedom of movement and lubricate them with a chain lubricant. A good method for doing this is to make a cup around the top of the cable using a piece of plastic. Pour or spray the lubricant into the cup until it begins to drip out of the bottom of the cable.

2. Inspect the handlevers for smooth operation and replace, grease, or file them down until they do operate smoothly.

3. Inspect the handlebar for a bent or cracked condition and replace them as necessary. Although bent bars can be straightened, they should be replaced as repeated bending may fatigue the metal and cause it to break at an inopportune time.

4. Inspect all the switches for proper operation, and examine all the leads for a damaged condition. If any portion of the switch is damaged, it should be replaced. These units are designed with replacement rather than repair in mind. If it becomes necessary to replace a switch, you'll find it easiest if you lubricate the leads sleeve, tape the lead ends together, and pull the leads through the bars with a piece of mechanic's wire.

Installation

1. Position the handlebar lower holder, rubber bushings for the handlebars, the

turn signals (if applicable), the handle-bars, and the handlebar upper holder (if applicable). Temporarily secure the bars to make the rest of the procedures easier.

2. Lubricate the handlebar with fresh grease where the throttle grip rides. Connect the cables in the reverse order of removal. It helps to have as much play as possible when connecting the cables. The clutch and brake cables can be attached to the levers and then the levers can be installed. Adjust all cables as described in chapter two.

3. Connect all of the electrical leads inside the headlight shell, then install the light and make sure everything works correctly. The leads are color-coded to make connecting them simpler. In instances where there is a different colored plastic sheath over the female connector, or a different colored band near the male connector, the color of the sheath or band stands for a tracer color.

4. Secure the handlebars. On the steel tube type models the serrated portion of the bars should be centered between the two holders and the punch mark should be at the junction of the two holder halves. Tighten down the securing bolts evenly.

STEERING STEM

The front suspension units are attached to the frame at the steering stem. The forks ride on ball bearings which are located in cone-shaped races at the top and bottom of the steering stem itself. It is not necessary to disassemble the front suspension components to work on the stem, and if you can raise the front of the motorcycle enough, it is not even necessary to remove the front wheel (although this is the accepted practice).

Disassembly

Leading Link Type Forks

1. Block up the motorcycle so the front wheel can be removed, then remove the front wheel.

2. Remove the handlebar assembly as described in the "Handlebars" section. It is not necessary to disconnect all of the cables, and you may wish to disconnect only those which will interfere with the removal of the forks.

3. Remove the headlight rim, lens, and

Removing the headlight shell

1. Headlight shell   2. Mounting bolts

case. The case is secured by two bolts and a screw on the inside.

4. Remove the steering stem head nut and the two, 8 mm bolts, then remove the fork top bridge.

5. Remove the steering head top thread using a suitable, 36 mm hook spanner or a suitable substitute.

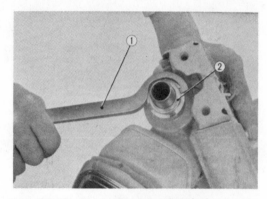

Removing the steering head top thread

1. 36 mm hook spanner   2. Steering head top thread

6. Pull out the fork from the bottom of the steering head. Keep a pan ready to catch the steering head bearings as they will probably fall out of the bottom race.

Telescopic Type Forks

1. Remove the handlebar assembly as described in the "Handlebars" section.

2. Remove the two fork bolts and the steering stem nut, then remove the fork top bridge.

3. Remove the headlight rim, lens, and shell assemblies, then remove the left and right front fork covers.

4. Block up the motorcycle and remove the front wheel assembly, then remove the

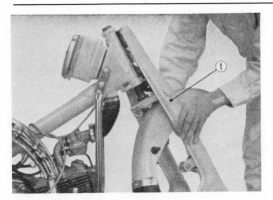

Removing the front fork
1. Front fork

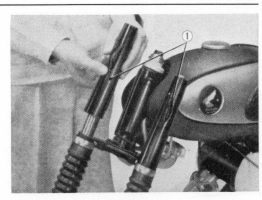

Removing the fork covers
1. Fork ears

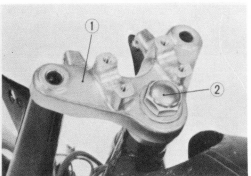

Removing the fork top bridge
1. Fork top bridge   2. Steering stem nut

Removing the front fender
1. Fender mounting bolts

Removing the headlight shell
1. Headlight shell mounting bolts

Removing the front fork legs
1. Fork legs

front fender. Remove the horn assembly from between the two fork legs (if applicable).

5. Loosen the front cushion mounting bolts from the lower triple clamp, then drop out the front fork assembly.

6. Remove the steering head top thread using a suitable, 36 mm hook spanner or a suitable substitute, then pull the stem out through the bottom of the head. Keep a pan ready to catch the steering head bearings as they will probably fall out from the bottom race.

Inspection and Repair (all Models)

1. Clean all steering head components in a suitable solvent and blow them dry.

2. Inspect the bearings for a worn, dam-

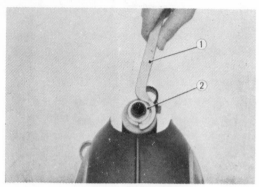

Removing the steering head top thread

1. 36 mm hook spanner   2. Steering head top thread

Removing the steering stem

1. Steering stem

aged, or pitted condition, and replace them as necessary. Bearings must be replaced as complete sets.

3. Inspect the steering stem for a worn, warped, or otherwise damaged condition and replace it as necessary. In some cases the stem may be repaired. Consult your dealer for additional information.

4. Inspect the steering head top and bottom cone races for wear, score marks, deep scratches, or any other damage, and replace them as necessary by drifting them out from their opposite sides using a suitable drift. The new cone races are then drifted into position. If the races are in bad shape, or if they look like they will be in an unserviceable condition soon, they should be replaced at this time. If you replace the bearings, you should consider replacing the races even if they look pretty good.

Assembly

1. Assembly is basically the reverse order of disassembly.

2. Install the steering stem bearings in the races after applying fresh grease to the races. There should be no more than 1–2 mm (0.040–0.080 in.) of clearance left between the bearings after they all have been installed.

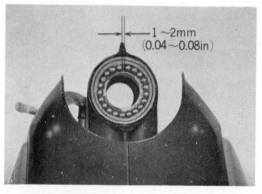

Steering head bearings

3. Tighten down the steering stem so that only a slight amount of pressure is required to start the wheel moving in either direction under its own weight when the wheel is raised off the ground. The front forks should rotate smoothly on the bearings, and there should be no noticeable play in the forks in the fore and aft direction with the wheel raised off the ground.

4. Make sure everything is adjusted properly before test-riding the vehicle.

FRONT FORKS

Leading Link Type Forks

DISASSEMBLY

1. Remove the front wheel as described in the "Wheels and Tires" section.

2. Remove the 6 mm lockpin and the 7 mm locknut, then remove the front cushion joint washer and joint rubber A (as illustrated). The front cushion and suspension arm can be removed as a unit by removing the front arm pivot bolt and the hex bolt.

3. Remove the front arm rebound stopper by removing the 8 mm hex nut and bolt.

4. Separate the front cushion and the front suspension arm by removing the 8 mm hex nut and the front cushion lower securing bolt. Take care not to loose the front cushion lower dust seal cap, seal, and

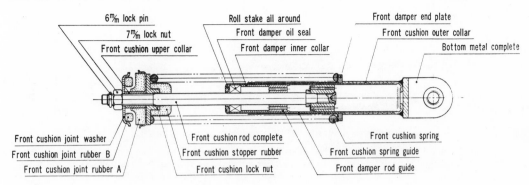

Front cushion sectional diagram

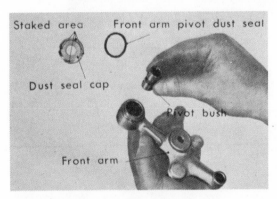

Pivot dust seal

spacer collar. The dust seal can be removed by unlocking the staking.

5. The suspension unit is now ready to be dismantled. The lower portion of the cushion is a sealed unit which cannot be rebuilt, and which must be replaced if weak or damaged. Disassemble the cushion by removing the locknut and spring. The spring guide, seat, stopper rubber, and outer collar are now free to be removed.

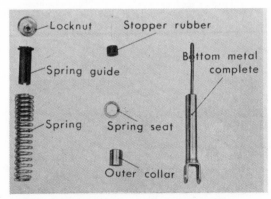

Cushion components

INSPECTION AND REPAIR

1. Clean all parts in a suitable solvent and blow them dry. The dust seals should be replaced as a matter of course.

2. Inspect the damper unit for oil leaks, warpage, or inefficient damping characteristics, and replace it as necessary.

3. Inspect the suspension and fork components for a worn or damaged condition and replace them as necessary. If the fork legs are bent slightly they can usually be straightened. Consult your local dealer for additional information.

4. Measure the free-length of the spring and replace it if collapsed, worn, or damaged.

ASSEMBLY

1. Assembly is basically the reverse order of disassembly.

2. Lubricate the suspension arm with grease and apply engine oil to the dust seal.

3. Lubricate the assembly when the assembly process is complete, by applying grease through the grease fitting using an automotive type grease gun.

Telescopic Type Forks

DISASSEMBLY

1. Remove the handlebars, headlight assembly, and the fork top bridge. The fork ears are now free to be removed.

2. Raise the motorcycle so the front wheel can be removed, then remove the wheel and fender assemblies. The fender is secured by four hex bolts located on the fork legs.

3. Remove the fork pinch bolts from the lower triple clamp and pull the fork assemblies down and out of the clamp.

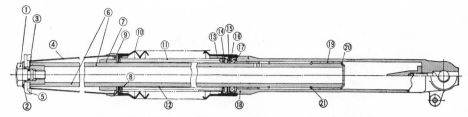

Front fork diagram (90 cc models except for the SL90)

1. Front fork filler bolt	8. Fork cover lower seat	15. Circlip
2. Washer	9. Fork cover lower seat packing	16. Front fork oil seal
3. O-ring	10. Front fork boot	17. Front fork leg guide
4. Front fork ear	11. Front cushion spring	18. Front fork slider
5. Fork top bridge plate	12. Front cushion spring guide	19. Front fork piston
6. Front fork leg	13. Front cushion under spring guide	20. Front fork piston snap ring
7. Fork bottom bridge	14. Front cushion spring under seat	21. Piston stopper ring

(CB100, CB125S)

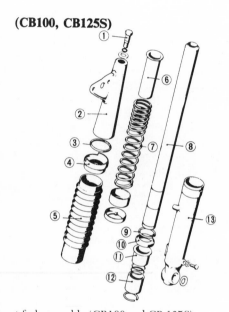

(CL100, CD125S)

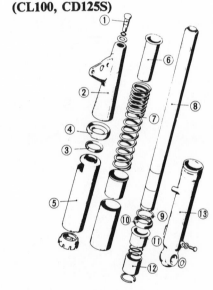

Front fork assembly (CB100 and CB 125S)

1. Fork filler bolt	7. Fork spring
2. Fork ear	8. Fork leg
3. Fork ear lower seat bushing	9. Circlip
4. Fork ear lower seat	10. Fork oil seal
5. Fork boot (CB models)/fork cover (CL and CD models)	11. Fork leg guide
6. Fork spring guide	12. Fork piston
	13. Fork slider

Front fork assembly (CL100 and CD125S)

1. Fork filler bolt	7. Fork spring
2. Fork ear	8. Fork leg
3. Fork ear lower seat bushing	9. Circlip
4. Fork ear lower seat	10. Fork oil seal
5. Fork boot (CB models)/fork cover (CL and CD models)	11. Fork leg guide
6. Fork spring guide	12. Fork piston
	13. Fork slider

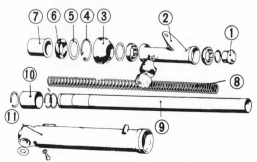

1. Fork filler bolt
2. Fork ear
3. Fork dust seal
4. Circlip
5. Back-up ring
6. Oil seal
7. Fork leg guide
8. Fork spring
9. Fork leg
10. Fork piston
11. Fork slider

Front fork assembly (SL models)

Disassembling the forks

1. Fork filler bolt   2. Pinch bolt

4. Allow the forks to drain into a suitable receptacle. The forks can be drained by merely inverting them.

5. Remove the fork boot or spring cover and the associated cover mounting apparatus, then remove the spring and spring guide.

6. Remove the circlip using a set of snap-ring pliers, then remove the fork piston, stop-ring, and oil and dust seal assemblies from the fork legs. The fork tube can be separated from the fork leg by securing the fork leg to something and pulling sharply on the tube.

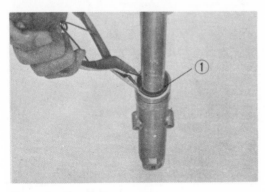

Removing the circlip

1. Circlip

7. Make sure you keep the assemblies separate so they can be reassembled with their original fork legs.

INSPECTION AND REPAIR

1. Clean all parts other than the oil seals in a suitable solvent, and blow them dry. The oil seals must be handled gently if you intend to reuse them, but if possible they should be replaced whenever they are removed.

2. Inspect all the components for an obvious worn or damaged condition and replace them as necessary. If the fork tubes are bent or scored, they can probably be turned down or straightened for considerably less money than the cost of replacements. If the threads, however, are damaged or stripped, the tubes will have to be replaced. Consult your dealer for additional information or the name of someone who is qualified to straighten the legs.

3. Inspect the front spring for a worn, collapsed, or damaged condition and replace it if necessary. The spring should be replaced if shorter than the specified free-length, or if tilted at a greater than acceptable angle.

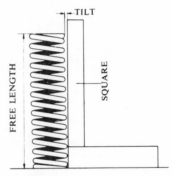

Spring inspection

4. Inspect the fork piston for wear or damage and replace it if worn past its serviceable limit. The piston should be measured with a micrometer.

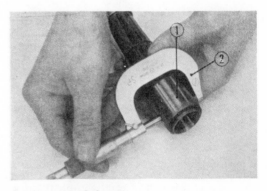

Measuring the fork piston

1. Fork piston   2. Micrometer

5. Carefully inspect the circlips and oil and dust seals if you plan to reuse them. The oil seals will just make the front end

look sloppy if they leak, but if the dust seal leaks it will allow dirt into the fork oil which will score the fork tubes and legs, and cause the oil seals to leak. If the rubber fork boot leaks, the same results will occur. If the circlips fail it's a whole new story. A broken circlip will almost certainly damage the fork legs and tubes, and incapacitate the front end.

ASSEMBLY

1. Assembly is basically the reverse order of disassembly.

2. Apply petroleum-resistant grease, or a suitable substitute, between the main and dust lips of the front oil seal, then install the seal into the bottom of the fork leg. An oil seal driving guide (tool no. 07054-07401) is available to prevent damage to the seal while driving it into the fork leg.

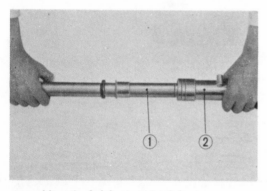

Assembling the fork leg into the slider

1. Fork leg   2. Fork slider

3. Install the circlips into their respective grooves, making sure they are correctly seated in the groove.

4. On internal spring type forks, install the spring into the fork leg so the smaller pitch of the spring is at the bottom of the fork leg. On the exposed type forks, and on the SL 100 and 125, install the spring with the larger pitch to the bottom of the fork leg.

5. Install each fork leg through the triple clamps so the top of the tube is flush with the top of the fork bridge. Remember to install the rubber boot or dust cover, and position the fork ears before running the fork tubes through the clamps. A fork

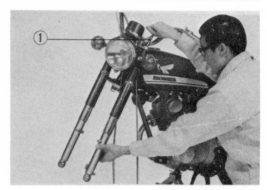

Installing the forks

1. Fork puller

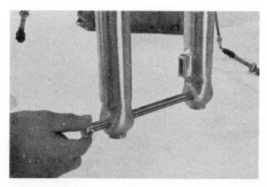

Aligning the forks

leg puller is available to assist in the operation, but is not essential.

6. Slip the axle into position to align the forks, then secure the pinch bolts at the lower triple clamp. The pinch bolts must be secure when the filler bolts are installed. The filler caps can be used to draw the fork tubes into position.

7. When the forks are completely installed and assembled, fill each fork tube with the recommended amount of fork oil, then make all necessary adjustments to the controls.

8. Check the operation of the forks by applying the front brake severely, without locking it, while exerting very little pressure on the handlebars. If everything else is in alignment, the forks should dip down evenly and the bike shouldn't tend to swerve to either side. Don't do this at high speeds or on any but the smoothest available road to preclude the possibility of going over the handlebars.

Rear Suspension

REAR SHOCK ABSORBERS

DeCarbon type shock absorber units are used on all of the 100 and 125 cc models, and also on all of the SL models covered in this guide. These units differ from conventional, double-damping hydraulic shocks in that they incorporate a chamber filled with nitrogen gas which is under high pressure. The pressurized nitrogen effectively prevents the hydraulic fluid from aerating and losing efficiency; however, it also means that the shock absorber cannot be rebuilt because of the danger of explosion. Do not attempt to disassemble the shock absorber, other than to remove the spring. If these units fail, they can be replaced with the factory replacements or by one of several substitute units which can be rebuilt and which may prove more effective for certain types of usage.

The 50–90 cc models, except for the SL models, use a more conventional, oil-dampened type of rear shock unit. These shocks, like the DeCarbon type shocks,

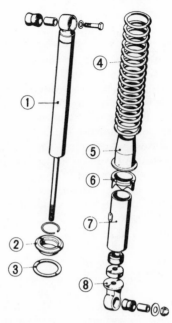

External spring type rear shock assembly (shown is a SL100 unit)

1. Shock absorber unit
2. Spring seat stopper
3. Spring upper seat
4. Spring
5. Spring guide
6. Spring adjuster
7. End case
8. Bottom mounting metal

cannot be rebuilt, however the springs, covers, and bushings are replaceable. All of the exposed, spring type shocks covered in this guide come equipped with a three-position cam adjuster which can be used to compensate for rider weight or for the kind of riding for which the machine is going to be used. The first position is used for solo street riding. The second is for two-up riding, heavy solo riding, or mild off-road riding. The third position is for two-up riding with heavy riders or for strenuous dirt riding. (The average rider is considered to weigh 150 lbs.) Adjustment is made with the hook spanner which comes in the tool kit.

To check the effectiveness of the shock absorber, compress and extend it by hand (after the spring has been removed of course). More resistance should be encountered on the extension stroke than on the compression stroke if the shock is operating correctly. Replace the unit if leaking or if the damping is unsatisfactory. You may find that the shock is working just fine but the ride is still not to your liking. This is entirely possible as the units mounted at the factory are often not up to handling

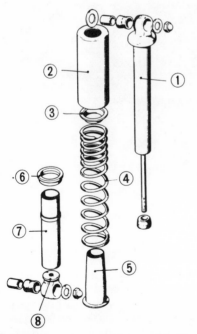

Covered spring type rear shock assembly (shown is a CB 100 unit)

1. Shock absorber unit
2. Upper case
3. Upper seat
4. Spring
5. Spring guide
6. Spring seat
7. Lower seat
8. Bottom mounting metal

the load put on them by a hard-riding, heavy rider. In this case you'll have to replace the shock with one of the fine competition units that are available. Most replacement shocks are designed to use the same spring that comes from Honda, and will work fine with this spring.

Disassemble the shock after removing it from the two mounting studs by setting it on the softest adjustment, then compressing the spring by hand until the locking nut can be removed. The shock can usually be compressed by one person, but it is a good idea to have someone there to remove the locking nut. Replace any worn or broken parts, and replace the spring if collapsed or if shorter than the specified length. When reassembling the shock, always install the spring so the smaller pitch of the coil is down as positioned on the bike. If you plan to store the shocks for any reason, make sure you store them in the position they are normally in on the motorcycle. This will keep the seals dry and thereby preserve them.

Removing the rear shock absorber
1. Cap nuts   2. Shock absorber

REAR SWING ARM

The rear fork is of the "swinging arm" design and is mounted to the frame through a rubber-bushed hinge at the rear of the frame, and by the rear shock absorber units which are attached to both the frame and the swing arm. When the rear wheel strikes a bump, the swing arm pivots on its rubber bushings while the shock absorber absorbs the shock. As the shock returns to its normal riding position, the swing arm is pushed down into its normal operating position. The swing arm is so designed that it does not affect chain tension when it pivots.

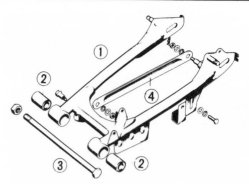

Swing arm assembly (shown is the fork from a CB 100)
1. Swing arm   3. Pivot bolt
2. Pivot rubber bushing   4. Rear brake stopper arm

Disassembly

1. Place the motorcycle on its centerstand and remove the rear wheel and drive chain. If the machine has a chaincase, that too must be removed.

2. Remove the lower mounting bolts from the shock absorbers and detach the units from the swing arm.

3. Remove the fork pivot bolt nut and pull the pivot bolt out. The swing arm is now free to be removed.

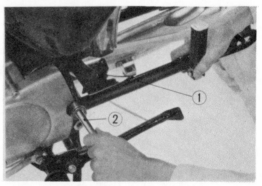

Removing the swing arm assembly (shown is a CB100)
1. Swing arm   2. Pivot bolt

Inspection and Repair

1. Clean all parts in a suitable solvent and blow them dry.

2. Replace all the bushings and the chaincase (if applicable) gasket. The bushings may be reused but as long as you've got it all apart you may as well replace them. If you decide to retain the bushings, use them only if they are in perfect condition, and exhibit no signs of wear, cracking, or age.

3. Inspect the fork pivot bolt for a scored, warped, or otherwise damaged condition, and replace it as necessary. Rolling the bolt on a perfectly flat surface will indicate whether or not it is out of true.

4. Inspect the swing arm for cracks, bends, signs of fatigue, warping, or damage, and replace it as necessary. If the fork is slightly bent, it can be repaired. Consult your dealer for additional information. Consider this if you are thinking of repairing the swing arm: once metal is bent and rebent it is permanently fatigued at least a little. Once a break is welded, it is never as strong as it should be. If you repair a broken or badly bent swing arm, you are taking a big chance since the fork could easily break again.

Assembly

1. Assembly is basically the reverse order of disassembly.

2. Thoroughly grease the rubber bushings before installing them in the fork, and grease the pivot bolt before installing it in the frame.

3. Make sure the chaincase packing (if applicable) is correctly seated before you install the case.

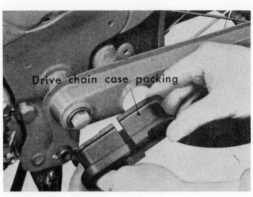

Installing the chaincase packing

Chassis Specifications

Model	C50 C50M S50 C65 C65M S65 Standard Value	Serviceable Limit
FRONT WHEEL AND SUSPENSION		
Cushion spring:		
free-length (in./mm)	5.14/130.7	4.72/120.0
spring compression (lbs/in.)	220.0/3.63	198/3.35
(kg/mm)	100.0/92.1	90.0/92.1
tilt	1°30′	4°
Damper:		
damping capacity (lbs/in./sec)	66–77/19.68/sec	——
(kg/mm/sec)	30–35/0.5/sec	——
Fork piston and bottom case:		
piston diameter (in./mm)	NA	NA
case inside diameter (in./mm)	NA	NA
stroke (in./mm)	NA	NA
damping capacity	NA	NA
Hub and axle assembly:		
front axle diameter (in./mm)	0.400/10.0	NA
front axle bend (in./mm)	0.008/0.2	0.02/0.5
brake drum inside diameter (in./mm)	4.33 ± 0.008/110.0 ± 0.2	4.33/100.0
brake lining shoe thickness (in./mm)	0.1417–0.1476/3.6–3.75	0.984/2.5
Steering geometry:		
trail length (in./mm)	2.95/75.0	——
caster angle	63°	——

Chassis Specifications (cont.)

Model	C50 C50M S50 C65 C65M S65	
	Standard Value	*Serviceable Limit*

REAR WHEEL AND SUSPENSION

Cushion spring:
free-length (in./mm)	9.260/209.8	7.874/200.0
spring compression (lbs/in.)	256/5.512	234/5.512
(kg/mm)	116.5/140.0	106/140.0
tilt	——	——
stroke	①	——

Damper:
damping capacity (lbs/in./sec)	55/19.68/sec	——
(kg/mm/sec)	25/0.5/sec	——

Hub and axle assembly:
rear axle diameter (in./mm)	0.4707–0.4720	——
rear axle bend (in./mm)	0.008/0.2	0.020/0.5
brake drum inside diameter (in./mm)	NA	——
brake lining shoe thickness (in./mm)	0.1378/3.5	0.0590/1.5

Swing arm pivot rubber bushing:
inside diameter (in./mm)	②	——

① C50, C50M	2.465/62.6	② C50, C50M, C65, C65M	O.D. 0.9055/23.0
C65, C65M	2.658/67.5	S50	O.D. 0.9842/25.0
S50, S65	2.492/63.6	S65	I.D. 0.4764/12.1

Model	C70 C70M	
	Standard Value	*Serviceable Limit*

FRONT WHEEL AND SUSPENSION

Cushion spring:
free-length (in./mm)	5.146/130.7	4.803/122.0
spring compression (lbs/in.)	264.6/3.386	——
(kg/mm)	120/86	——
tilt	1°30′	4°

Damper:
damping capacity (lbs/in./sec)	——	——
(kg/mm/sec)	——	——

Fork piston and bottom case:
piston diameter (in./mm)	NA	NA
case inside diameter (in./mm)	NA	NA
stroke (in./mm)	NA	NA
damping capacity	NA	NA

Hub and axle assembly:
front axle diameter (in./mm)	0.3923–0.3932/9.965–9.987	0.392/9.96
front axle bend (in./mm)	0.0020/0.05	0.008/0.2
brake drum inside diameter (in./mm)	4.323–4.339/109.8–110.2	4.448/113.0
brake lining shoe thickness (in./mm)	0.1417–0.1476/3.6–3.75	0.984/2.5

Steering geometry:
trail length (in./mm)	2.95	——
caster angle	63°	——

Chassis Specifications (cont.)

Model	C70 C70M Standard Value	Serviceable Limit
REAR WHEEL AND SUSPENSION		
Cushion spring:		
free-length (in./mm)	8.661/220.0	8.268/210.0
spring compression (lbs/in.)	187.4/5.512	——
(kg/mm)	85/140	——
tilt	1°30′	4°
Damper:		
damping capacity (lbs/in./sec)	——	——
(kg/mm/sec)	——	——
Hub and axle assembly:		
rear axle diameter (in./mm)	0.4704–0.4718/11.957–11.984	0.4705/11.95
rear axle bend (in./mm)	0.0020/0.05	0.008/0.2
brake drum inside diameter (in./mm)	4.323–4.339/109.8–110.2	4.448/113
brake lining shoe thickness (in./mm)	0.1417–1.1476/3.6–3.75	0.984/2.5
Swing arm pivot rubber bushing:		
inside diameter (in./mm)	0.398–0.406/10.1–10.3	0.411/10.45

Model	CL70 Standard Value	Serviceable Limit
FRONT WHEEL AND SUSPENSION		
Cushion spring:		
free-length (in./mm)	5.146/130.7	4.803/122.0
spring compression (lbs/in.)	264.6/3.386	——
(kg/mm)	120/86	——
tilt	1°30′	4°
Damper:		
damping capacity (lbs/in./sec)	NA	NA
(kg/mm/sec)	NA	NA
Fork piston and bottom case:		
piston diameter (in./mm)	1.1389–1.1402/28.93–28.96	1.1375/28.917
case inside diameter (in./mm)	1.1417–1.1430/29.0–29.033	1.1488/29.18
stroke (in./mm)	3.44/87.5	NA
damping capacity	——	——
Hub and axle assembly:		
front axle diameter (in./mm)	0.3923–0.3932/9.965–9.987	0.392/9.96
front axle bend (in./mm)	0.0020/0.05	0.008/0.2
brake drum inside diameter (in./mm)	4.323–4.339/109.8–110.2	4.448/113.0
brake lining shoe thickness (in./mm)	0.1417–0.1476/3.6–3.75	0.984/2.5
Steering geometry:		
trail length (in./mm)	2.76/70.0	——
caster angle	64°	——

Chassis Specifications (cont.)

Model	CL70 Standard Value	Serviceable Limit

REAR WHEEL AND SUSPENSION

Cushion spring:

free-length (in./mm)	8.224/208.9	7.874/200
spring compression (lbs/in.)	257.1/5.472	——
(kg/mm)	116.5/139.1	——
tilt	1°30′	4°

Damper:

damping capacity (lbs/in./sec)	——	——
(kg/mm/sec)	——	——

Hub and axle assembly:

rear axle diameter (in./mm)	0.4704–0.4718/11.957–11.984	0.4705/11.9
rear axle bend (in./mm)	0.0020/0.05	0.008/0.2
brake drum inside diameter (in./mm)	4.323–4.339/109.8–110.2	4.448/113
brake lining shoe thickness (in./mm)	0.1417–1.1476/3.6–3.75	0.984/2.5

Swing arm pivot rubber bushing:

inside diameter (in./mm)	0.476–0.484/11.957–11.984	0.490/12.45

Model	C90 CD90 CT90 (from F. no. 000001A) Standard Value	Serviceable Limit

FRONT WHEEL AND SUSPENSION

Cushion spring:

free-length (in./mm)	①	②
spring compression (lbs/in.)	③	——
(kg/mm)	④	——
tilt	1°	1°

Damper:

damping capacity (lbs/in./sec)	22.1/20.0/sec	——
(kg/mm/sec)	10.0/0.5/sec	——

Fork piston and bottom case:

piston diameter (in./mm)	NA	NA
case inside diameter (in./mm)	NA	NA
stroke (in./mm)	NA	NA
damping capacity	NA	NA

Hub and axle assembly:

front axle diameter (in./mm)	0.394–0.396/9.995–10.050	NA
front axle bend (in./mm)	0.008/0.2	NA
brake drum outside diameter (in./mm)	4.2992–4.3110/109.2–109.5	4.2323/107.5
brake lining shoe thickness (in./mm)	0.1575/4.0	0.1181/3.0

Steering geometry:

trail length (in./mm)	2.955/75.0	——
caster angle	⑤	——

① C90	5.2520/133.4	④ C90	47.5–52.5/112.6
CD90	5.886/149.5	CD90	76.0/117.0
CT90	8.0/203.0	CT90	23.5–26.5/119.6
② C90	4.73/120.0	⑤ C90	63°
CD90	5.32/135.0	CD90	63.5°
CT90	7.3/185.0	CT90	63.5°
③ C90	104.738–115.763/4.433		
CD90	167.58/4.606		
CT90	51.7–58.3/4.71		

Chassis Specifications (cont.)

Model	C90 Standard Value	Serviceable Limit

REAR WHEEL AND SUSPENSION

Cushion spring:		
free-length (in./mm)	8.313/212.0	7.48/190.0
spring compression (lbs/in.)	264.0/5.57	——
(kg/mm)	120.0/141.5	——
tilt	1.5°	2°
Damper:		
damping capacity (lbs/in./sec)	55–68/20/sec	——
(kg/mm/sec)	25–31/0.5/sec	——
stroke (in./mm)	2.46/62.4	——
Hub and axle assembly:		
rear axle diameter (in./mm)	0.472–0.515/11.984–12.957	——
rear axle bend (in./mm)	0.00/0.2	0.020/0.5
brake drum inside diameter (in./mm)	——	——
brake lining shoe thickness (in./mm)	0.5575/4.0	0.1181/3.0
Swing arm pivot rubber bushing:		
inside diameter (in./mm)	——	——

Model	CD90 Standard Value	Serviceable Limit

REAR WHEEL AND SUSPENSION

Cushion spring:		
free-length (in./mm)	8.313/211.0	7.48/190.0
spring compression (lbs/in.)	220.0/5.532	——
(kg/mm)	100.0/140.4	——
tilt	1.5°	2°
Damper:		
damping capacity (lbs/in./sec)	61.6–81.4/19.7/sec	——
(kg/mm/sec)	28–37/0.5/sec	——
stroke (in./mm)	2.41/61.2	——
Hub and axle assembly:		
rear axle diameter (in./mm)	0.472–0.515/11.984–12.957	——
rear axle bend (in./mm)	0.00/0.2	0.020/0.5
brake drum inside diameter (in./mm)	——	——
brake lining shoe thickness (in./mm)	0.5575/4.0	0.1181/3.0
Swing arm pivot rubber bushing:		
inside diameter (in./mm)	——	——

Model	CT90 Standard Value	Serviceable Limit

REAR WHEEL AND SUSPENSION

Cushion spring:		
free-length (in./mm)	8.776/222.9	8.16/207.0
spring compression (lbs/in.)	3.473/5.6181	——
(kg/mm)	157.5/142.7	——
tilt	1.5°	2°

Chassis Specifications (cont.)

Model	CT90 Standard Value	Serviceable Limit
REAR WHEEL AND SUSPENSION		
Damper:		
damping capacity (lbs/in./sec)	88–110/20/sec	——
(kg/mm/sec)	40–50/0.5/sec	——
stroke (in./mm)	①	——
Hub and axle assembly:		
rear axle diameter (in./mm)	0.472–0.515/11.984–12.957	——
rear axle bend (in./mm)	0.00/0.2	0.020/0.5
brake drum inside diameter (in./mm)	——	——
brake lining shoe thickness (in./mm)	0.5575/4.0	0.1181/3.0
Swing arm pivot rubber bushing:		
inside diameter (in./mm)	——	——

① CT90   2.49/62.4
   CT90 (after F. no. 000001A)   3.05/77.5

Model	SL90 Standard Value	Serviceable Limit
FRONT WHEEL AND SUSPENSION		
Cushion spring:		
free-length (in./mm)	——	——
spring compression (lbs/in.)	——	——
(kg/mm)	——	——
tilt	——	——
Damper:		
damping capacity (lbs/in./sec)	NA	NA
(kg/mm/sec)	NA	NA
Fork piston and bottom case:		
piston diameter (in./mm)	1.395–1.396/35.425–35.45	1.39/35.3
case inside diameter (in./mm)	1.399–1.400/35.53–35.57	1.405/35.7
stroke (in./mm)	——	——
damping capacity (lbs/in./sec)	——	——
(kg/in./sec)	——	——
Hub and axle assembly:		
front axle diameter (in./mm)	——	——
front axle bend (in./mm)	——	——
brake drum inside diameter (in./mm)	——	——
brake lining shoe thickness (in./mm)	——	——
Steering geometry:		
trail length (in./mm)	3.66/93.0	——
caster angle	61.5°	——

Chassis Specifications (cont.)

Model	SL90 Standard Value	Serviceable Limit
REAR WHEEL AND SUSPENSION		
Cushion spring:		
free-length (in./mm)	8.492/21.5	7.874/20.0
spring compression (lbs/in.)	——	——
(kg/mm)	——	——
tilt	——	——
Damper:		
damping capacity (lbs/in./sec)	——	——
(kg/mm/sec)	——	——
Hub and axle assembly:		
rear axle diameter (in./mm)	0.472–0.515/11.984–12.957	——
rear axle bend (in./mm)	0.00/0.2	0.020/0.5
brake drum inside diameter (in./mm)	4.32–4.34/109.8–110.2	4.41/112.0
brake lining shoe thickness (in./mm)	0.5575/4.0	0.1181/3.0
Swing arm pivot rubber bushing:		
inside diameter (in./mm)	0.472–0.480/12.0–12.2	——

Model	S90 CL90 CL90L Standard Value	Serviceable Limit
FRONT WHEEL AND SUSPENSION		
Cushion spring:		
free-length (in./mm)	7.789/197.7	7.013/178.0
spring compression (lbs/in.)	22.44/6.686	——
(kg/mm)	10.2/16.97	——
tilt	1°	1°
Damper:		
damping capacity (lbs/in./sec)	NA	NA
(kg/mm/sec)	NA	NA
Fork piston and bottom case:		
piston diameter (in./mm)	1.219–1.220/30.950–30.975	——
case inside diameter (in./mm)	1.22–1.223/31.0–31.039	——
stroke (in./mm)	——	——
damping capacity (lbs/in./sec)	22.1/20.0/sec	——
(kg/mm/sec)	10.0/0.5/sec	——
Hub and axle assembly:		
front axle diameter (in./mm)	0.394–0.396/9.995–10.050	——
front axle bend (in./mm)	0.008/0.2	——
brake drum outside diameter (in./mm)	4.2992–4.3110/109.2–109.5	4.2323/107.5
brake lining shoe thickness (in./mm)	0.1575/4.0	0.1181/3.0
Steering geometry:		
trail length (in./mm)	①	——
caster angle	②	——

① S90	2.955/75.0	② S90	65°
CL90, CL90L	2.87/73.0	CL90, CL90L	64°

Chassis Specifications (cont.)

Model	S90 Standard Value	Serviceable Limit
REAR WHEEL AND SUSPENSION		
Cushion spring:		
free-length (in./mm)	6.761/171.6	6.139/155.8
spring compression (lbs/in.)	257.4/3.983	——
(kg/mm)	117.0/101.1	——
tilt	1.5°	2°
Damper:		
damping capacity (lbs/in./sec)	55.125–77.175/19.68/sec	——
(kg/mm/sec)	25–35/0.5/sec	——
stroke (in./mm)	2.41/61.1	——
Hub and axle assembly:		
rear axle diameter (in./mm)	0.472–0.515/11.984–12.957	——
rear axle bend (in./mm)	0.00/0.2	0.020/0.5
brake drum inside diameter (in./mm)	——	——
brake lining shoe thickness (in./mm)	0.5575/4.0	0.1181/3.0
Swing arm pivot rubber bushing:		
inside diameter (in./mm)	0.472–0.480/12.0–12.2	——

Model	CL90 CL90L Standard Value	Serviceable Limit
REAR WHEEL AND SUSPENSION		
Cushion spring:		
free-length (in./mm)	6.7874/172.4	6.139/155.8
spring compression (lbs/in.)	2.280–2.571/4.6457	NA
(kg/mm)	103.4–116.6/118.0	NA
tilt	1.5°	2°
Damper:		
damping capacity (lbs/in./sec)	55.125–77.175/19.68/sec	NA
(kg/mm/sec)	25–35/0.5/sec	NA
stroke (in./mm)	2.11/53.6	NA
Hub and axle assembly:		
rear axle diameter (in./mm)	0.472–0.515/11.984–12.957	NA
rear axle bend (in./mm)	0.00/0.2	0.020/0.5
brake drum inside diameter (in./mm)	NA	NA
brake lining shoe thickness (in./mm)	0.5575/4.0	0.1181/3.0
Swing arm pivot rubber bushing:		
inside diameter (in./mm)	0.472–0.480/12.0–12.2	NA

Chassis Specifications (cont.)

Model	CB100 CL100 SL100 CB125S CD125S SL125 Standard Value	Serviceable Limit

FRONT WHEEL AND SUSPENSION

Cushion spring free-length: (in./mm)
CB100/CL100	7.2440/184.0	6.2992/160.0
SL100	19.0629/484.2	18.1102/460.0
CB125S/CD125S	8.0905/205.5	7.0866/180.0
SL125	18.9881/482.3	18.1102/460.0

Front fork piston outside diameter: (in./mm)
CB100/CL100/CB125S/CD125S	1.2174–1.2194/30.936–30.975	1.2165/30.9
SL100/SL125	1.3946–1.3956/35.425–35.450	1.2937/35.4

Stroke: (in./mm)
CB100/CL100	4.2716/108.5	NA
SL100	6.2992/160.0	NA
CB125S/CD125S	4.5000/114.3	NA
SL125	5.5118/142.0	NA

Brake drum inside diameter: (in./mm)
CB100/CL100/CB125S/CD125S	4.3229–4.3385/109.8–110.2	4.409/112.0
SL100/SL125	4.3307–4.3425/110.0–110.3	4.409/112.0

Brake lining shoe thickness: (in./mm)
All Models	0.1535–0.1614/3.9–4.1	0.0787/2.0

Trail length: (in./mm)
CB100	2.95/75.0	——
CL100	3.07/78.0	——
SL100	3.70/95.0	——
CB125S/CD125S/SL125	3.15/80.0	——

Caster angle:
CB100	64°	——
CL100	63°40′	——
SL100	61°30′	——
CB125S/CD125S	63°45′	——
SL125	60°	——

REAR WHEEL AND SUSPENSION

Cushion spring free-length: (in./mm)
CB100/CL100/CB125S/CD125S	7.1200/180.9	6.2992/160.0
SL100/SL125	7.4803/190.0	6.6929/170.0

Clearance between rear fork pivot bushing and bolt: (in./mm)
All Models	0.0031–0.0118/0.1–0.3	0.0196/0.5

Brake drum inside diameter: (in./mm)
CB100/CL100/CB125S/CD125S	4.3229–4.3385/109.8–110.2	4.409/112.0
SL100/SL125	4.3307–4.3425/110.0–110.3	4.409/112.0

Brake lining shoe thickness: (in./mm)
All Models	0.1535–0.1614/3.9–4.1	0.0787/2.0

9 · Troubleshooting

There are certain steps which, if followed, can transform the confusing task of troubleshooting into an exact science. Random efforts often prove frustrating, so a logical method of approach should be adopted. Troubleshooting is nothing more than a systematic process of elimination, tracing back and checking various components until the fault is located. In most cases this takes very little time and requires very few special tools.

Before you start, try to determine if this is a new problem or one that's been coming on gradually. If you are an aware rider you'll know whether or not performance has been diminishing, and consulting the troubleshooting guide in this section may provide an immediate answer. Also, whenever a problem shows up just after work has been done on the bike, check those areas that were involved first, regardless of the nature of the work.

When troubleshooting the engine, you will be concerned with three major areas: the ignition system; the fuel system; and the cranking compression pressure. The engine needs spark, fuel, and compression to run, and it will be your job to determine which of these it lacks and why. Let's say that your engine won't start one morning, but it was fine the night before. The most obvious thing to check first, but which is often overlooked, is the fuel supply. Keep in mind that even if there is gas in the tank, a low supply can sometimes make starting difficult. Check to see if you have fuel at the carburetor by unscrewing the float bowl plug. If so, you can be pretty sure that it is not a lack of fuel that is preventing the engine from starting.

As far as compression is concerned, there are only a few conditions that will cause a sudden loss of compression, and such an occurrence will normally only occur when the engine is running. You should be able to tell if you have sufficient compression simply by the way the engine sounds and feels as it cranks over. Or, if you have the spark plug out, cover the plug hole with your finger and kick the engine through. If the pressure forces your finger off the hole, there should be enough compression for the engine to start. Of course, the most accurate way to check compression is by using a compression gauge.

So, you have found that the engine has relatively normal compression and is getting fuel. The final area, and the one which is most likely to cause you to tear your hair out, is the electrical system. The first thing to do is to check to see if you are getting spark to the cylinders by removing the plug lead and inserting a metal object, such as a nail, into it. Using a piece of rubber as insulation, hold the nail about 1/8 in. away from the engine and crank it over with the ignition on. If you have spark at the plug leads, remove and check the spark plug for a fouled condition. A plug may look good but still be defective, and it may even come from the factory with hidden defects so it's a good idea to check things out with a new plug. If there is no juice at the plug lead, trace the ignition system back with a test light. (Make sure you use a test light with a self-contained power source because the bike's battery puts out a little too much juice for comfort.) Start by checking for electricity at the points while they are open. If you have juice there, the problem lies in the coil, spark plug wires, or the wires between the coil and the points. If you find that there is no supply of electricity to the coil, start looking for loose connectors in the wiring between the coil and the ignition switch. Speaking of connectors, whenever you have a problem with the electrical system they are the first things you should examine. These little devils have the habit of vibrating and pulling loose for no particular reason, and cause far more trouble and aggravation than any other part of the electrical system.

If you have a charging system problem, the most common faults to look for are loose connectors or a loose rectifier mounting nut. A large number of charging system problems experienced stem from simple things such as these. Honda builds fine charging systems and they don't often fail.

All of the above can be considered troubleshooting the engine to get it running, not troubleshooting to cure running faults. Once you have found the general location of the trouble, it is usually quite simple to make pinpoint checks or temporarily substitute new or improvised parts to determine exactly where the problem lies. The most important thing to remember is to try to remain rational and approach the troubleshooting procedures logically. If you do this, chances are that you'll find the source of all this unpleasantness and save yourself some time, money, aggravation, and embarrassment (when the mechanic tells you that you pushed the bike four miles and paid him five dollars to replace the fuse).

Troubleshooting an engine that is running poorly is often a bit trickier than trying to determine why an engine won't start. You will still be involved with the compression, fuel system, and electrical systems of your engine but the problems will be more subtle and harder to detect. It pays here, if you are making adjustments or are fine-tuning, to make one adjustment at a time, thoroughly check the results, and record the findings. Otherwise you will confuse yourself, ruin the results of one adjustment with another, and accomplish nothing.

Assuming your engine hasn't expired with a big bang, any mechanical difficulties that you suspect will have taken time to develop and are most often related to wear. Try to remember if a new sound shortly preceded the trouble, as sounds can often help trace the problems. Don't become paranoid about "new" noises though, because you can imagine all kinds of terrible sounds if you really try, and pretty soon you'll be looking under your bed before you get into it at night.

Remember, when trying to diagnose a running fault, to check all the parts related to the component you are examining. For example, suppose you are carefully scrutinizing a carburetor, expecting a revelation any moment. In the meantime don't forget to check the intake tube clamps, the air filter, and the fuel filter to make sure that the carburetor is not being sabotaged in one way or another by those components (too much air, or too little air and fuel). Or, if you are busy getting zapped by the high-tension lead while checking for sufficient spark, don't forget to check to make sure that the plug connector is tightly attached to the wire, that the insulation is not worn or cracked, etc., etc. Look for the little things, and do it systematically and thoroughly. In many cases a qualified mechanic may be able to help you with a specific problem without even having to look at the bike. He's seen it all before so don't hesitate to ask. The worst it can get you is a service appointment for next week.

Engine Noises

One of the first indications of change in the condition of your motorcycle is the sounds that emanate from it. A thoughtful rider will know that something is going wrong long before it happens and may be able to rectify the situation before it leads to costly repairs. Every machine has its own sounds and these sounds will remain constant until something begins to go wrong. Pay attention to this and whenever a new sound appears consult your local mechanic because he's the one who's heard them all before.

VALVE CLATTER

When tappet adjustment time comes rolling around you'll know it because the valves will tell you. They always make some noise, especially when cold, but will really get noisy when in need of attention. When listening to the tappets, keep in mind that when you can hear them they're alright. If you can't hear anything as soon as you start the bike, they're too tight and will cause damage to the valve train. One good way of listening to the valves is to place the metal tip of a screwdriver against the rocker box and listen through the handle.

PINGING

Poor-quality gasoline, advanced ignition timing, incorrect spark plug heat range, or a piece of metal or carbon in the combustion chamber can be causes of pinging.

Pinging sounds are generally associated with the top end, and occur at mid-throttle range during acceleration. Most of the time it is caused by preignition due to the use of low-octane fuel in a high-compression engine. The unnecessary detonation causes undue strain on piston assemblies and bearings.

If the ignition timing is advanced too far, the force of the combustion will try to force the piston down before it completes its rotation. This is another type of preignition and is as harmful as the use of poor fuel. When pistons end up with holes in them, it is often due to this, but may also be due to using the wrong heat range spark plug.

If the plug in use is too hot, it can't dissipate its heat quickly enough and begins

to act like a glow plug. This causes preignition also and can be corrected by using a colder plug.

Carbon or metal pieces in the combustion chamber can heat up and act like a glow plug. This is less common than the others and only occurs when the engine is running hot. The only way to quiet this type of pinging is through top-end surgery.

PISTON SLAP

Slap occurs most often at mid-throttle range during acceleration and requires top-end disassembly to eliminate it. The noise is metallic and is caused by excessive piston-cylinder clearance. If the noise goes away after the engine warms up, the condition is not urgent but you'd better start planning on rebuilding the top end quite soon.

KNOCK

If you hear a mighty knocking noise coming from the bottom end while accelerating, you can be pretty sure the main bearings haven't long to go. It also may be a crankshaft problem and is remedied in either case by taking down the entire engine.

RAP

When the connecting rod bearings start to go, rap develops. This is most often heard during decleration and increases in intensity with the speed of the engine.

DOUBLE RAP

This is caused by excessive piston/piston pin clearance and is most noticeable as a quick succession of raps at idle speeds.

WHINE

In the overhead-cam Honda engines, an unusually loud whine often indicates a loose cam chain. The noise may also come from a drive chain which is in need of lubrication or which is adjusted too tight.

Engine Troubleshooting

Problem	Probable Causes	Inspection and Remedy
Engine fails to start	Fuel starvation	Check fuel supply. Check to see that the fuel tap is turned on. Check the fuel filter and lines for obstruction.
	Fuel flooding	Remove and dry the spark plug. Check the carburetor float needle and seat for dirt and wear, and check the float level. Refer to chapter six, "Carburetor Overhaul" section.
	Insufficiently charged battery	Check the electrolyte level and recharge the battery. Investigate the cause of battery discharging. Refer to chapter seven, "Charging System."
	Fouled or improperly gapped spark plug	Clean and gap, or replace. Refer to chapter three.
	Badly oxidized, dirty, or improperly gapped ignition points	Clean and gap, or replace ignition points and condenser. Refer to chapter three, "Contact Breaker Points" section.
	Spark plug cable damaged	Replace high-tension wiring harness.
	Ignition timing out of adjustment	Reset timing, refer to chapter three, "Ignition Timing" section.
	Loose connection in ignition system	Check wiring harness connections.
	Ignition coil defective	Make sure that the ignition points, low-tension wire, and high-tension wire are in good condition. Check coil spark by inserting a metal object, such as a nail, into the spark plug wire connector, holding it about $\frac{1}{4}$ in. from the engine (with a cloth or other insulating material to prevent shock) and cranking the engine over with the ignition on. (The battery should have close to its normal amount of charge.) The coil should produce a fat, hot, consistent spark. Lack of spark or weak spark indicates a defective coil.
	Battery terminals loose or corroded	Clean and tighten.
	Low compression	If the engine can be turned over on the kick-starter with less than normal effort, perform a compression test and determine the cause of low compression. Refer to chapter three, "Compression Check" section.
Engine hard to start	Fuel starvation	Check fuel level. A minimal amount of fuel in the tank can sometimes make starting hard. Check float level. Refer to chapter six "Carburetor Overhaul" section. Make sure the fuel tank breather is not blocked. Check the fuel filter for obstruction. Check for intake air leaks. Make sure that the tube clamps are tight.
	Weak spark	Check ignition points, coil, ignition wires, and spark plug as described in chapter three.
	Contaminated fuel	Drain and replace the gas in the float bowls and fuel tank.

Engine Troubleshooting (cont.)

Problem	Probable Causes	Inspection and Remedy
Engine hard to start	Battery charge low	Check electrolyte level and recharge the battery. If discharging persists, investigate the cause. Refer to chapter seven "Charging System."
	Ignition timing improperly adjusted	Check and adjust timing. Refer to chapter three, "Compression Check" section.
	Low compression	If the engine can be turned over on the kick-starter with less than normal effort, perform a compression test and determine the cause of low compression. Refer to "Compression Check" section.
Engine dies while running	Lack of fuel	Check fuel supply. Check fuel lines and carburetor for leaking. Check fuel lines and fuel filter for obstructions.
	Lack of spark	Check electrical overload fuse that is located near the battery. Check ignition wiring harness connectors. Check battery terminal connections and ground cable frame connection. Check charging system wire connections and make sure that the rectifier mounting nut is tight.
	Mechanical failure	If the engine stops with a bang while running, it is time to thoroughly inspect your warranty policy and/or bank balance.
Engine idles poorly	Improper fuel mixture	Adjust carburetor air screw properly. Refer to chapter three, "Carburetor Adjustment" section. Remove and clean carburetor low-speed jet. Refer to chapter six, "Carburetor Overhaul" section. Check float level. Refer to chapter six, "Carburetor Overhaul" section. Check for intake air leaks. Make sure that the mounting bolts are tight.
	Weak spark	Check the spark plug. Clean and gap, or replace if necessary. Check ignition points. Clean and gap, or replace if necessary, and set ignition timing. Refer to chapter three. Check spark plug wire for worn or cracked insulation. Check the connectors for cracks and make sure they are securely attached.
	Valve sticking at low speeds	Check and adjust valve clearances if necessary. Refer to chapter three, "Valve Adjustment" section. Use a supplemental lubricant such as a top cylinder oil to free the valve.
Engine runs poorly at low- to mid-range throttle openings	Fuel mixture too lean	Check for intake air leaks. Make sure that the carburetor jet needle is positioned correctly. Refer to chapter six. Check for fuel contamination by draining the float bowl(s) and watching for water. Check spark plug, ignition points, ignition wires and connectors, and coil output. Check ignition timing and advance unit. Refer to chapter three.

Engine Troubleshooting (cont.)

Problem	Probable Causes	Inspection and Remedy
Engine misfires and runs poorly at full throttle	Improper fuel mixture	Clean air filter element. Check for fuel line or fuel filter obstruction. Check float level. Refer to chapter six, "Carburetor Overhaul" section. Check for intake air leaks. Make sure that the main jet is not loose and that they are the right size. Refer to chapter six.
	Fouled or worn spark plug	Carbon-fouled plug, or old plug, can sometimes cause high-speed misfire even though they look usable. If in doubt, try a new set. Make sure that you are using the correct heat range. Refer to chapter three, "Spark Plug" section.
	Ignition advance unit faulty	Check ignition timing with a strobe light. If the advance unit is not functioning properly, disassemble and inspect it. Refer to chapter three, "Ignition Timing" section.
	Weak spark	Check the ignition points and replace them, in any case, if they have been in service for more than 5,000 miles. Check coil output, ignition wires, and spark plug connectors. Refer to chapter three.
Loss of compression and power	Mechanical wear or failure, burnt valves, leaking head gasket, etc.	Refer to chapter three, "Compression Check" for analysis of compression test results.
Backfiring	Lean fuel mixture	Check for intake air leaks and exhaust leaks.
	Improper ignition timing	Check and adjust ignition timing. Make sure that the ignition advance unit is functioning properly. Refer to chapter three, "Ignition Timing" section.
Overheating, accompanied by pinging or spark knock	Ignition timing incorrect	Adjust
	Contaminated or poor-quality gasoline	Drain float bowl and fuel tank. Refill with fresh gas.
	Fuel mixture too rich	Examine and clean air filter element, if necessary. Check for worn main jet tube and jet needle. Make sure the needle is correctly positioned. Refer to chapter six, "Carburetor Overhaul" section.
	Weak spark	Check battery terminal connections and battery charge. Refer to chapter two, "Battery Section," and chapter seven, "Charging System."
	Lack of oil pressure, oil not circulating	Remove and overhaul oil pump. Refer to chapter three.
	Excessive carbon buildup in combustion chamber and on piston crown	Perform a top-end overhaul. Refer to chapter four.
	Incorrect spark plug heat range	Check for proper spark plugs in chapter three, "Spark Plug" and "Specification" sections.
	Lean fuel mixture	Check for intake air leaks.
	Lack of engine oil	Shame on you.

Engine Troubleshooting (cont.)

Problem	Probable Causes	Inspection and Remedy
Excessive oil consumption	Mechanical wear, piston, failure, etc.	Perform a compression test and analysis. Refer to chapter three, "Compression Check" section. If compression pressure is normal, oil burning is probably the fault of defective valve seals or worn valve seals or worn valve guides.
	Engine breather obstructed	Inspect and clean breather outlet.
Excessive vibration	Engine mounts loose or broken	Inspect and secure. Refer to chapter four, "Engine Removal and Installation" section.
	Incorrect ignition timing	Check and adjust.
	Misfiring, loss of compression, tight or sticking valves	Perform a tune-up.

Clutch Troubleshooting

Problem	Probable Causes	Inspection and Remedy
Clutch slippage	Improper adjustment	Perform full clutch adjustment. Refer to chapter two, "Clutch" section.
	Weak springs	Overhaul clutch unit. Refer to chapter four, "Clutch" section.
	Worn or glazed discs	See above.
Clutch chatter	Weak springs	Overhaul clutch unit.
	Warped plates	See above.
	Warped pressure plate	See above.
	Pressure plate rivets loose	See above.
Clutch drag	Improper adjustment	Perform full clutch adjustment. Refer to chapter two, "Clutch" section.
	Warped plates	Overhaul clutch unit.
	Defective release mechanism	Inspect and replace parts as necessary.

Transmission Troubleshooting

Problem	Probable Causes	Inspection and Remedy
Hard gear shifting	Improper clutch adjustment	Perform full clutch adjustment. Refer to chapter two, "Clutch" section.
	Damaged shift forks or drum	Overhaul shifter mechanism. Refer to chapter four, "Shifter Mechanism Service."
	Mainshaft and countershaft improperly aligned	Disassemble the transmission and replace the shafts or bearings as necessary. Refer to chapter four, "Transmission Service" section.
Excessive gear noise	Excessive backlash	Disassemble the transmission and check gear backlash. Refer to chapter four, "Transmission Service" section.
	Worn mainshaft or countershaft bearings	Overhaul the transmission unit. Refer to chapter four.

Transmission Troubleshooting (cont.)

Problem	Probable Causes	Inspection and Remedy
Transmission jumps out of gear	Worn shift forks or drum	Overhaul shifter mechanism. Refer to chapter four, "Shifter Mechanism Service" section.
	Worn main or countershaft splines or worn gears	Overhaul the transmission as described in chapter four.

Electrical System Troubleshooting

Complete testing, diagnosis, and repair procedures for the electrical system components will be found in chapter seven.

Battery Troubleshooting

Problem	Probable Causes	Inspection and Remedy
Sulfation The electrode plates are covered with white layer or in spots.	Charging rate is too small or else excessively large. The specific gravity or the mixture of the electrolyte is improper. Battery left in a discharged condition for a long period (left with the switch turned on). Exposed to excessive vibration due to improper installation. During cold season when motorcycle is left stored, the wiring should be disconnected.	When stored in a discharged condition, the battery should be recharged once a month even when the motorcycle is not used. Check the electrolyte periodically and always maintain the proper level 0.400–0.518 in. (10–13 mm) above the plates. In a lightly discharged condition, the battery may be restored by overcharging at 20 hours. Depending upon the condition, performing recharging and discharging several times may be sufficient.
Self discharge Battery discharges in addition to that caused by the connected load.	Dirty contact areas and case. Contaminated electrolyte or electrolyte excessively concentrated.	Always keep the casing clean. Handle the replenishing fluid with care.
Discharge rate large Specific gravity, gradually lowers and around 1.1, the turn signal lamp and horn no longer function.	The fuse and the wiring is satisfactory; the loads such as turn signal, lamp, and horn do not function. In this condition the motorcycle will operate but with prolonged use, both the + and − plates will react with the sulfuric acid and form lead sulfide deposits (sulfation) making it impossible to recharge.	When the specific gravity falls below 1,200 (20° C : 68° F), the battery should be recharged immediately. When the battery frequently becomes discharged while operating at normal speed, check generator for proper output. If the battery discharges under normal charge output, it is an indication of overloading; remove some of the excess load.
High charging rate The electrolyte level drops rapidly but the charge is always maintained at 100 percent and the condition appears satisfactory. A condition which is overlooked (specific gravity over 1.260).	The deposit will heavily accumulate at the bottom and will cause internal shorting, causing damage to the battery.	Check to assure proper charging rate. When an overcharge condition exists with the proper charging rate, place an appropriate resistor in the charging circuit.

Battery Troubleshooting (cont.)

Problem	Probable Causes	Inspection and Remedy
Specific gravity drops Electrolyte evaporates	Shorted Insufficient charging Distilled water overfilled Contaminated electrolyte	Perform specific gravity measurement. If the addition of distilled water causes a drop in specific gravity, add sulfuric acid and adjust to proper specific gravity.

Chassis Troubleshooting

Problem	Probable Causes	Inspection and Remedy
Excessive vibration	Loose, broken, or worn motor mounts	Tighten or replace as necessary.
	Loose axle nuts	Tighten as directed in chapter eight.
	Excessive hub bearing play	Replace as directed in chapter eight.
	Loose spokes	Tighten as necessary.
	Rear wheel out of alignment	Align the rear wheel as described in chapter two.
	Wheel rims out of true	Consult your dealer.
	Irregular or peaked front tire wear	Replace the tire and check the wheel run-out.
	Tires overinflated	Let some air out. Pressure should be checked when cold.
	Tire and wheel unevenly balanced	Consult your dealer.
	Worn steering head bearings	Consult chapter eight for replacement procedures.
	Worn rear shock bushings	Consult chapter eight for replacement procedures.
	Swing-arm bushings too tight or loose	Consult chapter eight for adjustment procedures.
	Excessive front-end loading	Unload the front end.
	Incorrectly adjusted ignition timing	Adjust the timing as directed in chapter three.
	Incorrectly assembled clutch mechanism	Consult chapter four for assembly details.
	Excessively worn crankshaft	Replace as directed in chapter four.
	Broken or bent frame, forks, or swing arm	Consult your dealer.
Uncertain or wobbly steering	Worn or bad steering head bearings	Consult chapter eight for replacement procedures.
	Worn swing-arm bushings	Consult chapter eight for replacement procedures.
	Worn or bad hub bearings	Consult chapter eight for replacement procedures.
	Tire improperly seated on rim	Reseat the tire.
	Wheels improperly aligned	Consult chapter two for alignment instructions.
Heavy or stiff steering	Low front tire pressure	Check the tire pressure.
	Bad steering head bearings or races	Consult chapter eight for replacement procedures.

Chassis Troubleshooting (cont.)

Problem	Probable Causes	Inspection and Remedy
Soft suspension	Loss of spring tension	Replace the spring as described in chapter eight.
	Excessive load	Reduce the load.
	Worn or leaky front oil seals	Replace as directed in chapter eight.
Hard suspension	Too much oil in the forks	Drain and replace the oil as described in chapter two.
	Fork oil too heavy	Drain and replace as described in chapter two.
Suspension noise	Cushion case rubbing	Consult chapter eight for repair procedures.
	Interference between cushion case and spring	Consult chapter eight for repair procedures.
	Damaged cushion stopper rubber	Replace as directed in chapter eight.
	Insufficient or diluted oil	Drain and replace as directed in chapter two.
Brakes do not hold	Brake pads glazed or worn	Consult chapter eight for repair procedures.
	Brake pads oil- or grease-impregnated	Replace as directed in chapter eight.
	Brake linkage improperly adjusted	Adjust as described in chapter two.
Brakes drag	Lack of play in the linkage	Adjust as described in chapter two.
	Weak return springs	Replace as directed in chapter eight.
	Dirt in the drum	Disassemble and clean as described in chapter eight.
	Rusted cam and lever shaft	Replace as directed in chapter eight.
Brakes make scraping noises	Worn out brake linings	Replace as directed in chapter eight.
	Broken brake shoe	Replace as directed in chapter eight.
	Dirt in the drum	Disassemble and clean as directed in chapter eight.
	Broken pivot	Replace as directed in chapter eight.
Chain whine	Chain too tight	Adjust as described in chapter two.
	Chain rusted	Lubricate or replace as directed in chapter eight.
Chain slap	Chain too loose	Adjust as directed in chapter two.
Pulls to one side	Faulty right or left rear shock	Replace as directed in chapter eight.
	Incorrectly adjusted drive chain	Adjust as directed in chapter two.
	Incorrect wheel alignment	Align as directed in chapter two.
	Incorrectly balanced tires and wheels	Consult your dealer.
	Defective steering head bearings	Replace as directed in chapter eight.
	Bent or damaged frame, forks, or swing arm	Consult your dealer.

Appendix

Thread Changes

NOTE: *Beginning in 1967, Honda (and many other manufacturers) began using nuts and bolts manufactured to the ISO metric standard rather than the earlier JIS standard that had been widely used in both Japan and Europe. ISO and JIS hardware is interchangeable in some sizes; however, the thread pitch in a few of the common sizes used has been changed and, in these cases, the hardware is not interchangeable. Note also that, except for the 10 mm size (6 mm diameter thread diameter), the width (across flats) of ISO nuts and bolts (relative to the thread diameter) has been reduced from that of JIS hardware. ISO parts are identified by an embossed dot on the bolt head or nut.*

Interchangeability Chart

Thread Diameter	Width Across Flats		Thread Pitch	
	ISO	*JIS*	*ISO*	*JIS*
3 mm	5.5	6	0.5	0.6
4 mm	7	8	0.7	0.75
5 mm	8	9	0.8	0.9
6 mm	10	10	1.0	1.0
8 mm	12	14	1.25	1.25
10 mm	14	17	1.25	1.25
12 mm	17	19	1.25	1.5
14 mm	19	21	1.5	1.5
16 mm	22	23	1.5	1.5
18 mm	24	26	1.5	1.5
20 mm	27	29	1.5	1.5

Inches to Millimeters—Units

Inches	0	10	20	30	40
0		254.0	508.0	762.0	1016.0
1	25.4	279.4	533.4	787.4	1041.4
2	50.8	304.8	558.8	812.8	1066.8
3	76.2	330.2	584.2	838.2	1092.2
4	101.6	355.6	609.6	863.6	1117.6
5	127.0	381.0	635.0	889.0	1143.0
6	152.4	406.4	660.4	914.4	1168.4
7	177.8	431.8	685.8	939.8	1193.8
8	203.2	457.2	711.2	965.2	1219.2
9	228.6	482.6	736.6	990.6	1244.6

One Inch—25.399978 millimeters
One Meter—39.370113 inches
One Mile—1.6093 KM
One Km—.62138 miles

Decimals to Millimeters— Fractions

1/1000		1/100		1/10	
inches	mm	inches	mm	inches	mm
0.001	0.0254	0.01	0.254	0.1	2.54
0.002	0.0508	0.02	0.508	0.2	5.08
0.003	0.0762	0.03	0.762	0.3	7.62
0.004	0.1016	0.04	1.016	0.4	10.16
0.005	0.1270	0.05	1.270	0.5	12.70
0.006	0.1524	0.06	1.524	0.6	15.24
0.007	0.1778	0.07	1.778	0.7	17.78
0.008	0.2032	0.08	2.032	0.8	20.32
0.009	0.2286	0.09	2.286	0.9	22.86

Millimeters to Inches— Fractions

1/1000		1/100		1/10	
mm	inches	mm	inches	mm	inches
0.001	0.000039	0.01	0.00039	0.1	0.00394
0.002	0.000079	0.02	0.00079	0.2	0.00787
0.003	0.000118	0.03	0.00118	0.3	0.01181
0.004	0.000157	0.04	0.00157	0.4	0.01575
0.005	0.000197	0.05	0.00197	0.5	0.01969
0.006	0.000236	0.06	0.00236	0.6	0.02362
0.007	0.000276	0.07	0.00276	0.7	0.02756
0.008	0.000315	0.08	0.00315	0.8	0.03150
0.009	0.000354	0.09	0.00354	0.9	0.03543

Millimeters to Inches—Units

mm	0	10	20	30	40
0		0.39370	0.78740	1.18110	1.57480
1	0.03937	0.43307	0.82677	1.22047	1.61417
2	0.07874	0.47244	0.86614	1.25984	1.65354
3	0.11811	0.51181	0.90551	1.29921	1.69291
4	0.15748	0.55118	0.94488	1.33858	1.73228
5	0.19685	0.59055	0.98425	1.37795	1.77165
6	0.23622	0.62992	1.02362	1.41732	1.81103
7	0.27559	0.66929	1.06299	1.45669	1.85040
8	0.31496	0.70866	1.10236	1.49606	1.88977
9	0.35433	0.74803	1.14173	1.53543	1.92914

mm	50	60	70	80	90
0	1.96851	2.36221	2.75591	3.14961	3.54331
1	2.00788	2.40158	2.79528	3.18891	3.58268
2	2.04725	2.44095	2.83465	3.22835	3.62205
3	2.08662	2.48032	2.87402	3.26772	3.66142
4	2.12599	2.51969	2.91339	3.30709	3.70079
5	2.16536	2.55906	2.95276	3.34646	3.74016
6	2.20473	2.59843	2.99213	3.38583	3.77953
7	2.24410	2.63780	3.03150	3.42520	3.81890
8	2.28347	2.67717	3.07087	3.46457	3.85827
9	2.32284	2.71654	3.11024	3.50394	3.89764